D1738695

Differences That
Make a Difference

Differences That Make a Difference

Examining the Assumptions in Gender Research

Edited by LYNN H. TURNER
and HELEN M. STERK

BERGIN & GARVEY
Westport, Connecticut • London

Library of Congress Cataloging-in-Publication Data

Differences that make a difference : examining the assumptions in
    gender research / edited by Lynn H. Turner and Helen M. Sterk.
        p. cm.
    Includes bibliographical references and index.
    ISBN 0–89789–387–5 (alk. paper)
        1. Communication—Sex differences. 2. Language and languages—Sex
differences. 3. Man-woman relationships. I. Turner, Lynn H.
    II. Sterk, Helen M.
    P96.S48D54   1994
    305.3—dc20   94–16453

British Library Cataloguing in Publication Data is available.

Library of Congress Catalog Card Number: 94–16453
ISBN: 0–89789–387–5

First published in 1994

Bergin & Garvey, 88 Post Road West, Westport, CT 06881
An imprint of Greenwood Publishing Group, Inc.

Printed in the United States of America

The paper used in this book complies with the
Permanent Paper Standard issued by the National
Information Standards Organization (Z39.48–1984).

10 9 8 7 6 5 4 3 2 1

Contents

Tables   ix

Introduction: Examining "Difference"
Lynn H. Turner and Helen M. Sterk   xi

PART I   EXPLAINING GENDER RELATIONS   1

1   Communication Competencies of Women Employees:
A Comparison of Self Ratings with Other Ratings
Cynthia Berryman-Fink   5

2   Gender Differences and the Use of Conflict Strategies
Barbara Mae Gayle, Raymond W. Preiss, and Mike Allen   13

3   Gender Differences in Critical Incidents Reported by
Elderly Health Care Consumers: A Narrative Analysis
Gary L. Kreps   27

4   Developmental Differences in MBA Students:
An Examination of Life Stories and Career Histories
Susan Schick Case and Lorraine Thompson   35

5   On the Origins of Gender-Linked Language Differences:
Individual and Contextual Explanations
Mary-Jeanette Smythe and Jasna Meyer   51

6   Effects of Sex Composition and Task Structure on Perceptions
of Gender-Linked Role Differentiation in Small Groups
Edward A. Mabry and Carolyn J. Sorgel   61

7   A Meta-Analysis of Gender Research in Managerial Influence   73
    Kathleen J. Krone, Mike Allen, and John Ludlum

8   Sex, Schemata, and Social Status: TV Character Identification
    and Occupational Aspirations among Adolescents
    Robert J. Griffin, Shaikat Sen, and Rhonda Plotkin   85

9   Interruptions and the Construction of Reality
    Sara Hayden   99

PART II   EVALUATING GENDER RELATIONS   107

10   The Image of Stepmothers in Children's Literature, 1980–1991
     Pamela J. Cooper   111

11   Women's Magazines: Confusing Differences
     Bren Ortega Murphy   119

12   Sport Sex: Toward a Theory of Sexual Aggression
     Sean Michael Gilmore   129

13   Courtroom Uses of Linguistic Analysis to Demonstrate
     a Hostile Work Environment for Women
     Susan Schick Case   137

14   "And If We Lose Our Name, Then What About Our Land?" Or,
     What Price Development?
     M. J. Hardman   151

15   Language Choice and Use: Influences of Setting and Gender
     Kathryn A. Remlinger   163

PART III   EXPANDING GENDER RELATIONS   175

16   Gender, Media, and Militarism
     Lisa Merrill and Denise Quirk   179

17   Difference, Dominance, and Dialectics: A Call for Change
     Linda A. M. Perry   187

18   Visionary Language: The Voice of Mary Robinson
     Kathleen B. Watters   195

19   Constructing a Postmodernist Ethic:
The Feminist Quest for a New Politics
Patricia A. Sullivan and Steven R. Goldzwig   203

20   Gender, Communication, and Community
Helen M. Sterk and Lynn H. Turner   213

Index   223

Contributors   229

Tables

2.1	Gender Differences and CMS Selection Vital Statistics	16
2.2	Effect Sizes	20
2.3	Average Effect Sizes	21
2.4	Binomial Effect Size Display	22
4.1	Group Comparison of Mean Length of Life Stories and Career Histories	40
4.2	Frequency of Occurrence of Code Themes by Gender	42
5.1	Twelve Language Variables Coded as Markers of Speaker Gender	54
5.2	Language Variables Displayed by Males and Females	56
5.3	Language Variables as Displayed within Dyads	57
6.1	Percent of Highest (#1) Rankings in Predominantly Female Group Compositions	66
6.2	Percent of Highest (#1) Rankings in Predominantly Male Group Compositions	67
7.1	Coding System for Meta-Analysis of Managerial Compliance-Gaining	74
7.2	Average Effect Sizes for the Relationship between Gender and Tactic Choice	80

8.1   Education, Occupation, and Television Character Identification
by Gender and Social Status   92

9.1   Conversation Transcription Key   100

15.1 Transcription Key   164

Introduction: Examining "Difference"

Lynn H. Turner and Helen M. Sterk

Analysis of current research into the complex relationships among gender, language, and communication forces acknowledgment that the concept of "difference" is unavoidable. Researchers continue to explore differences such as those that exist between women and men, those that mark the treatment of women and men, and differences that distinguish women at varying "standpoints" of life. However, the research literature is far from united in how it treats difference and what assumptions about difference ground it. In fact, there are profound distinctions among this book's contributors' understandings of and approaches to difference. To place the chapters of this book in a larger context, we will review the various ways that "difference" has grounded scholarship in the interdisciplinary intersection of gender, language, and communication and discuss how the essays gathered here fit into that framework.

When one of the editors first began graduate school, she told a professor that she was interested in examining women's and men's communication behaviors in an effort to understand the differences between them. He was not impressed. This eminent professor, who was to hold so much of her professional life in his hands, told her that while women and men may differ from one another in various ways, those differences were spurious; they made no significant difference in explaining human communication (and in her field, the phrase "no significant difference" was damning indeed). The professor rejected gender as a framework for understanding behavior. Despite the fact that he was a rather famous, well-respected, and well-established professor, and she was but a beginning graduate student, she continued to examine women's and men's communication because she was convinced that there was something to be observed, and more importantly, something to be learned about how gender affects people's life experiences and actions.

As both editors have continued their careers and research, they have had occasion to reexamine their initial, somewhat naive and enthusiastic, responses to the explanatory power of gender. Neither would argue, as the aforementioned professor did, that gender is a meaningless category creating only spurious differences. Less interested in the defining differences between women and men, now we are more conscious of the similarities between women's and men's *behaviors* and the differences in their *treatment*, and more interested in looking at women *without* comparing them to men.

However, difference remains an intriguing concept, one that continues to be foundational in communication, language, and gender research. It is instructive at this point to trace the meaning and utility of difference in feminist theory, as it has developed in the twentieth century. Just as difference has proved alternately useful and detrimental as a theoretical construct in feminist theory, so, too, has it waxed and waned in its academic applications.

The theme of difference has been sounded repeatedly in feminist thought since the early 1950s and the publication of de Beauvoir's *The Second Sex*. In the early days of American feminism, the question was, what are the grounds of difference between women and men? Are apparent gender differences the result of immutable physical forces or of cultural constructions? A lot rode (and still rides) on the answer. If women's domestic skills, including nurturing and caring for children and families, and men's aggression and ambition, which allowed them to succeed in the competitive public world, were a result of genetic "programming," then it would be at least inefficient and at most wrong to interfere with the natural order of things. On the other hand, if the differences between women and men were only apparent, brought on by differential treatment and training, then working to reform the gender system, which was marked by male power and female subordination, would benefit women and change culture in a way that would promote a just equality between the sexes.

With the rebirth of the women's movement in the 1960s, difference became a hotly debated topic. At that time, the popular press argued that the ascendence of feminism would sound the death knell of the very real differences between women and men. The claim was that the women's movement threatened the natural order of sex difference. The argument continued by pointing out that, as women gained equality with men, their femininity would fade and the two sexes would lose the differences that made them attractive complements to each other.

As Eisenstein observed, this argument responded to the feminist critique of masculinity and femininity which maintained that socializing females to femininity and males to masculinity was the way to keep women oppressed and patriarchy in place; "Obviously, one of the goals of the women's movement was to remove the obstacles to the full participation of women in all aspects of social life. A primary obstacle appeared to be the belief, and the argument, that women were 'different' and were limited by virtue of that difference to the domestic sphere" (Eisenstein, 1980, p. xvi). Eisenstein went on to point out that women were encouraged to minimize the differences among themselves through consciousness-raising groups that encouraged the sharing of life experiences, with a focus on their commonalities despite differences in social and demographic detail. In arguments such as Eisenstein's, what is now called the essentialist line of thinking was nurtured in feminist theory and Women's Studies as a distinct field of inquiry was born. In this movement the focus lay on the commonality of experience shared by all types of women that justified the use of "women" as a category.

In feminist theoretical developments in the 1970s and through the 1980s, the experiences women shared began to be seen less as necessary outcomes of oppression by men and more as sources of strength contained within women themselves. Thus, feminist theory moved into a period of valorizing the differences women shared that set them apart from men. Now men were positioned as the Other, and patriarchal structures were questioned not only because they oppressed women but because they were wrong, immoral, inaccurate, or distorted. Carol Gilligan's controversial book *In a Different Voice* (1982) is a classic example of writing in this vein. Out of this line of thinking developed critiques of compulsory heterosexuality and the hegemony of masculinity.

It is at this point that discussions of difference bifurcated, resulting in a heated, continuing debate about the utility of the difference construct. Recently, this debate has been featured in popular venues (i.e., Kaminer, 1993; Pollitt, 1993; Tannen, 1993; and Wolf, 1993), not the least of which is Naomi Wolf's *Fire With Fire: The New Female Power and How It Will Change the 21st Century*. Wolf argues that the logical, almost necessary outcome of difference feminism is what she calls "victim feminism." Instead, she advocates shunning the whole idea of difference and developing the political power that women now hold, whether they realize it or not. That power is starting what Wolf terms a "genderquake," one that "power feminism" can increase, leading women to take an equal place with men in politics, business, economics, religion, and other cultural institutions. Positions such as Wolf's are becoming more and more common, with the result that research pursuing understanding of differences between the sexes is devalued.

Forming the structure for much of these popular writings is the conflict between the positions of essentialists and theorists who espouse the multiplicities among women. As Wood (1992) explains, essentialists are those theorists who, following Carol Gilligan (1982), argue that there is something essentially female (and, for many theorists, superior) about all women that contrasts sharply with men's essentially male nature. Opponents of this position, such as Wolf, Pollitt, and hooks opine that women are too diverse a group to possess an essential nature, and other concepts such as race, ethnicity, and status, for example, play a much larger role than gender in shaping people's behavior. Further, these theorists maintain that the essentialist views cause more problems than they solve by obscuring the real differences *among* women and rendering women of color invisible (Wood 1992).

In brief, researchers who could be categorized as essentialists invariably direct their attention to the differences that exist between men and women while those who reject an essentialist stance are more interested in differences that exist among women and in the creation of the social construct of "gender." *Differences That Make a Difference* enters the difference debate with vigor. This book reflects the current state of communication, language, and gender research and its chapters represent one or the other stance toward difference. The essays in this book do not resolve the conflict between these two positions, but speak to important elements in the debate in many ways.

Part I of the book, Explaining Gender Relations, features articles by researchers who ask whether and how men and women differ on a range of communication behavior variables. In asking this question, researchers are drawn to the conclusion that there are some basic, important differences between the sexes. Then, the pressing issue becomes determining the most satisfying explanation for these differences. Several explanations are advanced, ranging from sexual stereotypes, situational variables, and gender schemata to cultural differences between the sexes.

Part II, Evaluating Gender Relations, includes chapters by researchers who imply that searching for differences in women's and men's behaviors is not of primary value to gender research because, regardless of women's similarities or differences from men, cultural hegemony works to their disadvantage. The analyses in this section show the workings of masculine hegemony and the limits upon female agency in the areas of children's literature, women's magazines, men's sexual language, and cross-cultural imposition of Western values.

These two sections contextualize Part III, Expanding Gender Relations, by warning us of the dangers of overexaggerating differences (the studies in Part I tend to find only small empirical differences between the genders) and cautioning us of the problems women may have, due to the cultural effects of even small differences.

Given this context, the chapters in Part III offer suggestions for reconceptualizing "difference" and how culture may be transformed and masculine hegemony challenged. The essays in this section offer an understanding of the ways in which structural features of cultural life exist in social institutions and how these institutions are and may be opened to include women alongside men.

Beyond being an intellectual exercise, an examination of what researchers mean by "difference" and what baggage the term brings with it is critical to both understanding their work and comprehending the trends in gender research. This book presents an array of current research in language, communication, and gender organized by research assumptions about difference. In this way, readers can examine their own assumptions and ask critical questions of each essay.

Further, this book indicates some of the promise of examining difference critically. Academic work on gender seems to be on the cusp between honoring and dishonoring the gifts and qualities of women. We believe that collapsing distinctions between women and men will work to the disadvantage of women. For that reason, this book features research which shows both women's strength as women (i.e., Kreps, Schick Case & Thompson, Hayden, Hardman, Remlinger, Perry, Watters, Sullivan & Goldzwig) and how women still starkly lack the power to create cultural meanings (i.e., Griffin & Sen, Cooper, Murphy, Gilmore, Schick Case, Merrill).

The collection poses stimulating questions about women and men and provides a three-part framework for understanding scholarship on gender. We believe that framework provides two things: (1) a mapping of the ways in which difference between women and men is assumed, explicated, rejected, or abdicated in favor of the diversity among women or in favor of the problems of patriarchy as an object of study in current research, and (2) a glimpse of the creative scholarly tension that exists between studies that look at actual, enacted gender relations and those that examine culturally constructed gender relations. In the studies that attend to enacted gender relations, we see a great deal of restraint voiced concerning the findings; that is, there are not as many clear-cut, definable, observable differences between women and men as we may have thought. In the chapters that analyze culturally constructed gender relations, we hear a more forceful voice articulating the harm that patriarchal structures of thought and action have done and can continue to do. Often, the tension between studies of enacted gender relations and culturally constructed relations is couched as a methodological debate (empiricists versus qualitative researchers), but we think it transcends methodology and focuses on the assumptive level, at the level of warrants which undergird the research. Further, we find it a creative tension or a dialectic. We do not favor one over the other, but rather we attempt to show in this volume how the two inform each other.

Women and men may not approach management, conflict, or small group discussion in radically different ways, but we live in a culture that reifies difference and the difference of biology is central to the ways in which we are understood by others and understand ourselves. As Wood (1994) argues, we live "gendered lives." Until we have changed society so that masculinity and femininity are not such salient features of social life, gender is a difference that makes a difference. It may not be the only difference or the most important difference to consider, but it cannot be ignored.

REFERENCES

de Beauvoir, S. (1953). *The second sex* (H. M. Parshley, Trans.). New York: Alfred A. Knopf. (Original work published 1949.)

Eisenstein, H. (1980). Introduction. In H. Eisenstein & A. Jardine (Eds.), *The future of difference* (pp. xv-xxiv). Boston: Barnard College Women's Center.

Gilligan, C. (1982). *In a different voice: Psychological theory and women's development.* Cambridge, MA: Harvard University Press.

hooks, b. (1981). *Ain't I a woman: Black women and feminism.* Boston: South End Press.

hooks, b. (1984). *Feminist theory: From margin to center.* Boston: South End Press.

hooks, b. (1989). *Talking back: Thinking feminist, thinking black.* Boston: South End Press.

Kaminer, W. (1993, October). Feminism's identity crisis. *The Atlantic Monthly,* 51-68.

Pollitt, K. (1993, September/October). Are women morally superior to men? *Utne Reader,* 101-109. (Original work published Dec. 28, 1992).

Tannen, D. (1993, September/October). Deborah Tannen responds. *Utne Reader,* 109.

Wolf, N. (1993) *Fire with fire: The new female power and how it will change the 21st century.* New York: Random House.

Wood, J. T. (1994). *Gendered lives.* Belmont, CA: Wadsworth.

Wood, J. T. (1992). Moving from woman's nature to standpoint epistemology. *Women's Studies in Communication, 22*, 1-24.

Part I

EXPLAINING GENDER RELATIONS

These essays presume that women and men communicate differently from one another. In this section, the essays are grouped by the framework they favor—implicitly or explicitly—to explain the differences. The first three chapters focus on sex or biological differences, while Chapter 4 draws upon psychological explanations for gender differences. Chapters 5 through 8 make the case that gender differences can be explained contextually, or by looking at the interaction of multiple factors. Finally, Chapter 9 puts forward the argument that power asymmetry helps to explain differences between women's and men's communication.

In Chapters 1 through 3, the authors look at how women and men differ in their communication behaviors. Cynthia Berryman-Fink studied how women and men rate themselves as competent communicators, contrasting those findings with how others rate those women and men. She found that women rated themselves less favorably than did other people. An intriguing finding in her research is that men rate themselves highly on commanding authority, while women rate themselves as being good nonverbal communicators and more empathetic than men. In Chapter 2, Barbara Gayle and Raymond Preiss analyzed women's and men's uses of different communication styles when faced with conflict. They found only small differences, but differences which correspond to sex-role expectations, namely, that men tend to choose competitive strategies and women tend to employ cooperative ones. In an interesting narrative analysis of how elderly women and men conceptualize their experiences with health care, Gary Kreps noted clear gender differences in how people view those experiences. He found women made more positive comments, focusing on the social and communicative aspects of health care, while men paid more attention to the negative aspects of their care, focusing on the results of that care. Kreps suggests the reason for the differences is that, in our culture, there are gendered expectations for the amount of control one can exert over a situation—women expect less control and therefore can accommodate themselves to situations where they are not in control, while men expect more control and as a result, are uncomfortable when they have to turn control over themselves to health caregivers.

In Chapter 4, Susan Schick Case and Lorraine Thompson present a detailed, nuanced study of how women and men M.B.A. students at a demanding midwestern university understand their lifework. They, too, find different understandings of what the world is like and how they fit in it between men and women. In self-descriptions of their lives, schooling and work, men tended to expand upon their acquisition and mastery of certain skills. In sharp contrast, women reflected on the many responsibilities they have to balance in their lives, including not only mastery of skills, but *also* personal development and family nurturing. Schick Case and Thompson suggest women's differing perceptions may be due to upbringing, expectations, and the reality that women who work outside the home must continue to work inside it as well.

Chapters 5 through 8 continue the trajectory marked by Schick Case and Thompson, developing ways in which many variables interact with gender to add nuance to our understanding of the forces creating gendered communication. Mary-Jeannette Smythe and Jasna Meyer argue that when communication patterns and styles are closely scrutinized, women and men are found to use the same ones. So, researchers should look at context, situations, tasks, and partners when trying to understand the communication choices made. In group discussions, say Edward Mabry and Carolyn Sorgel, women may find themselves at a disadvantage in groups with more men than women in them. In such groups, both women and men perceive the men as holding all the leadership positions—task and social. In female-dominated groups, women fare not much better, being perceived only half the time as holding leadership positions (even though they outnumber the men). Mabry and Sorgel suggest more than just gender affects these decisions. In a meta-analysis of studies seeking to know how managers get their people to do things, Kathleen Krone, Mike Allen, and John Ludlum found men tended to use both reward and punishment as incentives. In this study, women and men relied equally upon rational processes. Their conclusion suggests role effects and men's relative cultural power may affect the choices women and men managers make, but they say women "may be reconstructing what it means to enact power within organizations." (p. 82) Robert Griffin, Shaikat Sen, and Rhonda Plotkin present a study of adolescents and their choice of television role models to see what adolescents learn about career possibilities from television. Among other things, they posit that showing women in non-traditional (i.e., non-domestic) roles on television may help all of us to see new possibilities for women.

In the final chapter in this section, Sara Hayden tackles the problem of how interruptions function in conversation. Attending to women in a women's self-help group, Hayden argues that interruptions can be highly functional, enabling women to empower one another. Instead of operating competitively, these interruptions function as bridges, moving women from meaning to new meaning. Like Krone, Allen, and Ludlum, Hayden shows women developing new kinds of power, here, the power to support and sustain, rather than the power to make one's own meanings hold sway over those of another.

1

Communication Competencies of Women Employees: A Comparison of Self Ratings with Other Ratings

Cynthia Berryman-Fink

Evaluation of workplace performance has been a major area of study for several decades. As performance evaluations incorporate judgments from more raters, questions emerge about potential biases based on gender or organizational level of these raters. Despite the plethora of research investigating gender and status effects on performance appraisals, few conclusions can be drawn about the nature of those effects. The majority of studies reveal no effect of rater sex on judgments of performance (Griffeth & Bedeian, 1989; Mobley, 1982; Peters, *et al.*, 1984; Pulakos, Oppler, White, & Borman, 1989; Pulakos & Wexley, 1983). However, other studies have found female raters give more favorable evaluations of others' performance than male raters (Bartol & Butterfield, 1976; London & Poplawski, 1976; Wheeless & Berryman-Fink, 1985).

Relatively little research has examined the role of organizational status of the rater on judgments of performance. While Zalesny and Kirsch (1989) found that organizational position did affect performance appraisals, with peers rating employee performance significantly higher than did supervisors, this bias has not been demonstrated consistently. Expectations or suspicions of inflated ratings by peers and subordinates (Bernardin, 1986; McEvoy, Buller, & Roghaar, 1988) are more common than such empirically demonstrated leniency effects. There is no basis in the literature for concluding one group of raters (peer, subordinate, or superior) systematically gives more favorable ratings than another group.

Performance ratings increasingly include self-evaluations as well as ratings by superiors, subordinates, and peers, prompting questions regarding the relationship between self ratings and other ratings. The majority of studies reveal discrepancies between self-assessments and organizational assessments of performance (George & Smith, 1990; Martin & Klimoski, 1990; Staley & Shockley-Zalabek, 1986). Harris and Schaubroek (1988) report low correlations between self ratings and peer ratings and between self ratings and supervisor ratings. While self ratings and other ratings are likely to be discrepant, it is not clear whether self ratings are more favorable than others' ratings. Some studies show a tendency for self-ratings to be more inflated than other sources (Kraiger, 1986; Staley & Shockley-Zalabak, 1986), while others report that self-assessments are not more lenient than supervisors' assessments (Drory, 1988).

This study looks at organizational communication competency, specifically examining the effects of sex and rater level, the relationship between self ratings and other ratings, and the effect of sex on self-ratings. These factors are examined in relation to the evaluation of female employees. Research on workplace issues as they affect women, including perceptions of job performance for females, becomes increasingly important as labor force participation rates of women steadily increase (Larwood & Gutek, 1984; Staley & Shockley-Zalabak, 1986).

The following research questions are proposed:

RQ1: Do male and female raters differ in their evaluations of the organizational communication competency of female employees?

RQ2: Do superiors, subordinates, and peers differ in their evaluations of the organizational communication competency of female employees?

RQ3: Do female employees' self-evaluations of organizational communication competency differ from others' evaluations?

RQ4: Do male and female self-ratings of organizational communication competency differ?

METHOD

Participants

Data for this study were collected from individuals enrolled in several management and communication classes within the evening program of a large, metropolitan midwestern university. All participants were employed on a full- or part-time basis while taking evening college classes. Participants included 94 employees (62F; 52M) from a variety of types of organizations including medical (40% of sample), retail (15%), government (10%), as well as educational, utilities, financial, legal, entertainment, publishing, and miscellaneous organizations (5% each).

Procedures

All participants rated themselves on a test of organizational communication competency. Additionally, the female employees provided the name and address of a peer, superior, or subordinate who might also rate them on the same measure of communication competency. The workplace others designated by the female employees were contacted by mail, asked to complete a confidential evaluation of communication competency, and directed to return the evaluation to the researcher in a stamped, self-addressed envelope. Sixty-two completed responses were received.

Dependent Measure

Organizational communication competency was measured by a modified version of the Communication Competencies of Women Managers Scale (CCWMS) (Wheeless & Berryman-Fink, 1985; Berryman-Fink & Wheeless, 1986).

RESULTS

RQ1 asked if male and female raters differ in their evaluations of the organizational communication competencies of female employees. Of the 62 women rated, 39 (63%) opted to be rated by females while 23 (37%) opted to be rated by males. The *t*-test revealed no significant differences in the ways that male and female colleagues rated female employees ($t = .19$; $p < .85$). RQ2 asked if superiors, subordinates, and peers differ in their evaluations of the organizational communication competency of female employees. Thirty-two participants (52%) opted to be rated by superiors, 25 (40%) opted to be rated by peers, and 5 (8%) opted to be rated by subordinates. The one-way ANOVA revealed no significant differences in the ways that superiors, subordinates, and peers rated female employees ($F = 1.38$; $df = 2$; $p < .25$). RQ3 asked if female employees' self-evaluations of organizational communication competency differ from others' evaluations. The paired *t*-test revealed a significant difference between female employees' self-ratings and others' ratings of organizational communication competence ($t = 3.25$; $p < .002$). A comparison of means revealed that others' ratings were higher ($M = 129.2$) than self-ratings ($M = 122.1$). RQ4 asked if males and females differ in their self-ratings of organizational communication competency. The *t*-test revealed no significant difference between males' and females' self-ratings ($t = 1.77$; $p < .07$). Although the difference was statistically non-significant, examination of the means for each group showed a tendency for the women to rate themselves higher ($M = 122.1$) in organizational communication competency than the men rated themselves ($M = 117.6$).

Because the comparison between male and female self-ratings approached statistical significance, item-by-item *t*-tests were performed for each of the thirty questions. These analyses revealed nine items on which male and female employees' self-ratings were significantly different: nonverbal communication, empathy/sympathy, organization, openness/receptivity to others, sensitivity, sincerity, honesty, putting others at ease, and commanding authority. On all items except commanding authority, females rated themselves significantly higher than the males rated themselves.

DISCUSSION

The results of this study should be interpreted cautiously, due to the self-selection of other raters, the largely nonmanagerial sample, and the purpose of soliciting performance evaluations. The first research question asked if sex of rater affects judgments about the organizational communication competency of female employees. These results showed no difference in how males and females evaluate the communication competence of women in the workplace. This finding is consistent with previous literature.

The second research question asked if level of rater affects judgments about the organizational communication competency of female employees. These results showed no difference in how superiors, subordinates, and peers evaluate the communication competence of women in the workplace. It should be noted that of the sixty-two female participants, over half designated superiors to provide ratings. Perhaps employees are comfortable with superiors making performance appraisals, since this traditionally is the group with most responsibility in the performance evaluation process (Lane & Herriot, 1990). Forty percent of the women chose to have their communication rated by peers, while only 8% suggested subordinates to provide ratings. The lack of subordinate ratings is due to the fact that few of the women in this sample were managers with subordinates who could rate them.

The third research question asked if self evaluations differ from others' evaluations. These results showed a significant difference between the ways females rated their own communication competence and the ways others rated them. Such a finding is consistent with literature indicating discrepancies in self ratings and other ratings of job performance (George & Smith, 1990; Harris & Schaubroek, 1988; Martin & Klimoski, 1990). Additionally, these results corroborate discrepancies found between self and others' judgments of communication competence. Talley & Richmond (1980) report that people's perceptions of another's communication style often do not agree with the person's self-report and Staley and Shockley-Zalabak (1986) report a lack of agreement between a female professional and her supervisor regarding her communication competence.

When examining how self and others' judgments differed in this study, we found that females rated their organizational communication competency less favorably than others rated them. This result is somewhat puzzling to explain. Previous literature indicates no clear-cut directional difference in self ratings versus other ratings of performance. The present finding of more favorable ratings by others may be a function of this study's method. Self-selection of other raters might have led to the designation of favorable rather than objective or critical others. Likewise, the purpose of the evaluations may have affected the direction of ratings. Participants knew they were providing evaluations for research purposes only. Thus, colleagues who may perceive organizational rewards as zero-sum had nothing to lose by being generous in their ratings. Finally, raters may have attributed higher levels of communication competence to this female sample because sex-role stereotypes expect women to excel in expressive areas, including interacting with others (Wood, Polek, & Aiken, 1985).

The fourth research question asked if men and women rate themselves differently in organizational communication competency. These results showed no statistically significant difference between male and female self-ratings on the overall measure of communication competence in the workplace. Male and female self-ratings were significantly different on nine specific scale items, however. The women employees saw themselves as better nonverbal communicators, as more empathic/sympathetic, as more organized, as more open and receptive to others, as more sensitive, as more sincere, as more honest, and as more able to put others at ease than the men saw themselves. The male employees rated themselves significantly higher than the females on only one scale item: commanding authority. These sex differences in self-ratings are consistent with sex-role stereotypes that expect women to be sincere (Werner & LaRussa, 1985) sensitive (Arliss, 1991; Werner & LaRussa, 1985), and empathic (Pearson, Turner, & Todd-Mancillas, 1991), and with research that perceives women employees as more open than men employees (Lamude & Daniels, 1984) and men as using more command and control styles of leadership than women use (Rosener, 1990). These results also corroborate research on sex differences in actual behavior which reports women being more open and receptive at work (Putnam, 1983; Todd-Mancillas & Rossi, 1985) and more adept at nonverbal communication (Doyle & Paludi, 1991).

In summary, this research shows no effects of sex and organizational level of rater on evaluations of the communication performance of female employees. It does find a significant difference between self and others' assessments of performance with others' ratings being more lenient than the females' self-ratings. Finally, it indicates a tendency for male and female employees to assign sex-stereotypical characteristics to their own organizational communication performance.

Future studies might randomly select from a list of possible evaluators to provide assessments. Actual performance reviews completed within organizations by multiple raters including self, peers, subordinates, and superiors should be utilized in subsequent investigations. Future research which examines possible biases in performance evaluations, including the effects of gender, organizational position, and self-assessments, is necessary so organizations can determine the efficacy of their performance evaluation systems.

REFERENCES

Arliss, L. P. (1991). *Gender communication.* Englewood Cliffs, NJ: Prentice-Hall.

Bartol, K. M., & Butterfield, D. A. (1976). Sex effects in evaluating leaders. *Journal of Applied Psychology, 61,* 446-454.

Bernardin, H. J. (1986). Subordinate appraisal: A valuable source of information about managers. *Human Resource Management, 25,* 421-439.

Berryman-Fink, C., & Wheeless, V. E. (1986). The development and validation of the communication competencies of women managers scale. Paper presented at the Central States Speech Association, Cincinnati.

Doyle, J. A., & Paludi, M. A. (1991). *Sex and gender.* Dubuque, IA: William C. Brown Publishers.

Drory, A. (1988). Self versus superior assessment of social science research employees. *Employee Responsibilities & Rights Journal, 1,* 301-312.

George, D. I., & Smith, M. C. (1990). An empirical comparison of self-assessment in personnel selection. *Public Personnel Management, 19,* 175-190.

Griffeth, R. W., & Bedeian, A. G. (1989). Employee performance evaluations: Effects of ratee age, rater age, and ratee gender. *Journal of Organizational Behavior, 10,* 83-90.

Harris, M. M., & Schaubroek, J. (1988). A meta-analysis of self-supervisor, self-peer, and peer-supervisor ratings. *Personnel Psychology, 41,* 43-62.

Kalin, R., & Hodgins, D. C. (1984). Sex bias and occupational suitability. *Canadian Journal of Behavioral Science, 16,* 311-325.

Kraiger, K. (1986). An analysis of relationships among self, peer, and supervisory ratings of performance. Paper presented at the First Annual Conference of the Society for Industrial and Organizational Psychology, Chicago.

Lamude, K. & Daniels, T. D. (1984). Perceived managerial communicator style as a function of subordinate and manager gender. *Communication Research Reports, 1,* 91-96.

Lane, J., & Herriot, P. (1990). Self-ratings, supervisor ratings positions and performance. *Journal of Occupational Psychology, 63,* 77-88.

Larwood, L., & Gutek, B. A. (1984). Women at work in the USA. In M. J. Davidson and C. L. Cooper (Eds.), *Women at work* (pp. 237-267). New York: John Wiley and Sons.

London, M., & Poplawski, J. R. (1976). Effects of information on stereotype development in performance appraisal and interview contexts. *Journal of Applied Psychology, 61,* 199-205.

Martin, S. L., & Klimoski, R. J. (1990). Use of verbal protocol to trace cognitions associated with self- and supervisor evaluations of performance. *Organizational Behavior and Human Decision Processes, 46,* 135-154.

McEvoy, G. M., Buller, P. F., & Roghaar, S. R. (1988). A jury of one's peers. *Personnel Administrator, 33,* 94-101.

Mobley, W. H. (1982). Supervisor and employee race and sex effects on performance appraisals: A field study on adverse impact and generalizability. *Academy of Management Journal, 25,* 598-606.

Pearson, J. C., Turner, L. H., & Todd-Mancillas, W. (1991). *Gender and communication,* Dubuque, IA: William C. Brown Publishers.

Peters, L. H., O'Connor, E. J., Weekley, J., Pooyan, A., Frank, B., & Erenkrantz, B. (1984). Sex bias and managerial evaluations: A replication and extension. *Journal of Applied Psychology, 69,* 349-352.

Pulakos, E. D., Oppler, S. H., White, L. A. & Borman, W. C. (1989). Examination of race and sex effects on performance ratings. *Journal of Applied Psychology, 74,* 770-780.

Pulakos, E. D., & Wexley, K. N. (1983). The relationship among perceptual similarity, sex, and performance ratings in manager-subordinate dyads. *Academy of Management Journal, 26,* 129-139.

Putnam, L. L. (1983). Lady, you're trapped: Breaking out of conflict styles. In J. J. Pilotta (Ed.), *Women in organizations* (pp. 39-53). Prospect Heights, IL: Waveland Press..

Rosener, J. B. (1990). Ways women lead. *Harvard Business Review, 68,* 119-125.

Snyder, M., & Skrypnek, B. J. (1981). Testing hypotheses about the self: Assessment of job suitability. *Journal of Personality, 49,* 193-211.

Staley, C. C., & Shockley-Zalabak, P. (1986). Communication proficiency and future training needs of the female professional: Self-assessment versus supervisors' evaluations. *Human Relations, 39,* 891-902.

Talley, M. A., & Richmond, V. P. (1980). The relationship between psychological gender orientation and communicator style. *Human Communication Research, 6,* 326-339.

Todd-Mancillas, W. R., & Rossi, A. N. A. (1985). Gender differences in the management of personnel disputes. *Women's Studies in Communication, 8,* 25-33.

Werner, P. D., & La Russa, G. W. (1985). Persistence and change in sex-role stereotypes. *Sex Roles, 12,* 1089-1099.

Wheeless, V. E., & Berryman-Fink, C. (1985). Perceptions of women and their communicator competencies. *Communication Quarterly, 33,* 137-148.

Wood, W., Polek, D., & Aiken, C. (1985). Sex differences in group task performance. *Journal of Personality and Social Psychology, 48,* 63-71.

Zalesny, M. D., & Kirsch, M. P. (1989). The effect of similarity on performance ratings and interrater agreement. *Human Relations, 42,* 81-96.

2

Gender Differences and the Use of Conflict Strategies

Barbara Mae Gayle, Raymond W. Preiss, and Mike Allen

Results from twenty years of studies have not isolated consistent gender differences in the selection of conflict management strategies. While some studies[1] identify gender as a salient issue, researchers do not agree on patterns of, or situations involving, gender-related preferences for particular conflict management strategies. Other researchers[2] suggest that men and women employ quite similar conflict management strategies across a variety of situations and settings. This review summarizes the gender differences and conflict management strategy (CMS) selection literature meta-analytically, to elicit a unified perspective on the impact of gender upon CMS.

THEORETICAL ISSUES IN THE CMS LITERATURE

Two rationales have been advanced to account for the contradictory findings. One explanation argues that conflict strategy selection is affected by expectations based on sexual stereotypes. A second approach suggests that CMS selection is affected by situational, contextual, and personality variables.

Expectancy Theory Argument for CMS Selection

A popular explanation for male-female conflict differences is found in expectancy theory. This approach reasons that males and females communicate according to their perceptions of socially defined roles. From this view, males are expected to be more aggressive and dominating, and females are expected to be more submissive and pacifying (Burgoon, Dillard, & Doran, 1983). Support for the expectancy approach to CMS selection has been found in a variety of settings (organizations, universities) and sample populations (supervisors/subordinates, students, intimates).

However, no consistent pattern emerges from the literature attempting to identify gender differences in CMS selection. It is apparent that, even if researchers identify gender differences, the particular strategies attributed to male and female respondents differ. At this point, the direction of effects is equivocal and no attempt has been made to quantify the magnitude of outcomes linked to stereotypical expectations for conflict styles.

Interaction-Conflict Account for CMS Selection

The interaction-conflict perspective deals with the contextual, situational, and personality variables constituting the conflict situation. The rationale for this approach is based on the idea that situational determinants are more likely to account for behavior than gender differences (Eagly, 1987). The argument is that a broad range of variables play a role in determining male and female preferences for conflict behaviors (Shockley-Zalabak, 1981). Participants in conflict interactions make choices about conflict management strategy selection by considering their own and the other person's goals (Putnam & Wilson, 1982), or situational/contextual factors (Renwick, 1977; Shockley-Zalabak, 1981). If one of these factors is salient for either (or both) men or women, few differences in CMS would be anticipated.

The literature consistent with the interactional approach is difficult to interpret. The failure to find hypothesized, gender-linked conflict outcomes hardly justifies the conclusion that the context governs conflict management selection strategies. However, when a pattern of similar male-female outcomes is detected, it is reasonable to search for alternative interpretations. The interactional context explanation, if viable, must specify factors of the situation/context leading to similarities or differences in the selection of conflict strategies. However, no such elaboration of situational factors has emerged in the literature.

Our narrative review of gender differences in CMS selection reveals a fragmented body of literature replete with theoretical inconsistencies. Because meta-analysis can statistically synthesize a number of original studies and lead to generalizable conclusions (Rosenthal, 1984), investigating this literature meta-analytically may reconcile contradictory results and quantify the magnitude of gender differences associated with conflict management strategy selection.

METHOD

To explore the effect of biological sex on the selection of conflict management strategies, all existing studies relevant to this issue were aggregated meta-analytically.

Search Procedures

For this investigation, an extensive search of the literature was initiated by manual and computer searches.[3] Each study was subjected to inclusion rules for aggregation. A report was included if (a) it was an experimental investigation providing enough statistical information to allow calculation of an effect size, and (b) it reported a relationship relevant to the impact of biological sex on the selection of conflict management strategies.

The search procedures resulted in the location of 35 manuscripts with 37 studies relevant to the variables of interest. Basic information regarding each study is found in Table 2.1. Six studies did not provide sufficient statistical information to allow meta-analytic aggregation (Fitzpatrick & Winke, 1979; Monroe, DiSalvo, Lewis, & Borzi, 1989; Nowak, 1984; Rahim, 1983, Roloff & Greenberg, 1979; Sternberg & Soriano, 1984). The remaining 29 manuscripts with 31 separate studies were subjected to coding procedures.

Coding Procedures

Studies were coded using the definitions of the traditional five-factor model (Kilmann & Thomas, 1977) into categories of avoid, accommodate, compete, compromise, and collaborate. When categories differed, definitions were used to easily match those strategies with the ones used in the five-factor model. In the studies using the three-factor model (Putnam & Wilson, 1982; Schuekle & McDowell, 1990; Temkin & Cummings, 1986; Ting-Toomey, 1986; Ugbah & DeWine, 1986), the nonconfrontation strategy was entered as both accommodation and avoidance, the control strategy categorized as competitive, and the solution-orientation strategy was counted in both the compromising and collaborating categories.

Statistical Procedures

The summary statistics of each study were converted to correlations to quantify the magnitude of outcomes attributable to gender differences in CMS selection. A positive correlation (a randomly assigned designation) indicates that male means were higher on a particular strategy, while a negative correlation indicates female means were higher. The benchmark for evaluating the effect size is found in Cohen (1977): $r = .10$ is a small effect; $r = .30$ is a medium effect; $r = .50$ is a large effect.

The correlations were weighted for sample size and then averaged. Each average correlation was assessed to determine if the variance in the observed sample correlations was larger than expected by random sampling error (Rosenthal, 1984).

To detect a moderator, the sum of the squared error is assessed using a chi-square test. A nonsignificant chi-square indicates that the amount of variability is probably the result of chance, whereas a significant chi-square indicates that the amount of variability is probably the result of some type of moderator variable.

The search for moderator variables was guided by those issues frequently cited in the literature as potentially problematic. Issues such as the sample population used (Konovosky, Jaster, & McDonald, 1988), instruments and methods used to measure conflict management strategy selection (Womack, 1988), the gender of the author(s) (Eagly, 1987), and publication bias (Rosenthal, 1984) were coded.

Table 2.1
Gender Differences and CMS Selection Vital Statistics

Author(s) of Study	Year Completed	Sex Differences	Publication Status	Sample Population	Method Used	Author's Sex	Sample Size
Baxter & Shepherd	1978	Yes	Published	College Students	MODE	Female	57
Bell, Chafetz, & Horn	1982	Yes	Published	Married Couples	Interview	Both	60
Berryman-Fink & Bruner	1987	Yes	Published	College Students	MODE	Female	147
Chanin & Schneer	1984	Yes	Published	College Students	MODE	Both	94
Chusmir & Mills	1989	No/Yes	Published	Managers	MODE	Both	201
Euwema & Van de Vliert	1990	Yes	Convention	Employees	Survey	Male	215
Fitzpatrick & Winke	1979	Yes	Published	College Students	Survey	Both	170
Gayle	1991	Yes	Published	Managers/ Employees	OCCI	Female	304
Goering	1986	Yes	Convention	College Students	Survey	Female	22
Howell	1981	No	Dissertation	Managers & Employees	MODE	Male	52
Kilmann & Thomas	1977	Yes	Published	H. Sch. & College	MODE	Male	205
Kofron	1986	Yes	Dissertation	Managers & Employees	MODE	Male	300

Author	Year		Publication	Sample	Method	Gender	N
Konovsky, Jaster & McDonald	1988	Yes	Convention	Employees	MODE	Both	586
Monroe, DiSalvo, Lewis & Borzi	1989	Yes	Published	Managers & Employees	Describe	Male	381
Nadler & Nadler	1988	Yes	Convention	Managers & Employees	Scenario	Both	160
Nowak	1984	No	Dissertation	Married Couples	Interview	Female	40
Papa & Natalle	1989	Yes	Published	Employees	Observe	Both	26
Putnam & Wilson	1982	Yes	Published	Employees	OCCI	Both	120
Rahim	1983	Yes	Published	Managers	Survey	Male	100
Renwick	1977	No	Published	Managers	Survey	Female	95
Revilla	1984	No	Dissertation	Employees/Managers	MODE	Female	113
Roloff & Greenberg	1979	Yes	Published	High School Students	Survey	Male	175
Rossi & Todd-Mancillas	1987	Yes	Published	Managers	Scenarios	Both	80
Ruble & Stander	1990	Yes	Convention	Employees	MODE	Male	62
Schuekle & McDowell	1990	No	Convention	Students	OCCI	Male	217
Schockley-Zalabak	1981	No	Published	Managers	Survey	Female	69

Table 2.1 (continued)

Author(s) of Study	Year Completed	Sex Differences	Publication Status	Sample Population	Method Used	Author's Sex	Sample Size
Schockley-Zalabak & Morley	1984	No/Yes	Published	College Students	MODE	Both	61
				Managers & Employees	MODE	Both	100
Sone	1981	Yes	Dissertation	Employees	Survey	Male	110
Sternberg & Soriano	1984	No	Published	College Students	Survey	Male	32
Temkin & Cummings	1986	No	Published	Managers & Employees	OCCI	Both	162
Thomas	1971	Yes	Dissertation	Managers	Survey	Male	253
Ting-Toomey	1986	Yes	Published	College Students	OCCI	Female	303
Ugbah & Dewine	1986	Yes	Convention	College Students	Survey	Both	175
Yelsma & Brown	1985	Yes	Published	Married Couples	Survey	Male	182
Zammuto, London & Rowland	1979	Yes	Published	College Students	Survey	Male	106

RESULTS

Overall findings revealed a small average effect size for each of the five conflict strategies. The effect sizes for each conflict management strategy reported in all studies are listed in Table 2.2. In Table 2.3, the effect sizes are grouped into conflict management strategy categories and displayed.

In the 26 studies employing 4,210 respondents, the average effect size of gender differences in avoiding strategy section was very small ($r = -.045$). No moderator variables were detected ($X^2 = 23.35$, $df = 26$, $p > .05$).

In the 25 studies employing 3,490 respondents, the average effect size of gender differences in accommodating strategy selection was very small ($r = -.046$). No moderator variables were detected ($X^2 = 17.34$, $df = 25$, $p > .05$).

In the 29 studies employing 4,396 respondents, the average effect size of gender differences in competitive strategy selection was small ($r = .115$). No moderator variables were detected ($X^2 = 34.84$, $df = 29$, $p > .05$).

In the 30 studies employing 4,520 respondents, the average effect size of gender differences in compromising strategy selection was small ($r = -.114$). No moderator variables were detected ($X^2 = 31.82$, $df = 30$, $p > .05$).

In the 28 studies, employing 4,418 respondents, the average effect size was very small ($r = -.054$). No moderator variables were detected ($X^2 = 36.70$, $df = 28$, $p > .05$).

DISCUSSION

In this investigation, the magnitude of the average effect sizes varied substantially. Gender-based differences were detected for the strategies of competition and compromise. Although the average effects were small, males employed more competitive strategies and females employed more compromising strategies. These results may be interpreted using the Binomial Effect Size Display (Rosenthal & Rubin, 1982) (see Table 2.4). Our meta-analysis reveals that males are 27% more likely than females to use competitive strategies and females are 27% more likely than males to use compromising strategies. In these areas, the meta-analysis offers limited support for expectancy theory.

The search for moderator variables did not reveal any conclusive evidence that the sample population, type of instrument used to measure CMS selection, method employed, gender of the author(s), or publication status, influenced the findings in any way. Thus, the findings of this study lend some credence to the idea that individuals employ stable conflict management strategies across varying situations and contexts.

The conflict model that emerges suggests that compromising and competitive strategies may be separate orientations intrinsically tied to gender roles rather than processes that emerge over the length of the conflict interaction.

Table 2.2
Effect Sizes

Author(s) of Study	Effect Size By Strategy				
	AV[1]	AC	CP	CM	CL
Baxter & Shepherd	-.001	-.106	.394	-.106	-.106
Bell, Chafetz, & Horn			.270		
Berryman-Fink & Bruner	-.020	-.074	.171	-.180	-.130
Chanin & Schneer	.012	.042	.064	-.297	.220
Chusmir & Mills	-.114	.028	.086	.091	-.084
	.016	.007	.040	-.102	-.010
Euwema & Van de Vliert	-.052	.007	.166	-.132	-.007
Gayle	-.106	-.055	.212	-.147	-.001
Goering				-.520	
Howell	.071	-.233	.209	-.081	-.235
Kilmann & Thomas	.069	-.069	.098	-.104	.098
Kofron	-.119	-.070	.173	-.070	.005
Konovsky, Jaster & McDonald	-.080		-.005	-.040	-.040
Nadler & Nadler	.153		.181	-.199	-.224
Papa & Natalle		.016	.070	.129	.172
Putnam & Wilson	-.013	-.013	.030	-.129	-.129
Renwick	-.155	.056	-.075	-.200	.152
Revilla	-.191	.034	.071	.028	.019
Rossi & Todd-Mancillas			.001	-.210	
Ruble & Stander	-.125	-.125	.250	-.329	-.125
Schuekle & McDowell	-.002	-.002	.123	-.200	-.200
Schockley-Zalabak	-.001	.001	.001	-.001	.001

Table 2.2 (continued)

Author(s) of Study	AV	AC	CP	CM	CL
Schockley-Zalabak & Morley	.001	.001	.235	-.289	-.001
	.001	-.001	.112	-.057	.001
Sone	-.042	-.246	.157	-.172	-.098
Temkin & Cummings	-.001	-.001	.001	-.001	-.001
Thomas	-.033	-.040	.154	-.126	.044
Ting-Toomey	.001	.001	.160	-.108	-.108
Ugbah & Dewine	-.189	-.189	.059	-.189	-.184
Yelsma & Brown			-.088	-.088	
Zammuto, London & Rowland	-.034	-.164	.261	-.017	-.164

[1]AV = Avoid; AC = Accomodation; CP = Compete; CM = Compromise; CL = Collaboration

Table 2.3
Average Effect Sizes

	r	N	K	X^2
Avoid	-0.045	4210	26	23.35
Accomodate	-0.046	3490	25	17.34
Compete	0.115	4376	29	34.84
Compromise	-0.114	4520	30	31.82
Collaborate	-0.054	4418	28	36.70

NOTE: In these tables a positive correlation (randomly assigned designation) indicates that male means were higher on a particular strategy, while a negative correlation indicates female means were higher.

Perhaps females relate to other individuals in conflict situations first on the basis of stereotypes. In any case, the predisposition for females to employ slightly more relationally oriented or compromising strategies and males to use slightly more win-lose type of competing strategies as the foundation of their conflict management repertoire suggests a starting point for developing a processual model of conflict interactions. The real question is when and why males and females move beyond those stereotypes and what makes that movement possible.

Table 2.4
Binomial Effect Size Display

Compromise:

Female	56%	44%
Male	44%	56%
	High	Low

$r = -.114$

Compete:

Female	56%	44%
Male	44%	56%
	High	Low

$r = .115$

NOTE: A positive correlation (randomly assigned designation) indicates male means were higher on a particular strategy, while a negative correlation indicates female means were higher.

NOTES

1. Studies finding sex-based differences are Baxter and Shepherd (1978); Bell, Chafetz, and Horn (1982); Berryman-Fink and Bruner (1987); Chanin and Schneer (1984); Euwema and Van de Vliert (1990); Fitzpatrick and Winke (1979); Goering (1986); Kilman and Thomas (1977); Kofron (1986); Konovosky, Jaster, and McDonald (1988); Nadler and Nadler (1988); Putnam and Wilson (1982); Rahim (1983); Roloff and Greenberg (1979); Rossi and Todd-Mancillas (1987); Ruble and Stander (1990); Schuekle and McDowell (1990); Shockley-Zalabak and Morley (1984); Sone (1981); Thomas (1971); Ting-Toomey (1986); Ugbah and DeWine (1986); Yelsma and Brown (1985), and Zammuto, London, and Rowland (1979).

2. Studies failing to find sex-based differences are Chusmir and Mills (1989); Gayle (1991); Howell (1981); Nowak (1984); Renwick (1977); Revilla (1984); Shockley-Zalabak (1981); Shockley-Zalabak and Morley (1984); Sternberg and Soriano (1984); and Temkin and Cummings (1986).

3. Searches of *Social Sciences Citation Index, Psychological Abstracts, Dissertation Abstracts International, ERIC, ABI/Inform, Management Contents Database, Business Index,* and *Index to Journals in Speech Communication* from 1965 to 1990 were conducted. Other studies were identified by searches of the International Communication Association, Speech Communication Association, and Western States Communication Association convention programs from 1986 to 1990.

REFERENCES

Baxter, L. A., & Shepherd, T. L. (1978). Sex-role identity, sex of other, and affective relationship as determinants of interpersonal conflict-management styles. *Sex Roles, 6.* 813-825.

Bell, D. C., Chafetz, J. S., & Horn, L. H. (1982). Marital conflict resolution: A study of strategies and outcomes. *Journal of Family Issues, 3,* 111-131.

Berryman-Fink, C., & Brunner, C. C. (1987). The effects of sex of source and target on interpersonal conflict management styles. *The Southern Speech Communication Journal, 53,* 38-48.

Burgoon, B. R., Dillard, J. P., & Doran, N. E. (1983). Friendly or unfriendly persuasion: The effects of violations of expectations by males and females. *Human Communication Research, 10,* 283-294.

Chanin, M. N., & Schneer, J. A. (1984). A study of relationship between Jungian personality dimensions and conflict-handling behavior. *Human Relations, 37,* 865-879.

Chusmir, L. H., & Mills, J. (1989). Gender differences in conflict resolution styles of managers: At work and at home. *Sex Roles, 20,* 149-163.

Cohen, J. (1977). *Statistical power analysis for the behavioral sciences.* New York: Academic Press.

Eagly, A. H. (1987). *Sex differences in social behavior: A social-role interpretation.* Hillsdale, NJ: Erlbaum.

Euwema, M. C., & Van de Vliert, E. (1990, June). *The influence of sex on managers' perception attribution, stress and behavior in conflict with their subordinates.* Paper presented at the meeting of the International Association for Conflict Management, Vancouver, BC

Fitzpatrick, M. A., & Winke, J. (1979). You always hurt the one you love: Strategies and tactics in interpersonal conflict. *Communication Quarterly, 27,* 3-11.

Gayle, B. M. (1991). Sex equity in workplace conflict management. *Journal of Applied Communication, 19,* 152-169.

Goering, E. M. (1986, November). Context, definition, and sex of actor as variables in conflict management style. Paper presented at the meeting of the Speech Communication Association, Chicago, IL.

Howell, J. L. (1981). *The identification, description and analysis of competencies focused on conflict management in a human services organization: An exploratory study.* Unpublished doctoral dissertation, University of Massachusetts, Amherst, MA.

Kilmann, R. H., & Thomas, K. W. (1977). Developing a forced-choice measure of conflict-handling behavior: The "mode" instrument. *Educational and Psychological Measurement, 37,* 309-323.

Kofron, C. P. (1986). *A structural perspective of interpersonal conflict management.* Unpublished doctoral dissertation, Saint Louis University, Saint Louis, MO.

Konovsky, M. A., Jaster, F., & McDonald, M. A. (1988, November). Using parametric statistics to explore the underlying structures of the Thomas-Kilmann conflict MODE survey. Paper presented at the meeting of the Speech Communication Association, New Orleans, LA.

Monroe, C., DiSalvo, V. S., Lewis, J. J., & Borzi, M. G. (1989). Conflict behaviors of difficult subordinates: Interactive effects of gender. *Southern States Communication Journal, 54,* 12-23.

Nadler, M. K., & Nadler, L. B. (1988, November). Sex differences in perceptions of and orientations toward conflict resolving behaviors in the organizational environment. Paper presented at the meeting of the Speech Communication Association, New Orleans, LA.

Nowak, M. (1984). *Conflict resolution and power seeking behavior of androgynous and traditional married couples.* Unpublished doctoral dissertation, Michigan State University, Ann Arbor, MI.

Papa, M. J., & Natalle, E. J. (1989). Gender, strategy selection, and discussion satisfaction in interpersonal conflict. *Western Journal of Speech Communication, 53,* 260-272.

Putnam, L. L., & Wilson, C. E. (1982). Communicative strategies in organizational conflicts: Reliability and validity of a measurement scale. In M. Burgoon (Ed.), *Communication Yearbook 6* (pp. 629-652). Beverly Hills: Sage.

Rahim, A. (1983). A measure of styles of handling interpersonal conflict. *Academy of Management Journal, 26,* 368-376.

Renwick, P. A. (1977). Effects of sex differences on the perception and management of conflict: An exploratory study. *Organizational Behavior and Human Performance, 19,* 403-415.

Revilla, V. M. (1984). *Conflict management styles of men and women in higher education.* Unpublished doctoral dissertation, University of Pittsburgh, Pittsburgh, PA.

Roloff, M. E., & Greenberg, B. S. (1979). Sex differences in choice of modes of conflict resolution in real-life and television. *Communication Quarterly, 27,* 3-12.

Rosenthal, R. (1984). *Meta-analytic procedures for social research.* Beverly Hills: Sage.

Rosenthal, R., & Rubin, D. B. (1982). A simple general response display of magnitude of experiential effect. *Journal of Educational Psychology, 74,* 166-169.

Rossi, A. M., & Todd-Mancillas, W. R. (1987). Male and female differences in managing conflicts. In L. P. Stewart & S. Ting-Toomey (Eds.), *Communication, gender, and sex roles in diverse interaction contexts* (pp. 96-104). Norwood, NJ: Ablex.

Ruble, T. L., & Stander, N. E. (1990, June). *Effects of role and gender on conflict-handling styles.* Paper presented at the meeting of the International Association for Conflict Management, Vancouver, BC.

Schuekle, D., & McDowell, E. (1990, May). A study of the relationship between willingness to communicate and preferred conflict strategy: Implications for teaching communication and conflict. Paper presented at the International Communication Association Conference, Chicago.

Shockley-Zalabak, P. (1981). The effects of sex differences on the preference for utilization of conflict styles of managers in a work setting: An exploratory study. *Public Personnel Management Journal, 10,* 289-295.

Shockley-Zalabak, P., & Morley, D. D. (1984). Sex differences in conflict style preferences. *Communication Research Reports, 1,* 28-32.

Sone, P. G. (1981). *The effects of gender on managers' resolution of superior-subordinate conflict.* Unpublished doctoral dissertation, Arizona State University, Tempe, AZ.

Sternberg, R. J., & Soriano, L. J. (1984). Styles of conflict resolution. *Journal of Personality and Social Psychology, 47,* 115-126.

Temkin, T., & Cummings, H. W. (1986). The use of conflict management behaviors in voluntary organizations: An exploratory study. *Journal of Voluntary Action Research, 15,* 5-18.

Thomas, K. W. (1971). *Conflict-handling modes in interdepartmental relations.*

Unpublished doctoral dissertation, Purdue University, West Lafayette, IN.

Ting-Toomey, S. (1986). Conflict communication styles in black and white subjective cultures. In Y. Y. Kim (Ed.), *Interethnic communication: Current research* (pp. 75-88). Newbury Park, CA: Sage.

Todd-Mancillas, W. R., & Rossi, A. (1985). Gender differences in the management of personnel disputes. *Women's Studies in Communication, 8*, 25-33.

Ugbah, S. D., & DeWine, S. (1986, November). Conflict management and relational disengagement: Are the communication strategies the same? Paper presented at the meeting of the Speech Communication Association, Chicago.

Womack, D. F. (1988). A review of conflict instruments in organizational settings. *Management Communication Quarterly, 1*, 437-445.

Yelsma, P. & Brown, C. T. (1985). Gender roles, biological sex, and predisposition to conflict management. *Sex Roles, 12*, 28-32.

Zammuto, M. L., London, M., & Rowland, K. W. (1979). Effects of sex on commitment and conflict resolution. *Journal of Applied Psychology, 64*, 227-231.

3

Gender Differences in Critical Incidents Reported by Elderly Health Care Consumers: A Narrative Analysis

Gary L. Kreps

In comparison with other age groups, the aged are disproportionately high users of health care services. They comprise an extremely important population of health care consumers whose lives are dramatically affected by the health care system, especially those elders who receive long-term care in nursing homes (Callahan, 1987; Dunkle & Kart, 1990; Koff, 1988; Kreps, 1990; Nussbaum, 1990; Pegels, 1981; Verbrugge, 1984). To ensure that elderly health care consumers are receiving the best possible care, it is important to evaluate the effectiveness of the health care system in serving the aged. Since women live longer than men, they comprise a larger proportion of the population of elderly health care consumers (Verbrugge, 1989). Yet, there is little information about the comparative health care experiences of elderly men and women (Markides, 1989). The field research program reported here is designed to identify and examine key events, from the unique perspectives of elderly male and female health care consumers, that have increased or decreased their satisfaction with health care services.

RESEARCH DESIGN

This study combines survey research and ethnographic research methodologies to examine the health care experiences of elderly individuals. While the study is designed to describe the perspective of a particular population (elderly health care consumers), it also attempts to provide a deeper understanding of the patterns of interaction and significant symbols that make up the health care culture for male and female elderly health care consumers in order to determine whether this culture is the same for men and women. In-depth, open-ended, critical incident interviews were conducted with elders in institutional (nursing home) and noninstitutional (home) contexts, to elicit personal narratives from them describing satisfying and dissatisfying health care events they had experienced.

The Critical Incident Technique (CIT) is an innovative research strategy rarely used by health communication researchers, but has the potential to generate valid and reliable communication data that can be easily used to address practical problems. CIT combines survey and ethnographic methods to gather data about specific populations. It involves gathering self-report data (using either interviews or questionnaires) about respondents' most memorable positive and negative experiences within a specific social context (Flanagan, 1954). It is a straightforward, powerful, systematic, tightly controlled, yet adaptive qualitative research strategy. This method is particularly effective in gathering narrative data from health care consumers and/or providers to assess the quality of health care practices (Andersson & Nilsson, 1964; Ronan & Latham, 1974; Stein, 1981).

The narrative paradigm suggests that the telling of stories is a fundamental and universal human activity (Fisher, 1987). People tell stories to recount and account for their experiences, using narratives to constitute social reality. Smith (1987) explains that "it is through the telling of stories about ourselves and the events around us that we define reality, explain who we are to one another, and set the stage for future action. As we listen to the stories others tell us we learn what is important to them, what they believe is memorable, who in their stories is what kind of person, and what kinds of values justify decisions and actions" (p. 17). The use of CIT in health communication research is theoretically grounded in the narrative paradigm, since such research is designed to collect and examine the stories individuals tell about their most satisfying and dissatisfying experiences as consumers and/or providers of health care. Analyses of the stories gathered through CIT can identify the issues that are of greatest concern in providing effective and satisfying health care. The personal nature of narrative accounts of reality can reveal the unique voices and gender-specific experiences of elderly male and female health care consumers.

During the spring semester of 1989 (January 1989 through May 1989), 29 health communication students (both undergraduate and graduate students) at Northern Illinois University were paired with elderly residents of the DeKalb County Nursing Home. The residents were selected by the director of the nursing home based upon their interest in receiving visitors, their abilities to communicate, and their willingness to participate in this study. Students made weekly, friendly visits to the residents over the course of the semester to share information and establish relationships with the residents. At the end of the semester, each student conducted a critical incident technique interview with the resident. (In four cases, students were unable to successfully complete the interviews with a nursing home resident, because the residents were unable or unwilling to participate in the interview, and the students were encouraged to interview other noninstitutionalized elders, providing an opportunity to compare the health care experiences of institutionalized and noninstitutionalized elders.) The weekly visits increased rapport, respect, and understanding between students and residents, which helped the students to elicit full and candid responses from the elders in the critical incident interviews.

ANALYSIS AND RESULTS

Interviews were conducted with twenty-five nursing home residents and four noninstitutionalized elders in late April and early May 1989. The interviews were tape-recorded, transcribed, and submitted to CIT incident classification system analysis. Three general content categories for critical incidents were identified for this sample: (1) Satisfaction or dissatisfaction with communication, including positive or negative judgments of listening behaviors, caring, sensitivity, information giving, as well as whether communication is rude, soothing, supportive, or irritating. (2) Satisfaction or dissatisfaction with facilities, including positive or negative evaluations of cleanliness, food, equipment, expenses, staffing, or any special activities (such as arts and crafts or parties). (3) Satisfaction or dissatisfaction with treatment, including positive or negative judgments of the competence of health care providers, knowledge of personnel, conscientiousness and responsiveness of personnel, the effectiveness of treatments, and whether their health conditions were getting better or worse.

A content-analytic coding scheme was developed where three general judgments, reflecting the incident categories, were to be made by coders: 1. Is this critical incident a predominantly positive or negative incident? 2. Does this critical incident pertain predominantly to: a. Characteristics of a health care facility? b. Characteristics of health care treatment? c. Characteristics of communication? 3. Within each critical incident that was judged to pertain to communication, is each communication incident described primarily with or from: a. Health care staff? b. Nursing home residents or health care consumers? c. Family or friends? d.Media (radio, television, etc.)? e. Young children (including grandchildren)?

The transcripts of all 29 interviews were content analyzed by the researcher. A random sample of the transcribed interviews was selected and submitted to analysis by a trained coder to test the reliability of the coding scheme. Inter-rater reliability between this coder and the researcher was very high, with the two coders agreeing on 24 out of 25 coding judgments, accounting for a .96 level of agreement.

Demographic Data

Demographic data concerning the respondents' sex, age, health condition, and living context (institutionalized or noninstituionalized) were tabulated. There were eight male respondents and 21 female respondents. Respondents' ages ranged from 52 to 99. Mean age for male respondents was 76, while mean age for female respondents was 79. The respondents were divided into two subgroups based upon age: (1) Young-old respondents (below 80 years of age) $n = 12$; (2) Old-old respondents (80 years of age and above) $n = 17$. Only four of the respondents were living at home; the other twenty-five respondents were nursing home residents. Only seven of the respondents reported having no major health problems, while the vast majority of the respondents ($n = 22$; 76%) reported having serious, long-term ailments such as multiple sclerosis, strokes, paralysis, heart disease, epilepsy, arthritis, diabetes, cataracts, and broken hips.

Critical Incidents

Analysis of the twenty-nine interviews generated 151 separate critical incidents. Of these 151 incidents, seventy-seven were judged to be positive critical incidents (describing satisfying health care situations), and seventy-four were judged to be negative critical incidents (describing dissatisfying health care situations). The vast majority of the critical incidents generated in the study pertained to communication issues, as opposed to facility or treatment issues, with communication accounting for 71 of the 151 incidents (47%). Facilities' critical incidents accounted for 32% of all critical incidents, and treatment critical incidents accounted for 21% of all critical incidents. Chi-square tests indicated that respondents identified communication concerns significantly more frequently than they identified facility concerns, where X^2 (1) = 4.44, $p <. 05$. Furthermore, respondents identified communication issues significantly more often than treatment issues, where $X^2(1) = 14.76$, $p < .05$.

Male/Female Respondents Data

Female respondents reported 116 of the 151 total critical incidents (77%) which is 5% higher than their representation within the research sample (72%). Females were also more likely to report positive critical incidents than negative incidents (61+, 55-), accounting for 79% of the positive incidents generated (7% higher than their representation in the sample). Males, conversely, were more likely to report negative critical incidents than positive incidents (16+, 19-), accounting for 26% of the negative incidents (2% more than their representation in the sample).

Females reported 86% of all communication critical incidents (14% higher than their representation in the sample). Interestingly, they were more likely to describe positive communication incidents (94% of all positive communication incidents; 22% above their representation in the sample) than negative communication incidents, although they reported 77% of all the negative communication incidents (5% above their representation in the sample). Males, conversely, reported more negative communication incidents (23% of all negative communication incidents) than positive communication incidents (6% of all positive communication incidents), although they were underrepresented in both categories in respect to their percentage of the sample.

Males and females reported combined positive and negative facilities critical incidents in close proportion to their respective representations in the sample (females accounted for 75% and males accounted for 25% of these incidents). But, their tendencies to report positive and negative facilities incidents varied dramatically. Males were more likely to describe negative facilities critical incidents (accounting for 32% of the negative facilities incidents; 4% above their representation in the sample), while females were more inclined to report positive facilities incidents (83% of all facilities incidents; 11% above their representation in the sample).

Males reported a greater percentage, proportionally, of treatment critical incidents (40% of all treatment incidents; 12% above their percentage of the sample) than females. Males were particularly more likely to report positive incidents concerning treatment (50% of all positive treatment incidents; 22% above their representation in the sample), while their presentation of negative treatment incidents was closely in proportion with their representation in the sample (accounting for 29% of all negative treatment incidents). While females reported negative treatment incidents in proportion to their representation in the sample (71% of all negative treatment incidents), their description of positive treatment incidents was very low proportionally (accounting for only 50% of positive treatment incidents; 22% below their representation in the sample). Chi-square tests indicated that these differences between males and females across the communication, facility, and treatment categories were significant; that is, X^2 (1) = 8.87, p < .05.

Representative Critical Incidents

Several of the critical incidents gathered in this study attest to the importance of effective health communication between health care providers and elderly health care recipients in enhancing the quality of care elders receive. Due to the significantly higher presentation of communication themes in the study, several exemplar communication critical incidents will be presented here.

Positive Communication Incident 1

A 69 year old female nursing home resident, who was recovering from a stroke, recounted the following positive critical incident describing the therapeutic influences of supportive touching behaviors and cheerful smiles from health care staff members.

> I'll tell you, half the battle is having nice people to work with because a smile from a nurse and an arm around a body makes you feel like it's all worth it. In fact, I had one nurse, came in, coming in the morning and dress me, and she was a pretty girl, and I said she had a nice smile. And I said always keep that smile because that's half the battle for people getting well. It really is. It makes you feel good.

Positive Communication Incident 2

A 92-year-old female nursing home resident with heart problems recounted this critical incident, describing how health care staff members communicated sensitively and caringly with her in times when she felt particularly vulnerable. Note her recurrent references in this critical incident to the descriptors "kind" and "considerate."

> Oh, twice (I had something). I had nightmares and they came in and took care of me and satisfied. It's after I, that happened since I've been here. They were very kind about it - never referred to it again. It was a nurse. They were so kind and considerate—which is wonderful. It's the attention. They, they treat you as though you're a person. That's considerate. You aren't just a someone who's paying out money and they just have to take care of you. They don't make you feel that way.

Negative Communication Incident 1

Ineffective communication in health care is a serious impediment to achieving health care goals, and several critical incidents described ineffective communication between health care providers and residents. An 85 year old male nursing home resident, who was partially paralyzed, recounted the following critical incident that illustrates the lack of concern and respect with which his health care providers treated him, and also indicates the negative reactions he had to this insensitive interaction.

> Well, I'm not very happy with my doctor. Well, the doctor we had died from cancer and we had to get a new doctor. So, I went down to the clinic and got a new doctor. I told him what the other doctor was giving me and my wife, and he would not listen to me at all. And he wouldn't go to the old doctor's office and get the papers and the girl there wouldn't give it to him. I was unhappy with that doctor. I told him, "get the hell out of here," one day. So he didn't come back again. He does. You gotta have a doctor. So, he comes in once a month and looks at me and asks "how are you doing?" I say "ok" and he goes. They know it. You don't know anything. The patient don't know anything.

Negative Communication Incident 2

An 80-year-old male nursing home resident with heart problems and recovering from a stroke recounted the following disturbing critical incident about insensitive health communication where the health care provider does not provide him with relevant health information nor receive his informed consent for a very delicate and potentially uncomfortable treatment. The negative reaction this form of health communication engenders is made abundantly clear in this critical incident.

> They're all ignorant. They just don't have no respect for nobody. A couple of days ago a little girl, a little lady named Dawn, she came in to my room and said "Jeff, you're getting a suppository." I'm laying in bed naked on my side and she shoved a suppository up my asshole. She didn't ask me if I wanted it or nothing. She didn't tell me anything and it makes me pissed off. I haven't shit yet either.

DISCUSSION

The sample used in this study is the greatest limitation in this research, both in terms of the limited size of the total sample and the limited numbers of male respondents. This study examined the critical incidents that satisfy and dissatisfy elderly health care consumers. This is a very small sample of the total population of elderly health care consumers, with most of the respondents residing in the same nursing home. Moreover, the sample was not randomly selected, but represents a purposive sample of elders who were willing and able to provide critical incident data. Due to the sample limitations, care must be taken in generalizing these findings beyond the sample studied. Future research can help to validate and expand upon these findings by studying additional elderly consumers in different geographic areas and in different social contexts.

This study clearly illustrates the differences in the ways male and female elders interpret critical incidents in health care and communicate narratives about those incidents. Females are more likely to focus on social communicative aspects of health care, while males are more likely to dwell on the functional instrumental aspects of health care, supporting past research about traditional sex-role differences, where females have been shown to be more sensitive to communication issues than males and where males have been conditioned to adopt instrumental rather than affective perspectives on reality. Males were also more likely to dwell on negative incidents in this study while females focused on more positive incidents, indicating a greater level of personal adjustment to health care systems among female elders than among males. This may be due to female elders' higher levels of communicative involvement in health care and the greater number of female residents within nursing homes, providing females with better abilities and more opportunities to receive social support than their male counterparts and enhancing their positive interpretations of the health care system. These findings may also indicate gender differences in locus of control, where female elders demonstrate greater adaptability to their loss of personal control within the health care system than their male counterparts, who have been socialized over the course of their lives to maintain high levels of personal and social control and find it very difficult to give up this control.

Combining the data generated by the male and female elders, this study clearly illustrates the importance of sensitive and informative communication in health care for the elderly. Communication is the greatest single source of satisfaction and dissatisfaction for the total sample of elderly health care consumers studied. Health care providers must recognize the impact of effective and ineffective communication on the quality of health care for aged consumers. Care must be taken to design health care facilities and train health care providers to meet the unique communication needs of elderly health care consumers.

REFERENCES

Andersson, B., & Nilsson, S. (1964). Studies in the reliability and validity of the critical incident technique. *Journal of Applied Psychology, 48* (6), 398-403.

Callahan, D. (1987). *Setting limits: Medical goals in an aging society.* New York: Simon and Schuster.

Dunkle, R. E., & Kart, C. S. (1990). Long-term care. In. K. F. Ferraro (Ed.), *Gerontology: Perspectives and issues* (pp. 225-246). New York: Springer.

Fisher, W. R. (1987). *Human communication as narration: Toward a philosophy of reason, value and action.* Columbia, SC: University of South Carolina Press.

Flanagan, J.C. (1954). The critical incident technique. *Psychological Bulletin, 51* (July), 327-357.

Frey, L. R., Botan, C. H., Friedman, P. G., & Kreps, G. L. (1991). *Investigating communication: An introduction to research methods.* Englewood Cliffs, NJ: Prentice- Hall.

Koff, T. H. (1988). *New approaches to health care for an aging population.* San Francisco: Jossey-Bass.

Kreps, G. L. (1990). A systematic analysis of health communication with the aged. In H. Giles, N. Coupland, & J. M. Wiemann (Eds.), *Communication, health care, and the elderly* (pp. 135-154). Manchester, England: University of Manchester Press.

Kreps, G. L., & Thornton, B. C. (1992). *Health communication: Theory and practice* (2nd ed.). Prospect Heights, IL: Waveland Press.

Markides, K. S. (1989). Aging, gender, race/ethnicity, class and health: A conceptual overview. In K. S. Markides (Ed.), *Aging and health: Perspectives on gender, race, ethnicity, and class* (pp. 9-21). Newbury Park, CA: Sage Publications.

Nussbaum, J. F. (1990). Communication and the nursing home environment: Survivability as a function of resident-nursing staff affinity. In H. Giles, N. Coupland, & J. M. Wiemann (Eds.), *Communication, health care, and the elderly* (pp. 155-171). Manchester, England: University of Manchester Press.

Pegels, C. C. (1981). *Health care and the elderly.* Rockville, MD: Aspen Systems.

Ronan, W. W., & Latham, G. P. (1974). The reliability and validity of the critical incidents technique: A closer look. *Studies in Personnel Psychology, 6,* 53-64.

Smith, D. H. (1987, February). Stories, values, and patient care decisions. Paper presented to the University of South Florida Communicating With Patients conference, Tampa, FL.

Stein, D. S. (1981). Designing performance-oriented training programs. *Training and Development Journal, 35,* 12-16.

Verbrugge, L. M. (1984). Longer life but worsening health? Trends in health and mortality of middle-aged and older persons. *Milbank Memorial Fund Quarterly, 62,* 475-519.

Verbrugge, L. M. (1989). Gender, aging, and health. In K. S. Markides (Ed.), *Aging and health: Perspectives on gender, race, ethnicity, and class* (pp. 23-78). Newbury Park, CA: Sage Publications.

4

Developmental Differences in MBA Students: An Examination of Life Stories and Career Histories

Susan Schick Case and
Lorraine Thompson

Traditionally, the population from which business schools have drawn applicants was the same as that from which businesses drew their white collar employees: a relatively homogeneous pool of white American males. So, the curricula of business schools have been designed to meet the needs of these students. However, the composition of the American workforce has changed dramatically over the last thirty years. In 1980, 43% of the total workforce was women. Throughout the 1990s, 85% of the net growth in the American labor pool will be comprised of white women, people of color, and immigrants, with a projection that by the year 2000, these groups will comprise approximately 50% of the total workforce (Johnston & Packer, 1987). This shift in the demographics of the labor force is not reflected in the nation's top business schools, which have experienced a decline of 25% or more in female enrollment since 1990 (when women received 34% of all MBAs awarded in this country), while male enrollment has been slightly up. The percentage of women in incoming classes in 1992 ranged from 16% to 30% (Cowan, 1992; Fuchsberg, 1992).

This increasing trend in the diversity of the workforce has important implications for managerial education. Gallos (1993) found that traditional methods of teaching such as transmitting facts and knowledge, introducing theories and models, developing reasoning skills, discussing frameworks, cases, and readings were not sufficient for the needs of her female students. She found that "the women had clear expectations that all of their learning would touch the core of their central identities" (Gallos, 1993, p. 9). Other researchers have similarly indicated that women are developmentally different from men (Belenky, Clinchy, Goldberger & Tarule 1986; Gallos 1990; Gilligan 1977). All of this research sounds a similar theme. Women's conceptions of themselves, their lives, and the world around them are constructed differently from those of men. Effective graduate programs will recognize and accommodate these differences.

This study explores the career development experiences of MBA students. Our goal was to examine the gender-based developmental differences in men's and women's approaches to career assessment and development through a structured, thematic analysis of life stories and career histories. Our study suggests MBA women and men approach their own managerial development quite differently.

RELEVANT LITERATURE

Traditional theories of career and personal development focus on the centrality of work to identity and the need for separation and individuation in the search for maturity and personal empowerment (Erikson, 1968; Gallos, 1990; Levinson, 1978). Adult development has typically meant increased autonomy and separation from others as a means of strengthening identity, empowering the self, and charting a life course (Gallos, 1990).

It has already been established that attachment to significant other people is an important source of identity, maturity, and personal power for women (Bateson, 1989; Eichenbaum & Orbach, 1988; Josselson, 1987). The central role that attachments and relationships play in women's identity formation and in their conceptions of mature adult selves is incongruent with traditional theories of career and personal development. In earlier studies (Erikson, 1968; Kohlberg, 1976), women's focus on intimacy, intense attachments, concern for relationships, and context-based decisions were cited as deficient behaviors with respect to developing as an adult. Barnett and Baruch (1980) have reframed these perspectives, not as deficiencies but as differences, and have noted the importance to women of stressing both relationships and personal achievement over the course of a lifetime.

In contrast to men's development, which focuses on the primacy of the occupational role, development for women is tied to understanding and strengthening the self in relationship to others. Attachments and relationships color how they see themselves, their lives, their careers, and their ongoing responsibilities to those around them. Berzoff (1985) found that valued female friendships promoted self-definition, catalyzed change, and provided experiences of self-continuity over time. A similar recurring theme in Hancock's (1989) study of women's life stories was growth and development within the context of relationships. Tannen's (1990) discussion of how boys and girls learn to handle complexity describes boys as learning in terms of complex rules and activities and girls as learning in terms of complex networks of relationships.

Thus, interdependence and a combining of attachment and accomplishment seem key to women's life content and phases. But in addition to playing an important role in the development of women's identities, relationships with others have been found to affect professional development. Stewart and Gudykunst (1982) showed that women perceived both the help of friends and spending a lot of time communicating with their supervisors to be important to their career success. They also found that the perceived importance of skills in obtaining promotions was much greater for men than for women. Similarly, Gallos (1993) noted that support, encouragement, and acceptance from others were critical for women's learning. In their study of how women managers learn from experience, Velsor and Hughes (1990) said "although a manager's tendency to learn from work assignments and hardships does not appear to be gender-related, the capacity of the women to learn from other people is remarkable." Roberts (1991) found in achievement settings women's self-evaluations were more responsive to the valence of the evaluative feedback which they received than were those of men. The lessons women learned after feedback from reflecting on their own behavior helped them perceive themselves as more competent (Valliere, 1986; Velsor & Hughes, 1990). Men, on the other hand, were more responsive to evaluations of their ability when interacting with those who were clearly superiors, "such as coaches or advisors" (Roberts, 1991, p. 305).

This suggests there may be gender-specific ways in which women and men develop. Studies of the effects of relationships on women's career development have shown women's career gains and professional accomplishments to be complements, rather than substitutes, for strong, interdependent relationships (Abramson & Franklin, 1986; Baruch, Barnett, & Rivers, 1983; Bateson, 1989; Gallese, 1985; Gallos, 1993; Hardesty & Jacobs, 1986; Keele, 1986; Roberts & Newton, 1986).

Building on the notion that the centrality of others affects women's definitions of achievement, other studies (Astin & Leland, 1991; Case 1988; Hegelson, 1990; Rosener, 1990; Velsor & Hughes, 1990) have suggested women bring different skills and abilities to the work environment, including a concern for, and attachment to, others. The centrality of others for women, and their desire to balance personal and professional development simultaneously, greatly affects the nature of, though certainly not the value of, women's contributions to their work environments.

Independence, self-sufficiency, and an emphasis on a work career underpin life phases for men, whereas interdependence and a struggle to combine attachment and accomplishment are keys to explaining women's life content and phases. Biological factors related to the different roles men and women play in the reproductive process would be expected to affect career development outcomes and to interact with socially constituted elements of gender roles. Research has already shown us that women's development is not as sequential and predictable as men's nor is it as singularly focused on work and career (Abramson & Franklin, 1986; Bateson, 1989; Gallese, 1985; Gallos, 1990; Hardesty & Jacobs, 1986; Josselson, 1987; Powell & Mainiero, 1992; Roberts & Newton, 1986). As a result, women tend to consider all aspects of their lives as providing valuable insight to their own personal development.

The major means by which task achievements are stressed in the broader context of life is through self-reflection. Bateson (1989) found that women have been particularly interested in the notion of reflexivity, of looking inward as well as outward as a means for personal development. In their study on the development of managers, Velsor and Hughes (1990) found that men tended to focus on achieving skill mastery without feedback or self-reflection, whereas women both sought out feedback and reflected on it. Gallos (1993) found that women made "little distinction between professional learning and personal development. . . . The women had clear expectations that all of their learning would touch the core of their central identities"

(p. 9). Real learning for women implied personal growth.

Researchers (Eccles, 1987; Veroff & Feld, 1970) have emphasized the importance of providing women the flexibility to develop their own conceptions of achievements. Eccles stressed the importance of societal influence on definitions of achievement and its assignment of differential worth to various forms of activities. Similarly, Veroff and Feld (1970) have also noted differences in how men and women choose to express their achievement motives, suggesting that gender-role definitions may play a major role in these choices, with relational components prevalent in women's achievements.

Women focus on the multi-arenas of responsibility and obligations in their lives, juggling and prioritizing, committed to doing everything well. In attempting to strike a balance between their relationships with others and their personal achievements at work, women seek levels of personal satisfaction in both areas. Women still primarily handle family responsibilities in dual-career marriages. As a result, the ability to shift from one arena to another, to divide one's attention, to improvise in new circumstances, has always been important to women. Women appear to compose lives that will honor all their commitments and still enable them to express all their potentials.

HYPOTHESES

In light of the findings outlined above, and based on the hypotheses which follow, our current study attempts to identify, through a structured, thematic analysis of MBA career assessment materials, significant differences in approaches to managerial development that could influence the effectiveness of the MBA program on the development of its participants' managerial skills for their future careers. The written career histories and life stories of a sample of 125 first-year MBA students were analyzed for this study.

Hypothesis 1: The centrality of relationships with others is more critical in women's career development for their learning. than to men's career development.

Interactions with others are necessary for much of women's learning. Because women learn from interacting with others, they not only seek out evaluative feedback but are also more responsive to it. In this study we examined three dimensions of the centrality of others concept, which described the importance of others to career development and learning. These dimensions were: learning from interactions with others, impact of another, and family and friends.

Hypothesis 2: Women focus more on personal development within the context of their careers than do men.

Personal development was defined as task achievement in the broader context of life, not just work achievement. Three particular dimensions were examined in this study: self-reflection, self-confidence, and personal learning.

Hypothesis 3: Women develop their career roles from both work assignments and interactions with others, while men rely more heavily on task assignments for learning their career roles.

The role development concept stressed task achievements in the work context and dealt with two dimensions: achievement through self and tasks involving people.

Hypothesis 4: Women stress both personal achievements and relationships throughout their career, while men focus primarily on personal achievements as their main arena of responsibility.

METHODOLOGY

The initial population for this study consisted of 126 part-time students and 105 full-time students in their first year of an MBA program at a private midwestern university. All students were required to take a 14-week course entitled "Managerial Assessment and Development" their first semester. Excluded from the sample were 26 students who denied permission to use their data for research and those from other cultures (identified by scores on the TOEFL exam), since we assumed that cultural differences in non-English-speaking countries would be too great for comparison across gender. We divided the remaining students by part-time or full-time status, as well as by gender, thus creating four groups to be compared and contrasted.

The mean age of the students surveyed was 27. Since there were only 32 full-time, English-speaking males available for the sample, we used a random number table to randomly select 32 subjects from each of the three remaining groups. Twelve assessment instruments and exercises were used by participants during the first three weeks of this course. From the group of twelve instruments, we selected two for further study, the Career History and the Life Story (Dreyfus, 1991).

In writing their Career History, students were asked to: "Begin with your current job and list the jobs going backward in time. Indicate the dates, the name of the organization, the title of the job, the primary responsibilities or duties of the job, and what, if anything, you learned while you had that job. Use additional pages if necessary. Please include all jobs, full-time and part-time, since you began working."

In the first part of the Life Story exercise, students were asked to: "Think of your life as if it were a book. Most books are divided into chapters. Each chapter tells a kind of story; that is, it has a plot. Think about this, then divide your life into chapters, give each chapter a name and for each provide a short plot summary in two to four sentences. Try to think about the major events in your life as 'turning points' leading from one chapter to the next."

A second part of the exercise required the students to write about a peak and a nadir experience in their lives.

A preliminary code was developed after a thematic analysis of both the Career Histories and Life Stories. To develop this code, a sample of these written assessment instruments was taken from four men and women not in this study sample, but from the same MBA class. In the Career History, the analysis was performed on the section entitled "What I Learned." A content analysis of the complete Life Story was performed. This preliminary analysis led to the development of a specific coding scheme for both instruments. Every occurrence of codable themes, words, and actions was counted.

To obtain reliability information for the code, the Career Histories and Life Stories of sixteen individuals who were involved in the pilot of the Managerial Assessment and Development course were coded by two independent coders. An initial interrater reliability of 86% was obtained between the two coders for both documents for all sixteen individuals. After discussion between the two coders about where the differences in coding had occurred, an additional sample of four histories was coded with 100% reliability. Any reference to the subjects' names or genders had been eliminated by the course administrative assistant from both documents used in this study, before they were coded. Thus, all coding was performed with the coders blind to the gender of the subjects (see Table 4.1).

Table 4.1
Group Comparison of Mean Length of Life Stories and Career Histories

Group[1]	Life Story			Career History		
		Group Difference			Group Difference	
	Avg. No. of Words	t-test (2-tailed)	U^2	Avg. No. of Words	t-test (2-tailed)	U
Part-time	784			132		
		...0.98	168		0.28	167.5
Full-time	685			144		
Women	725			139		
		...0.19	198		0.06	162.5
Men	744			137		

1. Sample: $N = 40$, with 10 of each of the following: part-time men, part-time women, full-time men, full-time women.
2. U was obtained using 2-tailed p corrected for ties. No significant differences were found.

RESULTS AND DISCUSSION

For all of the results presented below, the sample was collapsed, comparing it across gender, since analysis across full-time and part-time status did not reveal any significant differences. Tests were performed using ANOVA for two-way interactions between gender and type of program for each variable, with task achievement found to be statistically significant. For all the analyses performed, a criterion value for statistical significance of p....05 was used. To assess distributional differences between men and women, the subjects were grouped into low, medium, and high levels of the individual traits or variables. This grouping of subjects allowed comparisons of the proportions of men and women in each category as well as identification of those levels in which men and women, respectively, were most highly concentrated.

Hypothesis 1: No significant differences were found in the mean number of statements about the centrality of others made by men and women. Women were coded more frequently than men for learning through interactions of others as well as for impact of another at nearly significant levels (see Table 4.2).

Twenty-eight percent of the men were concerned with impact of another, in contrast to 32% of the women. This finding was contrary to our previous expectations. To be coded for impact of another, a person had to write about the explicit impact a particular individual had on his or her life at a specific time. The authors had initially expected to find a greater number of men making statements about the impact one other person had made on them because of more frequent mentorship of men by others (Kram, 1985).

There were no significant differences found between men and women for the separate learning from interactions, although there was greater variance within the subsample of women on learning from interactions than there was within the male subsample. Our findings did not support those of Velsor and Hughes' (1990) study in which women were found to be more likely than men to learn from others. This may be an artifact of the environment in which this study took place. The men and women in this sample were first-year MBA students in their first semester of the program. They had just spent the major part of ten weeks giving and receiving feedback in a group of twelve people. Furthermore, they were strongly encouraged by the groups' facilitators and the course's instructors to use one another as resources for information.

Additionally, seven of the twenty-two managerial abilities, many of which the students focused on developing, were clearly interaction-oriented. These were empathy, persuasiveness, networking, negotiating, group management, development of others, and oral communications. It may be that in looking for ways to develop skills which clearly involve other people, men as well as women in this sample turned to other people. This may have carried over to the goal and action management abilities (such as planning and efficiency orientation) and the analytical reasoning abilities (such as systems thinking and pattern recognition) which the students also selected to develop.

The lack of a clear gender-split in these findings may also be a reflection of changing societal norms. There are an increasing number of men who are rebelling

Table 4.2   Frequency of Occurrence of Code Themes by Gender

Variable	Frequency of Occurrence	Mean Frequency of Occurrence				Group Difference (1-tailed)	Variance[1] Homogeneity
		Female[2]	SD	Male[3]	SD	t-test	F-value
Personal Development[4]		10.49	5.63	8.41	5.28	2.12**	1.13
Self-Reflection	563	5.33	3.57	3.72	2.84	2.78*****	1.58**
Confidence.	73	0.59	0.82	0.59.	0.90	-0.02	1.22
Personal Learnings	538	4.57	3.97	4.10	3.44	0.71	1.33
Role Development[5]		11.19	8.96	9.63	6.90	1.09	1.69**
Achievement through Self	866	7.38	6.31	6.38	5.36	0.96	1.39
Tasks Involving People	445	3.81	3.58	3.25	2.75	0.98	1.69**
Centrality of Others[4]		14.83	11.96	12.57	7.94	1.24	2.27****
Achievement through Others	302	2.74	3.05	2.11	2.17	1.32+	1.98*****
Impact of Another	55	0.56	1.15	0.33	0.57	1.39+	4.06****
Family/Friends	1322	11.52	10.53	10.13	7.26	0.85	2.11*****
Arenas of Responsibility[4]	67	0.78	0.92	0.34	0.63	3.04*****	2.15*****

1. Variance among women is greater in this sample than that of men.   2. $N = 64$.   3. $N = 64$.   4. Coding from both the Life Story and Career History.
5. Coding from the Career History

$+ p < .10$ $* p < .05$ $** p < .025$ $*** p < .01$ $**** p < .005$

against the stereotype of what it means to be a man in America. Stoltenberg's *Refusing to Be a Man* (1990) is unprecedented in its outright rejection of domination masculinity. Brod (1987, p. 1), one of the pioneers of the men's studies movement, writes of nothing less than a fundamental "deconstruction and reconstruction of masculinity." Other men propose new ways of defining "masculinity" that are more stereotypically "feminine" (Coltrane, 1988; McGill, 1985). Men are turning down promotions that involve relocating in order to accommodate their spouses' careers and/or to prevent the disruption of their children's lives. These trends all reflect a different form of concern for others which has not traditionally been part of the male sex role.

Hypothesis 2: A comparison of the mean frequency of occurrence revealed that women mentioned personal development in the context of their career role development significantly more frequently than men did ($p < .025$, $df = 122$, $t = 2.12$). Men primarily mentioned role development. Examination of the component variables--self-reflection, personal learning, and self-confidence--showed that the greater number of occurrences of statements of personal development for women was largely due to the highly significant self-reflection component of this category ($p < .005$, $df = 122$, $t = 2.78$). Women were significantly more self-reflective about the consequences of their actions in developing their careers, while men focused on achieving skill mastery without reflection. There were no significant differences found between men and women for the individual personal learning and self-confidence variables.

Statements of self-reflection that were coded involved a person taking time to stop and think about the consequences (including emotional reactions) of his or her actions. In examining the data, it appeared that there were distributional differences by gender ($X^2 = 8.02$, $df = 3$, $p \ldots .01$); significantly more of the women made statements of self-reflection than did the men (86% of the women as compared to 67% of the men). Men were less likely to engage in self-reflection, whereas women were more likely to use it. Only 14% of the women in our sample did not engage in any self-reflection when telling their life stories; in contrast, almost 33% of the men did not engage in any self-reflection. At the high frequency use end of the scale (5 or more occurrences), 21% of the women in our sample used self-reflection, as opposed to only 8% of the men. Of the total number of individuals who engaged in self-reflection at this level, 72% of them were women, in contrast to 28% who were men. This indicates that not only are women significantly less likely to not use self-reflection, but that when they do use self-reflection, one-fifth of them will do so frequently.

Velsor and Hughes (1990) suggested that women see a greater need for personal development through self-reflection than men do because the criteria for being a good manager are not as clear to them. Several studies have shown that general descriptions of women are less congruent with corresponding descriptions of men, the latter of which are congruent with descriptions of managers (Brown, 1979; Heilman, Block, Martell, & Simon, 1989; Schein, 1975). This suggests that the women in our sample, enrolled in a school of management at the time of this study, would be more likely to spend time thinking about what actions are appropriate for a managerial environment.

With respect to the self-confidence variable, statements in which the student explicitly mentioned a need to develop more confidence were coded, as were statements of possessing confidence. As can be seen in Table 4.2, the mean number of statements concerning self-confidence made by men and by women was the same. Of the women who wrote about confidence, 60% of the statements indicated having confidence, whereas 40% were about the need to develop it. In contrast, 82% of the statements by men were positive ones, with only 18% of the sample indicating low self-confidence, but they were as equally concerned as women with their need to develop more confidence. An alternative explanation is that women were not less confident, but simply more willing to state when they did not feel confident.

Hypothesis 3: No significant differences were found between the number of times that men and women wrote statements concerning role development ($t = 1.09$, $df = 116$, $p ... .25$), as shown in Table 4.2. The component variables of this category were achievement through self and tasks involving people. Those statements in which people listed activities which they planned to accomplish alone were coded as task achievements. There was no significant difference ($t = 0.96$, $df = 123$, $p ... .177$) in the mean number of statements coded for task achievements by gender, as shown in Table 4.2. Both men and women focused on task achievements as a major part of their career role development. Maccoby and Jacklin's (1974) classic study on sex differences found no evidence in their research that boys would be more interested in task achievement than girls. Because women are concerned with personal development and maintaining relationships, an erroneous assumption is that their task achievements are fewer. It was evident that this component variable was largely responsible for the mean frequency of the overall role development category. Also, as expected, our findings confirmed that men engaged in task achievements without reflection, which was in accordance with findings of Velsor and Hughes (1990) .

An analysis of variance of this variable showed that there was a significant two-way interaction effect of gender and the type of program (whether the student was in the full-time or part-time program) at the $p ... .05$ level with the part-time women making the greatest number of statements of task achievements followed by full-time women. Of those who spoke of task achievements nine or more times (one standard deviation above the mean) 42% were part-time women, followed by 25% of the full-time women, and 19% and 16% for the part-time and full-time male samples, respectively. It may be that women, in general, and part-time female students in particular, are aware that they have to achieve more and perform better in order to achieve the same career success as their male colleagues (Hardesty & Jacobs, 1986).

These results bring into question studies that suggest women define achievements differently than men (Eccles, 1987; Veroff & Feld, 1970). Our overall results suggest women's definitions for achievement encompass not only traditional ones such as high task performance, but also include more relationship-oriented definitions such as enabling co-workers to feel satisfied and accomplished on the job.

The second component variable of role development was tasks involving people ("group management," "employee motivation"). There were again no significant differences by gender, but patterns similar to those described above emerged. Of those who mentioned tasks involving people eight or more times (one standard deviation above the mean), 83% were women, while only 17% were men. Sixteen percent of the women in the sample were at this level in contrast to 3% of the men. It is clear that both groups develop role-related tasks involving people, but the contrast between women and men at high levels of usage suggests a need for further study.

Hypothesis 4: Statements coded under the arenas of responsibilities category were ones in which the person wrote about doing multiple tasks simultaneously or expressed a need to maintain a balance among a variety of roles. There was a significant difference in the mean number of statements concerning arenas of responsibilities made by the women and men in the sample. Forty-nine percent of the women made such statements, while only 28% of the men did ($p < .01$, $X^2 = 10.00$), thus suggesting that women see themselves as having responsibilities and obligations in a variety of areas in their lives, their career being just one. The differences in frequency of use of this variable by men and women is important in understanding a major difference in career development by gender. Women appear to focus on multi-arenas of responsibility far more frequently than do men and at the same time try to be responsible in all of the arenas. Men appear to be less likely to refer to concerns about doing multiple tasks or balancing a variety of roles.

At the high frequency use end of the scale (one standard deviation above the mean), 24% of the women referred to a concern with doing multiple tasks as opposed to 5% of the men. Of the total number of individuals who wrote about multiple tasks and balance at this level, 72% were women, while only 28% were men. This supported the research by Abramson and Franklin (1986), Barnett and Baruch (1980), and Gallese (1985), which found that women's professional accomplishments complement other areas of responsibility.

SUMMARY AND IMPLICATIONS

Our examination of written life stories and career histories in a sample of male and female MBA students yielded four important findings.

First, our expectation that women engage in self-reflection about their actions and their consequences more frequently than men do was verified. In contrast, men focused on achieving skill mastery without reflection. That women discussed engaging in self-reflection significantly more often than men did suggests that, for women, reflecting on their own actions enables them to get a more accurate depiction of their role in events that occurred. Self-reflection serves as an important mode of understanding life experiences.

Second, as hypothesized, women seemed to consider their careers to be but one component of their lives. Women tended to discuss their lives as comprised of many complementary parts, including their careers, which parts are continually balanced and together form a whole. In contrast, men did not discuss a need similarly to balance areas other than work and school.

Third, the prediction that women would focus on career task achievement as well as personal development was also supported. Women tended to think about task achievement on the job as often as men do. This finding, coupled with the finding that women tend to be responsible in multi-arenas of their lives, is important in that it shows that although women are very concerned with balancing the many components of their lives, their concern does not interfere with task achievements. The expectation that women would make more statements regarding personal development than men was supported. It seems that men focus primarily on role development through skill mastery, whereas women's development occurs as an interaction between self-reflection and expression of feelings on one hand and skill mastery and task achievements on the other.

Fourth, our hypothesis that women focus on task achievements as a means of skill development as often as men was confirmed. A closer examination of the data showed that women in the part-time program engaged in task achievements significantly more than the men (both full-time and part-time). We suspect that one factor which may account for this finding is that part-time women have learned that they must outdo their male colleagues at work to obtain recognition whereas an academic classroom setting is more merit-based.

Our findings indicated that, contrary to our earlier expectations, women did not mention the need to develop more self-confidence any more frequently than men. Both were concerned with its increased development for career success, yet women mentioned the importance of personal development in the context of their career role development significantly more frequently than men. Previously, we elaborated on the environmental factors (e.g., setting) which may have affected the self-confidence finding. Further investigation is necessary to determine the strength of the effects which such factors may have on this variable as well as our finding of a significant two-way interaction of gender and type of program.

Although we found significant overall differences between men and women in several developmental areas, it is crucial that these findings be viewed in an appropriate context. Women are not a homogeneous mass in which each member is identical to the others. While we have presented data which show some differences between men and women, we expect that, as we continue to examine the data by generational cohorts, both historic circumstances and the positioning of women in their reproductive life cycles may have important implications for understanding the developmental differences both within and between groups of men and women. Indeed, our study revealed a greater variance in the subsample of women than of men. Many of the most substantively interesting results were found by examining differences at the high and low frequency ends of the variable ranges, as well as our finding of a significant, two-way interaction of gender and type of program.

While studies of managers have revealed that for many managers, personal and family time was sharply curtailed and that personal identity was indistinguishable from work (Halper, 1988; Mintzberg, 1973), managers suggested that such sacrifices were costs they were willing to pay for career achievement (Halper, 1988). More recently, Hegelson (1990) found that women were more likely than men to view their jobs as just one element of who they were and were not willing to sacrifice themselves to their careers. Our findings confirm those of Hegelson. Powell and Mainiero (1992) take the notion of complementarity one step further and suggest that in balancing the multiple arenas of work and personal lives, women tend to seek some desired level of satisfaction with both realms. They argue that this *satisfaction* with their multiple arenas of responsibility may make women better equipped for coping with the trials and tribulations of management than those who focus on more objective measures of career success. That is, managerial success in this ever-changing business climate may be becoming dependent upon the ability to measure career success subjectively and flexibly rather than in rigidly objective terms.

Understanding the developmental differences both confirmed and suggested in this study is also important for business schools in designing their curricula and delivering their instruction. Schools need to recognize differences in developmental needs of women and men MBA students, as the need to maximize all employees' productivity continues to be an important issue. Business schools are now faced with the demands of a student population which includes larger proportions of women than ever and, as we found, women rely on assessment both by themselves and by others, and seek feedback and dialogue with others as conscious elements of the learning experience. MBA education must take the developmental needs of female students into account in order to prepare business students adequately for their responsibilities as managers. Not only must students themselves be provided with substantial and frequent feedback, but they also must be taught to recognize the importance of providing opportunities for such feedback and corresponding dialogue when they hold authority.

The result of the discovery of developmental differences between men and women is that not only must MBA programs be designed to meet the needs of their female students, but male and female students alike must be prepared for managing, while at the same time encouraging such differences in the workplace. Currently, most MBA programs focus on providing students with functional reasoning skills (i.e., learning *how* to achieve their goals). However, in many instances, managers do not actually spend the majority of their time using functional reasoning skills; rather, they spend more time using substantive reasoning (i.e., choosing priorities, determining why it is important to do something, integrating multiple tasks). Ethical questions arise at intersections of professional and private lives; thus, instruction in critical thinking—that which management programs seek to provide—must address these intersections if it is to influence behavior. Although conversations about ethical questions necessitate skills which many are not accustomed to using in the classroom, it is deliberations on such matters which give purpose to learning. It would then seem that women, with their tendency to focus simultaneously on issues of personal development as well as career development, may be particularly well suited to addressing and resolving ethical questions.

We also need ways to design and describe professional work that include professional and nurturing roles over time, including simultaneous high achievement and high relations for both men and women. Insights such as these are useful for managing a diverse workforce of the 1990s, which will most likely include a large number of women. Implicit in understanding individual career motivation are strategies for effective supervising and maximizing productivity. Such strategies include the importance of more frequent feedback from others for self-reflection, flexibility in job design, recognition of balance needs, and assignment of important task responsibilities to women, since they learn through task accomplishment just as men do.

Not only is the nature of work changing, but the nature of people who work is changing, too. They are concerned with growth opportunities and happiness at work. They do not want inhumane and stifling jobs. Managers are called upon to appreciate the legitimate differences which exist in how individuals develop, both personally and professionally, and to devise organizational structures that encourage and nurture human growth. It is through this approach that people may be made to feel that they are bringing something of value to their organizations and that they are being judged, as they should be, on their organizational contributions.

ACKNOWLEDGMENT

The authors acknowledge the financial support of the National Center of Adult Learning and of a Case Western Reserve University Research Initiation Grant in the preparation of this manuscript. The authors thank Richard Boyatzis, Melina Forthofer, Mike Hitt, Laurie Larwood, Bob Mason, and Don Wolfe for comments on an earlier version of this chapter.

REFERENCES

Abramson, J., & Franklin, B. (1986). *Where are they now.* New York: Doubleday.

Astin, H. S., & Leland, C. (1991). *Women of influence, women of vision: A cross-generational study of leaders and social change.* San Francisco: Jossey-Bass.

Barnett, R., & Baruch, G. (1980). On being an economic provider: Women's involvement in multiple roles. In D. McGuigan (Ed.), *Women's lives: New theory, research and policy* (pp. 69-83). Ann Arbor: University of Michigan Center for Continuing Education of Women.

Baruch, G., Barnett, R., & Rivers, C. (1983). *Life prints: New patterns of love and work for today's women.* New York: New American Library.

Bateson, M. (1989). *Composing a life.* New York: Plume Books.

Belenky, M., Clinchy, B., Goldberger, N., & Tarule, J. (1986). *Women's ways of knowing.* New York: Basic Books.

Berzoff, J. (1985). Valued female friendships: Their functions in female adult development. (*Dissertation Abstracts International, 46,* 3890).

Brod, H. (Ed.). (1987). *The making of masculinities: The new men's studies.* Boston: Allen & Unwin.

Brown, L. (1979). Women and business management. *Signs: Journal of women in culture and society, 5* (2): 266-288.

Case, S. S. (1988). Cultural differences not deficiencies: An analysis of managerial women's language. In S. Rose & L. Larwood (Eds.), *Women's careers: Pathways and pitfalls* (pp. 41-63). New York: Praeger.

Coltrane, S. (1988). Father-child relationships and the status of women: A cross-cultural study. *American Journal of Sociology, 93* (5): 1060-95.

Cowan, A. (1992) For women, fewer M. B. A.'s. *The New York Times*, Sunday, September 27.

Dreyfuss, C. (1991). *Scientists and engineers as effective managers: A study of the development of interpersonal abilities.* Unpublished doctoral dissertation, Case Western Reserve University, Cleveland.

Eccles, J. (1987). Gender roles and women's achievement-related decisions. *Psychology of Women Quarterly, 11*: 135-172.

Eichenbaum, L., & Orbach, S. (1988). *Between Women.* New York: Viking.

Erikson, E. (1968). *Identity: Youth and Crisis.* New York: Norton.

Fuchsberg, G. (1992). Female enrollment falls in many top M.B.A. programs. *The Wall Street Journal*, September 25, B1,6.

Gallese, L. (1985). *Women like us.* New York: Signet.

Gallos, J. V. (1990). Exploring women's development: Implications for career theory, practice and research. In M. Arthur, D. Hall, and B. Lawrence (Eds.), *Handbook of career theory and development* (pp. 110-132). New York: Cambridge Press.

Gallos, J. V. (1993) Women's experiences and ways of knowing: Implications for teaching and learning in the organizational behavior classroom. *Journal of Management Education, 5* (1): 7-26.

Gilligan, C. (1977). In a different voice: Women's conception of self and morality. *Harvard Education Review, 47*: 481-517.

Gilligan, C. (1982). *In a different voice: Psychological theory and women's development.* Cambridge: Harvard University Press.

Halper, J. (1988). *Quiet desperation: The truth about successful men.* New York: Warner Books.

Hancock, E. (1989). *The girl within.* New York: Ballantine Books.

Hardesty, S., & Jacobs, N. (1986). *Success and betrayal: The crisis of women in corporate America.* New York: Franklin Watts.

Hegelson, S. (1990). *Female advantage: Women's ways of leadership.* New York: Doubleday.

Heilman, M., Block, C., Martell, R., and Simon, M. (1989). Has anything changed? Current characteristics of men, women and managers. *Journal of Applied Psychology, 74* (6): 935-942.

Johnston, W., & Packer, A. (1987). *Workforce 2000: Work and workers for the 21st century.* Indianapolis: Hudson Institute, Inc.

Josselson, R. (1987). *Finding herself: Pathways to identity development in women.* San Francisco: Jossey-Bass.

Keele, Reba L. (1986). Mentoring or networking? Strong and weak ties in career development. In Lynda L. Moore (Ed.), *Not as far as you think: The realities of working women* (pp. 53-68). Lexington, MA: Lexington Books.

Kohlberg, L. (1976). Moral stages and moralization: The cognitive-developmental approach. In T. Lickona (Ed.), *Moral development and behavior: Theory, research and social issues* (pp. 54-69). New York: Holt, Rinehart and Winston.

Levinson, D. (1978). *The seasons of a man's life*. New York: Knopf.

Maccoby, E., and Jacklin, C. (1974). *The psychology of sex differences*. Stanford, CA: Stanford University Press.

McGill, M. E. (1985). *The McGill report on male intimacy*. New York: Harper & Row.

Mintzberg, H. (1973). *The nature of managerial work*. New York: Harper & Row.

Powell, G., & Mainiero, L. (1992). Cross-currents in the river of time: Conceptualizing the complexities of women's careers. *Journal of Management, 18* (2): 215-237.

Roberts, P., & Newton, P. (1986). Levinsonian studies of women's adult development. Working paper. Wright Institute, Berkeley, CA.

Roberts, T. (1991). Gender and the influence of evaluations on self-assessments in achievement settings. *Psychological Bulletin, 109*, (2): 297-308.

Rosener, J. B. (1990). Ways women lead. *Harvard Business Review*, November-December: 119-125.

Schein, V. (1975). Relationship between sex role stereotypes and requisite management characteristics among female managers. *Journal of Applied Psychology, 60* (3): 340-344.

Stewart, L., & Gudykunst, W. (1982). Differential factors influencing the hierarchical level and number of promotions of males and females within an organization. *Academy of Management Journal, 25*: 586-597.

Stoltenberg, J. (1990). *Refusing to be a man*. New York: Meridian.

Tannen, D. (1990). *You just don't understand: Women and men in conversation*. New York: William Morrow and Company, Inc.

Valliere, P. (1986). Perceived academic competence in women in Ph.D. programs: Effects of feedback, self-esteem, and academic discipline. (*Dissertation Abstracts International, 47*, 4528).

Velsor, E., and Hughes, M. (1990). *Gender differences in the development of managers: How women managers learn from experience*. Greensboro, NC: Center for Creative Leadership.

Veroff, J., and Feld, S. (1970). *Marriage and work in America*. New York: Van Nostrand-Rineholt.

5

On the Origins of Gender-Linked Language Differences: Individual and Contextual Explanations

Mary-Jeanette Smythe and Jasna Meyer

For years, scholars in a number of disciplines have debated whether there are reliable linguistic markers of gender. Whether couched in the constructs of feminist criticism or pursued in clinical, laboratory or anthropological settings, the questions about differences have remained for the most part unresolved. The renewed enthusiasm for differences occasioned by the appearance of Tannen's (1990) popular examination of the issue is a vivid reminder of our deep and abiding interest in the ways sex and identity find expression through communication behaviors.

Within the discipline of communication, several constructs address these concerns about sex and identity as they are manifested in differences, actual or perceived, in the language used by women and men. Two such accounts are particularly useful in charting the nature and extent of differences. One, the gender-linked language effect, conceptualizes language behaviors as individual differences phenomena. Speech accommodation theory, on the other hand, provides a situational explanation for language behaviors.

Research on the gender-linked language effect, a construct positing that men and women exhibit characteristic patterns of verbal expression quite apart from any consideration of linguistic stereotype, has been completed largely by Mulac and his associates as an outgrowth of work with the Speaker Dialect Attitude Scale (1977). In a series of studies (Mulac & Lundell, 1980; 1982; Mulac, Lundell, & Bradac, 1985; Mulac, Bradac, & Mann, 1985; Mulac, Wiemann, Widenmann, & Gibson, 1988), these researchers identified differences in male and female language that were found in public speeches, in the dialogue of television programs, and even within the content of children's TV programs. Behaviorally, the gender-linked language effect finds expression in the appearance or absence of specific language features. It is not that case that these variables are sex-exclusive. Rather, it seems likely that both sexes use certain linguistic cues differently.

Thirteen language variables have been identified which appear to account for most of the between-sex differences in perceptions of language. Mulac and his associates (1986) further assert that the variables afford virtually perfect accuracy in predicting speaker gender by even untrained judges. The male predictors in the gender-linked language effect include syllables per word, first-person singular pronouns, present tense verbs, vocalized pauses, grammatical error, active voice verbs, judgmental adjectives, and references to people. These factors constitute a style that is egocentric, nonstandard, active and intense. Female predictors include adverbials beginning sentences, oppositions, rhetorical questions, references to emotion, and fillers. The researchers suggest this creates a style which is complex, tentative, and literate.

On balance, the gender-linked language effect studies constitute some of the most ambitious gender and language research. It is equally true, however, that these investigations provoke at least as many questions as they answer. For instance, the relationship between the language features and gender styles is ambiguous. The gender-linked language effect is essentially an attributional phenomenon, the consequence of listener/reader perceptions of language. How much or how often the specific variables appear in any individual's discourse is unknown. Moreover, there have been comparatively few attempts to place these features in any sort of social context, relating variables such as task or relational history to the appearance of language variables.

Numerous researchers have called for studies of the language/gender relationship which acknowledge the importance of context variables directly (Thorne, Kramarae, & Henley, 1983). Most studies of language differences have been conducted without regard for even the most basic of context concerns. A contextualist perspective argues that any and all sex differences displayed by women and men are powerfully affected by the social context in which they appear, and suggests the need to examine (at least) the direct and interactive effects of such elements as individuals, settings, tasks, and relationships that are present in all communication events. These concerns are to some degree addressed by speech accommodation theory (Giles & Powesland, 1975; Giles & Smith, 1979).

The relevance of speech accommodation theory to the study of gender differences in language is well reasoned. Considerable evidence suggests that participants in conversation are affected by the communicative behaviors of their partners (see Andersen and Andersen (1984) for comparisons across various influence theories). Much less agreement is apparent concerning the precise nature and extent of this mutual influence during same-sex or cross-sex dyadic interactions.

Speech accommodation theory posits that when interacting with individuals not of their own social group (e.g., female/male, African-American/Anglo-American, etc.), people adapt their speech styles in order to diminish real or imagined differences between themselves and their partners. This pattern, referred to as speech convergence, is anticipated when individuals desire the social approval of their partner, seek a high level of communicational efficiency, and the social norms are not perceived to dictate alternative speech strategies.

Based upon the foregoing, the present investigation addressed three issues of theoretical and methodological consequence in studies of gender linked language differences. Most of the studies of the gender-linked language effect have been concerned with transcripts of speech prepared by researchers rather than spontaneously recorded talk. Thus, our first consideration became one of devising a situation in which "normal" utterances of males and females might be obtained. In addition, the absence of attention to context variables in previous studies led us to include a task variable in the current study in an attempt to explore relationships among language, sex, and task considerations. Finally, the interaction of speaker sex and listener sex is a frequently confounding factor in studies of male and female language. For this reason, data on both the sex of a speaker *and* his or her conversational partner are required if any understanding of gender-linked language differences are to be achieved.

Taken together, the extant empirical evidence and explanatory models concerning the gender and language relationship suggest the following research hypotheses.

H1:   Male and female speakers will exhibit characteristically distinct language patterns conforming to the gender-linked language profiles.

H2:   Male and female speakers will exhibit speech accommodation by adapting their language cues to match those of their conversational partner.

H3:   Performance of a sex-typed (male or female) task will affect the characteristic language patterns of male and female speakers.

METHOD

In brief, the goal of this study was to locate and identify differences in male and female language as these occurred in the conduct of one of two similar discussion tasks. Three independent variables included sex, sex of partner, and task. The dependent measures were twelve language variables previous researchers (Mulac, Wiemann, Widenmann, & Gibson, 1988) have identified as reliable indicators of speaker gender (see Table 5.1).

Thirty dyads composed of students drawn from the enrollments of several large basic communication courses at a midwestern university were used in this study. Ten dyads were composed of women, ten of men, and the remaining ten were composed of a man and a woman. None of the previous interactants had met their task partner previously. Assignment to dyad pairing was randomized across subjects.

Data were collected in a carpeted seminar room located in a laboratory suite. One table and several chairs were located near the center of the room, opposite a one-way mirror. Subjects were videotaped from behind this mirror as they sat discussing their task.

Eagly (1987) has suggested that men and women alike exhibit different behaviors in response to the demands of the task or situation in which they find themselves. Few studies have attempted to explore this variable, however. Instead, most researchers

Table 5.1
Twelve Language Variables Coded as Markers of Speaker Gender

1. **FILLERS**
   Words or phrases used without apparent semantic intent
   (e.g., "well, y'know, like....")
2. **INTERRUPTIONS**
   Breaking into another person's speaking turn in an effort to seize the floor
   (e.g., Speaker A: "I like ice cream flavors that have candy and nuts...."
   Speaker B: "All the fat stuff, I can't stand that stuff, too rich for me.")
3. **ADVERBIALS BEGIN SENTENCE**
   Opening an utterance with an expression such as "Really, I cannot
   understand...."
4. **CONJUNCTIONS/FILLERS BEGIN SENTENCE**
   Opening an utterance with an expression such as "Well, OK now, let's get it
   together...."
5. **DIRECTIVES**
   One participant apparently orders the other around or appears to tell what
   to do (e.g.,"Why don't we try this approach?" or "Will you stop that now?")
6. **NEGATIONS**
   Statements that describe what is not the case (e.g., "It's not hard.")
7. **QUESTIONS**
   Utterances phrased as interrogatives (e.g., "What is your name again?")
8. **HEDGES/SOFTENERS**
   Language forms designed to mitigate listener impressions
   (e.g.,"sort of strange")
9. **INTENSIVE ADVERBS**
   Expressions intensified through modifiers (e.g., "Quite rightly," or "How
   maddeningly slow")
10. **JUSTIFIERS**
    Reasons provided for an utterance (e.g., "I'd prefer this option because....")
11. **ACTION VERBS**
    Form indicating movement (e.g., "shoving")
12. **PERSONAL PRONOUNS**
    Use of "I", "You", "We"

hold task constant and compare the reactions of men and women against a "neutral"
backdrop. In point of fact, there are probably no truly neutral tasks or topics. In the
current study, two discussion tasks were selected which were subtly sex-typed. They
were comparable in terms of the demands they placed on subjects' intellectual
capacities, and in terms of the time requirements. Neither task presumed any unusual
background, knowledge, or special skills.

The "male" task was *Lost on the Moon,* developed by NASA, which involved ranking a number of items a lost mission would require to survive until a rescue party could reach them. A set of correct answers exists for this test, by which group or individual decision-making may be assessed. The "female" task was *The Kidney Machine*, a familiar task used widely in T-group training, and involves selection of candidates to fill a limited number of treatment slots while awaiting transplant surgery. No single list of correct choices exists for this exercise. Judgments are achieved and evaluated subjectively. The linear, list-making requirements of the NASA task contrast with the more reflective, empathic judgments required by the T-group task. Pilot testing (N = 53) confirmed the sex-typing distinction of these two tasks in the perceptions of students similar to those who participated in the study.

When both participants were seated, the experimenter introduced herself and the participants to one another and explained the nature of their assigned task. In both instances, the individuals were told that they were to discuss, and reach agreement on their joint solution to the problem. They were then left to complete the task. Following completion of their discussions, the two participants were taken to separate rooms, where each completed a series of questionnaires and was debriefed.

RESULTS

Trained coders worked in various combinations of two and three person groups. Coders examined only one subject in a dyads and one measure at a time. Although the sex and dyadic pairing of each subject were obvious to the coders, they were kept blind to the specific research questions and relationships anticipated among the language cues (dependent measures).

Data relevant to research hypotheses were analyzed through analyses of variance. Hypothesis 1 was drawn from the gender-linked language differences literature that stipulates specific combinations of language cues for men and women. Only one significant main effect emerged from this analysis. As displayed in Table 5.2, the variable labeled "action verbs" was significantly different for men and women (F = 4.74 $p \le$ .05). Contrary to the expectations described in previous studies, however, women used more action verbs than men. Indeed, the only signs of support for the gender-linked language differences emerged from significant interaction effects, such as the finding that dyads composed of two females used significantly more adverbials than either of the other two dyadic combinations. Similar interactions involving questions and personal pronoun usage occurred.

Hypothesis 2 explored the speech accommodation construct, suggesting that males and females might adapt their language use to more closely approximate that of their interaction partner. Dyadic effects emerged on several key variables and lent support to the accommodation hypothesis. Specifically, a significant main effect emerged on hedges (F = 3.19, $p \le$ .05). Inspection of cell means indicated that hedges were most frequently used in FF dyads, consistent with the hypothesis expressed first by Hall (1984) that talk between same-sex pairs is often marked by increases in sex-specific displays. A like pattern of findings was noted on adverbials (F = 3.55, $p \le$ .05). On

Table 5.2
Language Variables Displayed by Males and Females

Variables	Females	Males
Fillers	9.16$_a$	8.83$_a$
Interruptions	2.25$_a$	2.54$_a$
Adverbials begin Utterance	1.38$_a$	1.25$_a$
Conjunctions begin Utterance	4.45$_a$	4.90$_a$
Directives	2.29$_a$	2.77$_a$
Negations	4.38$_a$	3.64$_a$
Questions	9.25$_a$	7.67$_a$
Hedges	1.96$_a$	1.87$_a$
Intensive Adverbs	1.58$_a$	1.29$_a$
Justifiers	3.87$_a$	5.12$_a$
Action Verbs	4.45$_a$	2.19$_b$
Personal Pronouns	29.35$_a$	23.74$_a$

Note: Means with uncommon subscripts are significantly different.

directives, FF dyads exhibited the lowest frequency of usage.

Similarly, support for Hypothesis 2 emerged from FM pairs. Significant main effects were obtained on questions ($F = 8.79$, $p \leq .05$), directives ($F = 3.50$, $p \leq .05$), adverbials ($F = 3.35$, $p \leq .05$). Interaction effects provided additional support, revealing that personal pronoun usage was highest in MF dyads ($F = 3.68$, $p \leq .05$) Inspection of cell means indicated that in each of these instances, accommodation was evident in the language use of the participants. In directives, for instance, the frequency of this type of statement was higher for females talking with males. By contrast, males increased their usage of questions when working with a female.

Hypothesis 3 was concerned with the impact of another context variable, tasks, upon the language behaviors of participants.

Table 5.3
Language Variables as Displayed within Dyads

Dyads	FF	FM	MM
Fillers	8.02$_a$	11.45$_a$	10.09$_a$
Interruptions	2.02$_a$	3.27$_a$	2.90$_a$
Adverbials begin Utterance	1.72$_a$	0.72$_b$	0.45$_b$
Conjunctions begin Utterance	3.87$_a$	7.27$_a$	5.00$_a$
Directives	1.97$_a$	3.72$_b$	3.36$_b$
Negations	3.86$_a$	3.81$_a$	4.72$_a$
Questions	8.30$_a$	9.90$_b$	7.63$_a$
Hedges	2.45$_a$	1.18$_b$	0.72$_b$
Intensive Verbs	1.52$_a$	1.36$_a$	1.18$_a$
Justifiers	4.52$_a$	4.36$_a$	4.54$_a$
Action Verbs	3.12$_a$	3.27$_a$	4.09$_a$
Personal Pronouns	24.20$_a$	33.36$_b$	28.27$_a$

NOTE: Means with uncommon subscripts are significantly different.

Three significant main effects emerged from the analysis. Task effects were most pronounced on questions ($F = 4.45$ $p \le .05$) and on hedges ($F = 4.25$, $p \le .05$). Questions were used more frequently during the Lost on the Moon task (masculine) and hedges were used more frequently on the kidney machine task (feminine). In both instances, these findings supported the hypothesis. Another main effect emerged for intensive adverbs ($F = 4.13$, $p \le .05$, indicating that the more extreme form of speech was elicited when working on the kidney machine task. Finally, a significant interaction effect emerged on the personal pronoun variable. Inspection of cell means revealed that this effect was limited to MF dyads, when working on the kidney machine task.

DISCUSSION

The pattern of findings reported here provide scant evidence of a gender-linked language pattern. The absence of strong sex differences in the twelve language phenomena chosen for observation can be viewed only as an argument against the utility of difference-driven models of the gender and communication behaviors relationship. Recall that there were virtually no statistically significant differences between males and females at all in this investigation. Moreover, the only significant difference that emerged from the analysis contradicted expectations based on the gender-linked language literature. Given this set of findings, it seems reasonable to argue that considerably more empirical work will be required to refine our conceptions of gender-based differences in language, if they are to prove useful in a descriptive sense. Predictive capabilities present another set of questions altogether.

The results of this investigation point rather more directly toward a contextualistic perspective on language usage, positing that individuals make choices based upon their assessment of important situational variables. In this instance, it seems clear that both females and males adapted their language use according the demands of their task as well as to the sex of their partner. While the differences observed were not overwhelmingly large, they argue against reductionist, sex-exclusive dichotomies and in favor of notions such as linguistic styles. This study extends previous investigations asserting the primacy of context in shaping language choices, and suggests further ways in which these differences and similarities might emerge. The speech accommodation explanation, in particular, seems to warrant closer scrutiny.

In some respects the results of the current study support the social-role-based analyses of communication behaviors provided by Hall (1984) and Eagly (1987). Hall's work has revealed that women deal with each other in a more accommodating manner than they do with men (Hall, 1984; Hall & Braunwald, 1981, Hall, Braunwald & Mroz, 1982). Female-female interactions, argues Hall, contrast with male-male interactions by an absence of a process of dominance-matching in which each male responds to the others' real or perceived dominance by behaving more dominantly himself. The possibility that the prototypic "feminine" behaviors are most obvious in same-sex interactions is a direct challenge to prevailing stereotypes of male-female interactions and to traditional concepts of complementary male and female roles. The glimmerings from this investigation, combined with previous studies reported by Mulac, Wiemann, Widenmann and Gibson (1988) and Pillon, Degauquier, and Duquesne (1992) suggesting that men and women adjust their language usage to more closely parallel that of their partner appear quite substantial. Our finding that men did as much of this as women seems particularly noteworthy and warrants further inquiry.

Participants in this study also appeared to adapt their language use as a function of the task that they completed with their partners. In general, the observed effects were consistent with expectations concerning the relationships among task, gender and communication behaviors. Questions are, after all, a very useful means of structuring interactions. Both men and women appeared to use questions in the masculine task ("Lost on the Moon") more frequently to direct the discussion, and seek their partners' views on the ordering of the choices on their final list. Similarly, the less definitive nature of the feminine task ("Kidney Machine") elicited discourse that was at once more tentative and dramatic. Speech was marked by more colorful language, as evidenced by the incidence of intensive adverbs, but was strongly qualified, as if the subjects were sensitive to the social consequences of their decision.

The absence of the stereotypic sex differences on these two linguistic features made the findings all the more compelling, and reinforced the idea that individuals adjust their language choices according to their perceptions of task expectations or demands. Whether intentionally or as part of a larger process of speech accommodation, both men and women in this study varied their language usage in ways suggesting they were influenced by the sex-typing of their experimental tasks. Men posed more questions and phrased their comments more tentatively than expected, and women displayed markers of the masculine style—intensive adverbs and personal pronouns—as described by the gender-linked language effect literature (Mulac, *et al.*, 1986) and in the gender-linked language differences literature, generally (Smythe, 1991).

Finally, the results of this study may be viewed as an argument against those popular, yet simplistic interpretations of complex social interactions. Tannen's (1990) anecdotal accounts of the coils and snares of conversations between the sexes have delighted the public, but have offered little to the community of scholars attempting to document the presence and degree of differences associated with sex and gender. Moreover, accounts like Tannen's in some subtle ways seem to echo and affirm differences between male and female speech that empirical researchers would, at best, characterize as undocumented. At worst, these accounts perpetuate inaccurate, stereotypical conceptions of sex differences in communication.

If the complex relationship between gender and language is ever to be understood, we must surely begin by tempering our endorsement of the differences hypothesis with an appreciation for the strategic and creative choices available to men and women during conversations. Empirical studies designed to explore those choices, as well as the individuals who make them are needed to document and describe the effects of these variables on the display of communication behaviors. Until these fundamental questions are fully examined, the nature of the relationships among gender and communication behaviors will remain a matter of speculation and our quest for a theory of gender will fail to advance.

REFERENCES

Andersen, P. & Andersen, J. (1984). The exchange of nonverbal intimacy: A critical review of dyadic models. *Journal of Nonverbal Behavior, 8,* 327-349.

Eagly, A.H. (1987). *Sex differences in social behavior: A social-role interpretation.* Hillsdale, N.J.: Erlbaum Associates.

Giles, H. & Powesland, P. (1975). *Speech style and social evaluation.* London: Academic Press.

Giles, H. & Smith, P. (1979). Accommodation theory: Optimal levels of convergence. In H. Giles and R. St. Clair (Eds.) *Language and social psychology* (pp. 45-65). Oxford: Blackwell.

Hall, J.A. (1984). *Nonverbal sex differences: Communication accuracy and expressive style*. Baltimore, Md: The Johns Hopkins University Press.

Hall, J. & Braunwald, K. (1981). Gender cues in conversations. *Journal of Personality and Social Psychology, 40,* 99-110.

Hall, J. A., Brunwald, K., & Mroz, B. (1982). Gender, affect, and influence in a teaching situation. *Journal of Personality and Social Psychology, 43,* 270-280.

Mulac, A., Bradac, J. & Mann, S. (1985). Male/female language differences and attributional consequences in children's television. *Human Communication Research, 11,* 481-506.

Mulac, A., Incontro, C., & James, M. (1985). Comparison of the gender-linked language effect and sex role stereotypes. *Journal of Personality and Social Psychology, 49,* 1098-1109.

Mulac, A. & Lundell, T. (1980). Differences in perceptions created by syntactic-semantic productions of male and female speakers. *Communication Monographs, 47,* 111-118.

Mulac, H. & Lundell, T. (1982). An empirical test of the gender-linked language effect in a public speaking setting. *Language and Speech, 25,* 243-256.

Mulac, A., Lundell, T., & Bradac, J. (1985). Male/female language differences and attributional consequences in a public speaking setting: Toward an explanation of the gender-linked language effect. Paper presented at Speech Communication Association, Denver, Colorado.

Mulac, A., Lundell, T., & Bradac, J. (1986). Male/female language differences and attributional consequences in a public speaking setting. *Communication Monographs, 53,* 115-129.

Mulac, A. & Rudd, M. (1977). Effects of selected American regional dialects upon regional audience numbers. *Communication Monographs, 44,* 185-195.

Mulac, A. Wiemann, J., Widenmann, S., & Gibson, T. (1988). Male/female language differences and effects in same-sex and mixed sex dyads: The gender-linked language effect. *Communication Monographs, 55,* 315-335.

Pillon, A., Degauquier, C., & Duquesne, F. (1992). Males' and females' conversational behavior in cross-sex dyads: From gender difference to gender similarities. *Journal of Psycholinguistic Research, 21,* 147-172.

Smythe, M.J. (1991). Gender and communication behaviors: A review of research. In B. Dervin & M. Voigt (Eds.) *Progress in Communication Sciences, 10* (pp. 173-216). Norwich, NJ: Ablex.

Tannen, D. (1990). *Men and women speaking: You just don't understand.* New York: Random House.

Thorne, B., Kramerae, C., & Henley, N. (1983). Language, gender, and society: Opening a second decade of research. In B. Thorne, C. Kramerae, & N. Henley (Eds.) *Language, gender and society* (pp. 7-24). Rowley, Mass: Newbury House.

6

Effects of Sex Composition and Task Structure on Perceptions of Gender-Linked Role Differentiation in Small Groups

Edward A. Mabry and Carolyn J. Sorgel

Small group researchers have found elusive any single explanation for the consistently observed differences in group participation of men and women. The most extensive and promising examinations of this issue are related to the study of social roles. Early research on sex differences in group participation (Parsons & Bales, 1955; Strodtbeck & Mann, 1956; Strodtbeck, James, & Hawkins, 1957) focused on the effects of socialization processes experienced by men and women. Male socialization was observed to emphasize responsibilities for organizing and initiating social action, such as decision making and problem solving. Thus, men were thought to be ascendant and to prefer *task-specialist* and leadership role opportunities. Conversely, the socializing experiences for women were seen as predisposing them to social practices aligned with supportiveness, cohesiveness, and social deference leading to their identification with a *social-emotional specialist* role.

Subsequent theoretical explanations have concentrated on factors that influence the mutual definition of group roles that men and women develop. Role expectation theories propose that differences in participation are caused by the reactions of men and women to gender-role congruent or incongruent forms of social interaction (Bradley, 1980; Meeker & Weitzel-O'Neill, 1977; Ridgeway, 1979, 1982; Ridgeway & Berger, 1986). Recent expansions of this perspective are seen in Kay Deaux' research (Deaux, 1986; Deaux & Major, 1987) on a *gender schema* theory of mutual role attribution processes, and Alice Eagly's more inclusive *gender role* theory, which focuses on the salience of internalized sex-roles in shaping expectations about role-appropriate interaction in social contexts (Eagly 1987).

Eagly's gender-role interpretation for observed differences in the group participation of men and women is promising. She and her associates have successfully accounted for the strength of the contribution of sex differences to group participation, leader emergence, and performance outcomes (Carli, 1989; Eagly & Carli, 1981; Eagly & Johnson, 1990; Eagly & Karau, 1991; Eagly & Wood, 1991; Wood, 1987; Wood &

Karten, 1986; Wood, Polek, & Aiken, 1985). Eagly (1987) employs two dimensions of social experience (agency and communion) as role precepts she posits are used to differentiate the social experiences of men and women. The *agentic* role typical of male gender stereotyping includes attributes of assertiveness, dominance, decisiveness, confidence, directness, and self-expansion. According to Eagly, women usually experience stereotyping consistent with a *communal* gender role projecting a concern for others attributed to emotional expressiveness, interpersonal sensitivity, and personal gentleness. Eagly proposes that the role stereotypes, while decidedly categoric, are not characterized by a high degree of empirical distinctiveness nor are they internalized evenly across men and women. She contends that societal values and attitudes lead to differential attributions about men and women and their allocated access to experiences congruent with the contents of these roles. How fully an agentic or communal gender role is enacted depends on the *salience* of that role for the context of interaction, compared to other social role enactments also deemed appropriate and important.

Gender-role theory differs from other theories of gender differences in two ways: (1) gender-role socialization is not postulated as a direct causal variable in female and male social interaction differences, and (2) role *salience* explains gendered role behavior observed in a particular social setting as codetermined by that setting's place in a broader social structure (e.g., work, family) and manifestations of role content (gender related and non-gender related) that characterize the local, normative constraints operating in the setting.

HYPOTHESES

Role theory orientations for explaining sex differences in interaction behavior in small groups generally focus on the behaviors of male or female members. The properties of small groups as social entities often are secondary variables of interest, even though certain variables have demonstrable effects on how men and women participate. Two variables that often are not linked together in studies of sex differences in group interaction are group tasks and the proportionate composition of men and women that constitute the group. The combined effects of both variables can significantly predict observed group interaction between men and women (Bartol & Martin, 1986; Dion, 1989; Mabry, 1985, 1987, 1989). However, the majority of sex-role theory studies do not control for the effects of one or both of these factors. The consequence of overlooking task and composition effects is important. For example, Eagly argues that interaction context influences role appropriations. Small group scholars are univocal on the importance of group composition characteristics and group tasks in defining the social context parameters of small groups (Mabry & Barnes, 1980; McGrath, 1984). Failing to fully account for these variables limits the generalizability of role theory findings.

This study examines the effects of social interaction on the development of female and male role impressions under varying task and group composition conditions. Two hypotheses are advanced. The first hypothesis accounts for the climate-making potential of the proportionate representation of men and women in a group.

Hypothesis 1: Predominately male groups will foster interaction climates conducive to gender-role differentiations that parallel traditional or "expected" stereotypical perceptions of men and women, compared to predominately female groups that will enable female members to broaden their range of behaviors, thereby contributing to less stereotypical role perceptions.

The second hypothesis focuses on the social performance demands of group tasks. A structured task setting is expected to require more dominance behaviors than a more ambiguous setting. Highly structured tasks usually require more individual assertiveness for advancing opinions or solution proposals (when trained competency is held constant), because ideational involvement is easier to maintain but interaction access and gatekeeping is diminished.

Hypothesis 2: In light of the foregoing analysis, and in conjunction with Hypothesis 1's assertion on the evocative properties of male versus female skewed sex composition ratios, we would expect that women would be nominated as role occupants of task-specialist and idea-person positions more often in the structured than unstructured task condition in groups where they were in the majority.

METHODS

Small groups studied were a subset of groups involved in a broader experimental investigation of group sex composition and task structure (see Mabry, 1985, for a more complete description of procedures). A total $N = 30$ small groups, ranging in size of 3 to 5 members, with heterogeneous sex compositions were examined in this study. Groups were composed of undergraduate communication and liberal arts students who volunteered to participate in the study for minimal extra credit in a course. Assignment to groups was randomized within the constraints of the research design and participant availability. Overall, data from N = 89 subjects, n = 43 women and n = 46 men, were available for analysis.

Group Tasks

Task outcome structure was operationalized according to Shaw's (1963) conceptualization of "goal-path multiplicity" differences in small group experimentation. Two tasks differentiated outcome structure: a "human relations" case study task, and an "item ranking" task. Research indicates that case study tasks confront group participants with more responsibility and flexibility in defining task products, thereby creating a more ambiguous stimulus setting in contrast to the explicit and inflexible requirements of rank-ordered item task products (Shaw, 1981).

Instructions directed groups to reach a consensus decision on each task. The ranking task required group members to decide on the ordering of a ten-item list of social behaviors according to the perceived level of interpersonal or social incompetence implicated in each behavior listed. The case study problem focused on an executive secretary's misperceptions that were the likely source of a conflict regarding her efforts to shield a female superior from casual, unscheduled contacts with other department members during working hours. The order of task introduction was randomized across groups. One section of a questionnaire administered upon the completion of each task requested members to rate the task on its perceived difficulty, its goal-path multiplicity, and its intrinsic interest. A one-tailed t-test of goal-path multiplicity means was significant ($t = 4.01$, $df = 166$, $p < .001$), indicating group members perceived a difference in the outcome structure of the case study versus ranking task.

Participant Evaluation Instrument

Data for this study were obtained from items included on a post-task questionnaire section entitled: "Reactions to Group Members." All group participants were instructed to evaluate other group members by rank-ordering them (most to least) on the following four items:

(1) Rank your group's members according to the *quality* of the ideas they contributed to the group. (2) Rank the members of your group in terms of how much you thought they participated. (3) In any small group some members will have more influence on the group's final decision than others. Rank the members of your group in terms of the *amount of influence* you felt each had on your group's final decision. (4) One characteristic of small group discussions is that some members will contribute to the positive social climate, or atmosphere, of the group more than others. These are usually people we would find it pleasant to work with if we were in another group together. Rank the members of your group in terms of who you would *most* like to be with in another small group discussion.

The first and third questions elicit impressions about the "task-specialist" role, while the second question asks for the "idea person" in the group. Persons selected for either of these two roles would typically be members that concentrate on the task and are more aggressive and model the male sex-role stereotype. The fourth question inquires about the social maintenance contributions and likeability of group members ("best-liked" person) and thereby concentrates on social-emotional factors that typically model the female sex-role stereotype.

Procedures

Volunteers were randomly assigned to groups on the basis of schedules they provided to the researcher and received notices on participation about one week prior to their scheduled participation time. When people arrived at the laboratory room, they were greeted by an assistant, led into the room and seated at desks arranged in a discussion circle. Desks were letter-coded (A, B, etc.) to facilitate peer evaluations on questionnaires. Once at least three people reported, the assistant briefly discussed the general objectives of the study, sequences of events taking place in the session, and called attention to the presence of audio-tape recording equipment in the room (including the necessity for all participants to speak in a distinct manner for recording). After the orientation, materials for the first task were distributed, recording equipment was activated, and the assistant left the room. After twenty minutes, the assistant entered the room, turned off the equipment, collected the group's task decision sheet and other materials, and distributed questionnaires. The questionnaire contained items regarding the task, peer rating items, and perceptions of the group's work climate. After questionnaires were completed, the assistant distributed materials for the next task, activated the equipment, and left the room. At the conclusion of the second round of task deliberation and questionnaire completion, volunteers were debriefed and thanked.

Statistical Analysis

Sociometric questionnaire data were analyzed to determine frequencies of nominations for the highest ranked person under the structured and unstructured task conditions according to three sex or gender-role variables: Sex of the Rater, Sex of the Person Rated, and Composition of the Group (either predominately female or male). Only the sex of the top-ranked person was considered for these analyses. The final sample $N = 674$ nominations. Data varied slightly across groups due to incomplete responses from participants. A chi-square statistic was used as a test of significance on the frequencies of first-ranked nominations of men and women by same- and opposite-sex peers. The alpha level for the critical value of chi-square for all tests was set at $p < .05$.

RESULTS

Hypotheses 1 and 2 were not fully supported. Tables 6.1 and 6.2 clearly show that males were most often ranked first on the two "task-specialist" (1 and 3) and the "idea-person" (2) questions by their same-sex peers. Likewise, females were most often ranked first on all four questions by other women. Task structure did not seem to affect these outcomes. In fact, the clearest results are uniformly from comparisons of female and male raters within group sex compositions.

Generally nonsignificant or near significant results were obtained from Questions 2 and 3. Tables 6.1 and 6.2 show that in predominately female groups, females nominated males only slightly more often than they did females, and males in those same groups nominated females slightly more than they did other males. For the same questions in predominately male groups, the males were nominated more often by both males and females. This was true across both task conditions. Sex composition evoked more differences in gender-role differentiation than did group task structure.

Table 6.1
Percent of Highest (#1) Rankings in Predominantly Female Group Compositions

Tasks and	Sex of Rater and Person Rated*			
	Female Raters		Male Raters	
Questions	Females	Males	Females	Males
Structured Task				
Q1 Idea Quality	34.0% (18)	30.2% (16)	17.0% (9)	17.0% (9)
Q2 Participation	30.2% (16)	32.1% (17)	18.9% (10)	15.1% (8)
Q3 Influence	26.4% (14)	35.8% (19)	20.8% (11)	13.2% (7)
Q4 Likeability	30.2% (16)	34.0% (18)	20.8% (11)	13.2% (7)
Unstructured Task				
Q1 Idea Quality	37.7% (20)	28.3% (15)	22.6% (12)	9.4% (5)
Q2 Participation	34.0% (18)	28.3% (15)	22.6% (12)	11.3% (5)
Q3 Influence	35.8% (19)	28.3% (15)	20.8% (11)	13.2% (7)
Q4 Likeability	32.1% (17)	32.1% (17)	26.4% (14)	3.8% (2)

*Percentages equal cell percent-to-totals and frequencies = (n).

Question 1 (idea quality) resulted in a nearly significant chi-square for unstructured tasks in the predominately male group ($X^2 = 3.48$, $df = 1$, $p < .10 > .05$). Women in the group nominated males more frequently as the "task specialist" while the males' ranked nominations didn't favor either sex. This would be consistent with the logic of Hypothesis 1. No other significant effects were found for this question.

Question 4 (most liked) resulted in significant chi-square values for ratings in the unstructured task condition. As Tables 6.1 and 6.2 show, male raters in predominately female groups chose women as the "best-liked" member significantly more often ($X^2 = 8.31$, $df = 1$, $p < .01$). Within compositions, in the predominately female groups, men almost exclusively nominated women while women did not evidence a preference in their attributions of best-liked member ($X^2 = 6.49$, $df = 1$, $p < .02$). These findings are consistent with the expectations advanced in Hypothesis 2. When

Table 6.2

Percent of Highest (#1) Rankings in Predominantly Male Group Compositions

| Tasks and | Sex of Rater and Person Rated* | | | |
| | Female Raters | | Male Raters | |
Questions	Females	Males	Females	Males
Structured Task				
Q1 Idea Quality	11.4% (4)	17.1% (6)	20.0% (7)	51.4% (18)
Q2 Participation	8.6% (3)	20.0% (7)	11.4% (4)	57.1% (20)
Q3 Influence	11.4% (4)	17.1% (6)	25.7% (9)	45.7% (16)
Q4 Likeability	11.4% (4)	17.1% (6)	25.7% (9)	45.7% (16)
Unstructured Task				
Q1 Idea Quality	2.9% (1)	17.1% (6)	37.1% (13)	31.4% (11)
Q2 Participation	2.9% (1)	17.1% (6)	25.7% (9)	42.9% (15)
Q3 Influence	5.7% (2)	17.1% (6)	28.6% (10)	40.0% (14)
Q4 Likeability	8.6% (3)	14.3% (14)	25.7% (9)	42.9% (15)

*Percentages equal cell percent-to-totals and frequencies = (n).

unstructured and structured tasks were combined for Question 4, predominately female groups again showed a statistically significant chi-square value (X^2 = 5.775, df = 1, with $p < .02$). Males in these groups heavily nominated females as their "best-liked" member, while females divided their nominations between both sexes. Group task did not seem to affect nominations.

DISCUSSION

The objective of this study was to determine if perceived gender-role differentiation was affected by a combination of gender composition and task structure during small group interaction. The predictions were that in predominately male groups, traditional sex-role evaluations would more likely accrue to males, but in predominately female groups, women would also be perceived as enacting task-specialist and/or idea-person roles. Group tasks were thought to amplify these differences in that structured group tasks would better enable women to experience role expansion. The predictions for composition were partially supported. Except in the "best-liked" category in the predominately male groups, gender composition, not task structure, most significantly affected role attributions.

In male dominated groups, a male was nominated as the "task specialist," "idea person," and "best-liked" person more than 50% of the time under both task structures. It appeared that women were not really considered for either role in male dominated groups. The female dominated groups produced a more interesting pattern. Men and women equally nominated both sexes as the top-tanked person on the "task" or "idea" questions. The only significant difference occurred as females nominated both sexes almost equally on the "best-liked" category while the males nominated the females more often.

The results of this study clearly point to a gender composition effect predicated on more than the mere presence of both sexes in the composition of the task-oriented group. The question remains as to how this outcome can be formally explicated. The research literature on small group performance is a fertile ground from which to draw conceptual frameworks for explaining sociality. One such concept is the *assembly effect bonus* (see Shaw, 1981, for a useful summary). Assembly effects are beneficial consequences of composing (assembling) groups with members who possess particular skills, attitudes, personalities, or interests. Assembly *bonuses* represent latent performance advantages obtained from a unique combination of attributes created by the intended assembly of the specific attribute(s) desired in the group. Thus, assembling a team where all members possessed mathematics backgrounds, in order to provide task competence for a given project, also might bring together a team with above average interest in the project, because it represents a task members enjoy and have relatively high confidence in being able to complete successfully.

The study of gender-roles and group sex composition appear to share certain characteristics classifiable as assembly effect bonuses. One compelling piece of evidence can be found in the results of this study. The failure to validate a task effect on role attribution argues for the presence of some form of social synergy instrumental in creating a social context for interaction that shapes actors' perceptions independently of verbal instrumentalities needed in task completion. The cross-sex evaluations afforded by sex composition proved to be that synergy factor.

There is, of course, the consideration of whether groups with a preponderance of female or male members actually can produce a qualitative or quantitative *bonus* effect. Available evidence suggests that predilections of man and women may complement each other. Men as small group participants have been found to perform better on and prefer production tasks requiring high volumes of verbal or other outputs, while women appear to perform better on analytical discussion and negotiation tasks (Wood, Polek, & Aiken, 1985). Complementarity is a key factor in the assembly effect bonus in that most *bonuses* appear to be the products of compensatory integration rather than summative homogeneity of attributes. At this juncture of assessment, the primary point we want to emphasize is the lack of attention small group sex composition as an assembly effect bonus—or *gender-mix bonus*—has received.

Exploring the gender-mix bonus effects of small group sex compositions should provide researchers with a profitable starting point for conceptual development. Pruett's (1989) meta-analytic investigation of communicator style differences noted that men and women differ on most dimensions of communicator style and men are more likely to find their self-perception disconfirmed by others. One might inquire into the composition effects of communicator style and whether there are discernable style-by-sex (or gender-role) interactions. Smythe and Schlueter (1989) noted with some frustration the possible contaminating effects of laboratory experiment settings on the literature of sex differences in language use. They called for more naturalistic research. Such research could assess the potential confounding effects of contextual roles that may not be equitably or equally distributed among both sexes or the interplay between mixed-sex positional occupants in mutually interdependent positions, as either instance could stimulate gender-mix effect bonuses (or deficits).

In our attempt to isolate gender-linked small group role perceptions in mixed-sex groups, we have found that group sex compositions heavily weighted toward one sex appeared to affect group members' interaction role attributions of task-specialist, idea-person, and best-liked person (or social-emotional specialist). These findings are conceptually similar to those reported for small group performance assembly effect bonuses. The implications of this conceptualization for understanding the influence of communication on role development is only broached and must be left to future research to be explored in greater depth.

REFERENCES

Bartol, K. B., & Martin, D. C. (1986). Women and men in task groups. In R. D. Ashmore & F. K. Del Boca (Eds.), *The social psychology of female-male relations* (pp.259-310). New York: Academic Press.

Bradley, P. H. (1980). Sex, competence and opinion deviation: An expectation states approach. *Communication Monographs. 47*, 101-110.

Deaux, K. (1976). Sex: A perspective on the attribution process. In Harvey, W. J. Ickes, & R. F. Kidd (Eds.), *New directions in attribution research*, Vol. 1 (pp. 335-352). Hillsdale, N. J.: Erlbaum.

Deaux, K., & Major, B. (1987). Putting gender into context: An interactive model of gender-related behavior. *Psychological Bulletin, 94*, 369-389.

Dion, K. L. (1985). Sex, gender, and groups: Selected issues. In V. E. O'Leary, R. K. Unger, & S. B. Wallston (Eds.), *Women, gender, and social psychology* (pp. 293-347). Hillsdale, N. J.: Lawrence Erlbaum.

Eagly, A. (1987). *Sex differences in social behavior: A social-role interpretation.*

Hillsdale, N. J.: Lawrence Erlbaum.

Eagly, A., & Carli, L. L. (1981). Sex of researchers and sex-typed communication as determinants of sex differences in influenceability: A meta-analysis of social influence studies. *Psychological Bulletin, 90,* 1-20.

Eagly, A., & Johnson, B. T. (1990). Gender and leadership style: A meta-analysis. *Psychological Bulletin, 108,* 233-256.

Eagly, A., & Karau, S. J. (1991). Gender and the emergence of leaders : A meta-analysis. *Journal of Personality and Social Psychology, 60,* 685-710.

Eagly, A., & Wood, W. (1991). Explaining sex differences in social behavior:A meta-analytic perspective. *Personality and Social Psychology Bulletin, 17,* 306-315.

Mabry, E. A. (1985). The effects of gender composition and task structure on small group interaction. *Small Group Behavior, 16,* 75-96.

Mabry, E. A. (1987, November). *Sex, sex composition and task outcome structure effects on small group interaction.* Paper presented at the annual convention of the Speech Communication Association, Boston.

Mabry, E. A. (1989). Some theoretical implications of female and male interaction in unstructured small groups. *Small Group Behavior, 20,* 536-550.

Mabry, E. A., & Barnes, R. E. (1980). *The dynamics of small group communication.* Englewood Cliffs, N. J.: Prentice-Hall.

McGrath, J. E. (1984). *Groups: Interaction and performance.* Englewood Cliffs, N. J.: Prentice-Hall.

Meeker, B. F., & Weitzel-O'Neill, P. A. (1977). Sex roles and interpersonal behavior in task-oriented groups. *American Sociological Review, 42,* 91-105.

Parsons, T., & Bales, R. F. (1955). *Family, socialization and interaction process.* Glencoe, IL: Free Press.

Pruett, B. Mc. (1989). Male and female communicator style differences: A meta-analysis. In C. M. Lont & S. A. Friedley (Eds.), *Beyond boundaries: Sex and gender diversity in communication* (pp. 107-119). Fairfax, VA: George Mason University Press.

Ridgeway, C. L. (1978). Conformity, group-oriented motivation, and status attainment in small groups. *Social Psychology, 41,* 175-188.

Ridgeway, C. L. (1982). Status in groups: The importance of motivation. *American Sociological Review, 47,* 76-87.

Ridgeway, C. L., & Berger, J. (1986). Expectations, legitimation, and dominance behavior in task groups. *American Sociological Review, 51,* 603-617.

Shaw, M. E. (1963). Scaling group tasks: A method for dimensional analysis. *Technical Report No. 1,* ONR Contract NR 170-266, nonr-580 (11), University of Florida.

Shaw, M. E. (1981). *Group dynamics: The psychology of small group behavior* (3rd ed.). New York: McGraw-Hill.

Smythe, M. J., & Schlueter, D. W. (1989). Can we talk? A meta-analytic review of the sex differences in language literature. In C. M. Lont & S. A. Friedley (Eds.),

Beyond boundaries: Sex and gender diversity in communication (pp. 31-48). Fairfax, VA: George Mason University Press.

Strodtbeck, F., James, R. M., & Hawkins, C. (1957). Social status in jury deliberations. *American Sociological Review, 22,* 713-719.

Strodtbeck, F., & Mann, R. (1956). Sex role differences in jury deliberations. *Sociometry, 19,* 3-11.

Wood, W. (1987). Meta-analytic review of sex differences in group performance. *Psychological Bulletin, 102,* 53-71.

Wood, W., & Karten, S. J. (1986). Perceived sex differences in competence as a determinant of sex differences in interaction. *Journal of Personality and Social Psychology, 50,* 341-347.

Wood, W., Polek, D., & Aiken, C. (1985). Sex differences in group task performance. *Journal of Personality and Social Psychology, 48,* 63-71.

7

A Meta-Analysis of Gender Research in Managerial Influence

Kathleen J. Krone, Mike Allen, and John Ludlum

Questions related to gender and interpersonal influence in organizations have inspired considerable scholarly activity in recent years. One of the most frequently studied issues concerns similarities and differences in the communicative tactics male and female managers use when attempting to influence their employees' behavior. Many studies have investigated the impact of gender on compliance-gaining choices (see Table 7.1). While there appear to be many similarities in tactic choices among men and women, with only two exceptions (Kipnis, Schmidt, & Wilkinson, 1980; Riccillo & Trenholm, 1983), every study also reports some difference in tactic choice between the two groups.

Interpreting the meaning of these differences is difficult because of contradictory findings. For example, Instone, Major, & Bunker (1983), and Schlueter, Barge, & Blankenship (1990), report that under certain conditions women use more coercive behaviors than men, while Harper and Hirokawa (1988) and Offerman and Schrier (1985) report the opposite—men select coercive tactics significantly more often than women. Turner and Henzl (1987) report that women use more assertiveness than men, while Rizzo and Mendez (1988) claim men use more assertiveness than women. Some researchers report no gender differences in how often male and female managers use reward-based tactics (Hirokawa, Kodama, & Harper 1990), while others report men use rewards more often than women (Instone et al., 1983) and still others report that under certain conditions, upper-level female managers use rewards/promises more often than upper-level males (Schlueter et al., 1990).

Interpreting the research is further complicated by the variety of data collection procedures and measures of influence used. Laboratory studies in which students role-play managers attempting to influence must be compared to studies in which experienced workers respond to hypothetical influence situations. In some cases, researchers analyze participants' responses to pre-established lists of tactics (Kipnis, Schmidt, & Wilkinson, 1980; Offerman & Schrier, 1985; Riccillo & Trenholm, 1983; Rizzo & Mendez, 1988). In others, participants' written responses are analyzed (Harper & Hirokawa, 1988; Hirokawa et al., 1990; Schlueter et al., 1990). In fewer cases, what participants say they would say or do (Mainiero, 1986), or what they

Table 7.1
Coding System for Meta-Analysis of Managerial Compliance-Gaining

Study	Terms Used in Study	Code Used in Meta-Analysis
Harper & Hirokawa, 1988	reward-based	Reward
	punishment-based	Threat/Punishment
	altruism-based	Altruism
	rationale-based	Persuasion
Hirokawa, Kodama, & Harper, 1990	reward-based	Reward
	punishment-based	Threat/Punishment
	altruism-based	Altruism
	rationale-based	Persuasion
Instone, Major, & Bunker, 1983	reward	Reward
	coercion 1	Threat/Punishment
	coercion 2	Threat/Punishment
Mainiero, 1986	ingratiation	(not used)
	alternatives	Persuasion
	coalition formation	(not used)
	persuasion	Persuasion
	acquiescence	(not used)
Neuliep, 1985	ingratiation	(not used)
	promise	Reward
	debt	(not used)
	esteem	Altruism
	allurement	Reward
	threat	Threat/Punishment
	guilt	Altruism
	warning	Threat/Punishment
	direct request	(not used)
	explanation	Persuasion
	hinting	(not used)
	deceit	(not used)
Offerman & Schrier, 1985	reasoning	Persuasion
	indirect	(not used)
	withdrawal	(not used)
	reward/coercion	Reward and Threat
	pressure	Threat/Punishment
	unilateral	(not used)
	negotiation	Persuasion
	personal/dependent	Altruism

Table 7.1 (continued)

Study	Terms Used in Study	Code Used in Meta-Analysis
Riccillo & Trenholm, 1983		coercionThreat/Punishment
	persuasion	Persuasion
	reward	Reward
Rizzo & Mendez, 1988	assertiveness	(not used)
	reason	Persuasion
	friendliness	(not used)
	bargaining	Persuasion
	coalition	(not used)
	appeal to higher authority	(not used)
	sanction	Threat/Punishment
Rosen & Jerdee, 1973	threat	Threat/Punishment
	reward	Reward
	friendly-dependent	Altruism
	helping	Altruism
Schlueter, Barge,	reward-based	Reward
& Blankenship, 1990	punishment-based	Threat/Punishment
	altruism-based	Altruism
	rationale-based	Persuasion

actually say when attempting influence in an organizational simulation are analyzed (Turner & Henzl, 1987). Further, some studies examine the unmoderated effects of gender on managers' compliance-gaining choices while others also examine a range of variables as potential moderators. The degree of actual or perceived power a manager has in a particular organization appears to be an important situational variable affecting his or her compliance-gaining choices. However, very few studies include actual or perceived power as potential moderators of gender differences in influence tactic choice, and when they do, "power" often is operationalized differently across studies.

This chapter uses the technique of meta-analysis to clarify empirical research in the area of gender and managerial influence tactic choice. Recently, two impressive but more broadly focused meta-analyses attempted to clarify relationships between gender and organizational leadership behaviors (Eagly & Johnson, 1990; Wilkins & Andersen, 1991). Counter to gender-stereotypical expectations, Eagly and Johnson (1990) report evidence of *no* significant differences in the extent to which male and female managers lead in an interpersonally-oriented or in a task-oriented style.

However, results also are reported that are more consistent with gender-stereotypical expectations for male and female leaders. Specifically, women tended to adopt a more democratic, participative style, while men tended to adopt a more autocratic or directive leadership style. While this study is impressive in its scope, the authors intentionally excluded aspects of leadership style that are directly related to influence tactic choice, such as confronting errant employees or managing conflict. Wilkins and Andersen (1991) detected significant gender differences in male and female managers' influence choices, but concluded that the differences were too small to be of social significance. However, their research included only a small number of managerial influence studies. In analyzing broad ranges of leadership and managerial communication behavior, these meta-analyses completely exclude or include only a small number of studies directly related to managerial influence tactic choice. In the present study we assume that attempting to influence employees is a managerial activity of central importance in organizations, and thus, we focus specifically on managerial influence tactic choices: rational, coercion/punishment, altruism, and rewards.

EXPLAINING GENDER EFFECTS
IN MANAGERS' INFLUENCE CHOICES

Research reveals both similarities and differences in male and female managers' compliance-gaining choices. Gender similarities in managerial influence tactic choice can be explained by organizational socialization processes. According to this view, processes such as managerial selection and training are in place that ensure a certain degree of uniformity in managerial influence attempts. For instance, the accumulating research on interpersonal influence in organizations reveals that regardless of gender, the most commonly reported strategies involve the use of rationality and information-based persuasion (Kipnis et al., 1980; Krone, 1992; Krone & Ludlum, 1990). Put simply, part of becoming a manager involves learning how to exercise influence in ways that are judged to be both appropriate and effective in an organizational setting.

Research results that reveal gender differences in managerial influence choices are more difficult to explain. Sometimes these results are consistent with stereotypical sex-role expectations and thus may be attributed to traditional gender-role socialization processes. There are times however, when the pattern of differences is inconsistent with traditional sex-role expectations. A stereotypical gender socialization perspective on managerial compliance gaining predicts that male and female managers will attempt organizational influence differently because of differences in how they have been socialized to get their way. Male managers will be more task-oriented and use competitive and aggressive communication tactics in their influence attempts, while female managers will be more interpersonally inclined and use more cooperative tactics. Research results that support gender-stereotypical predictions include: (a) men use more assertiveness during their first influence attempts than do women (Rizzo &

Mendez, 1988), (b) men select coercive tactics significantly more often than women (Offerman & Schrier, 1985), (c) women and men in high dependency jobs (i.e., low power) acquiesce more than those in low dependency jobs, but women do so even more (Mainiero, 1986), (d) when confronting employees in an obligatory work situation (i.e., arriving late for work) men supplement their use of rationality tactics with harsher tactics such as issuing warnings and ultimatums, while women supplement their use of rationality tactics with softer strategies such as counsel (Harper & Hirokawa, 1988), and (e) women report using more altruism and disguised request than men (Schlueter et al., 1990).

Results that appear to contradict gender-stereotypical expectations include: (a) women use more coercion than men (Instone et al., 1983), (b) women use more assertiveness than men (Turner & Henzl, 1987), and (c) upper-level women report using threatening tactics more often than do upper-level men (Schlueter et al., 1990). This pattern of results could reveal that stereotypical, gender-role socialization and organizational socialization processes are not uniformly applied and evenly "absorbed" by all individuals. That is, there is hardly total societal consensus over what constitutes appropriate behavior for males and females or for what constitutes appropriate and effective ways for all organizational managers to influence their employees. Moreover, gender-role socialization and organizational socialization processes may not always complement one another. Males who have been socialized to be directive and authoritative must sometimes learn to act as participatory leaders in organizations. Females who have been socialized to be receptive and yielding must sometimes learn to act as aggressive and unyielding managers in organizational settings. Thus, the use of some managerial influence tactics may be more evenly conditioned by gender and organizational socialization processes than others.

Because research consistently reports that men and women use rationality tactics equally often in their managerial influence attempts, we expect meta-analytic results to reveal that:

H1: There will be no systematic differences in the extent to which male and female managers use rational, persuasive tactics in their compliance-gaining attempts with employees.

A gender-stereotypical perspective predicts that male managers will select harsher tactics such as punishment and threats more often than female managers. However, as was discussed previously, little empirical consensus exists concerning the extent to which men and women use coercive/punishment tactics during influence attempts with their employees. Some studies reveal no differences, another reveals that men use these tactics more often than women (Offerman & Schrier, 1985), while still other studies reveal that women use these tactics more often than men (Instone, et al., 1983; Schlueter et al., 1990). Because the empirical evidence is confusing, the following research question is posed:

RQ1: To what extent do male and female managers differ in their selection of coercion/punishment tactics in their attempts to influence employees?

To the extent that altruistic tactics reflect stereotypically feminine communication behaviors such as counseling and the use of disguised requests, a gender socialization perspective would predict that female managers use these tactics more often than their male counterparts. Available research reveals either no differences in the extent to which male and female managers use altruistic tactics in their influence attempts, or that women use more altruistic tactics in their managerial influence attempts than do men. Based on a gender-stereotypical perspective, meta-analytic results are expected to confirm the latter pattern.

H2: Female managers will report using more altruism in their compliance-gaining attempts than will males.

It is difficult to link gender-stereotypical expectations to female and male managers' use of rewarding strategies, since research results in this area are inconclusive. Studies either reveal no gender differences, that men use more rewarding tactics than women, or that women use more of these tactics than men. Because it is not clear that traditional sex-role socialization differentially affects the use of rewarding tactics by women and men, and because the existing research is inconclusive, the following research question is posed:

RQ2: To what extent do male and female managers differ in their use of rewarding tactics in their attempts to influence employees?

METHODOLOGY

Procedures

Meta-analysis was chosen to clarify this body of research, since it avoids problems associated with more traditional literature reviews (see Cooper & Rosenthal, 1980). Traditional reviews may prematurely conclude that an effect or a particular moderator exists based on the results of a single study. Traditional reviews also may overlook an effect or a moderator simply because a single experiment lacked sufficient statistical power to detect them. Meta-analysis avoids these problems by conducting systematic, statistical examinations across groups of studies. Statistical analyses were conducted by averaging effect sizes using algorithms developed by Hedges and Olkin (1985), and testing for homogeneity of the observed effects using a mainframe version of SPSS-X.

Literature Search

The *Social Sciences Citation Index* was examined for research related to social influence and compliance gaining in organizations. The term "gender" was useful in conducting the search, but it also was necessary to cast a wider net, since some research examined gender differences without referring to gender in the article's title.

As each published article was read, the references were examined for additional articles related to our topic. Several reviews of the literature also were examined (Krone & Ludlum, 1990; Ludlum & Krone, 1990; Seibold, Cantrill & Meyers, 1985) and relevant manuscripts obtained. Ultimately, ten research articles related to managerial compliance gaining were located that also reported the statistical information required in order to conduct a meta-analysis.

Coding for Influence Tactics

Managerial influence tactics have been conceptualized and measured in a variety of ways. To complete the meta-analysis, a single coding system was developed and used to recategorize influence tactics into four general categories: reward, threat/punishment, persuasion, and altruism. *Reward* consists in using promises, allurements, and positive self-esteem, while *threat/punishment* consists in giving warnings and ultimatums. *Persuasion* consists in giving rational explanations, exploring alternatives, and using negotiation. *Altruism* includes the use of counseling/helping, requesting favors, and appealing to the target's sense of duty.

RESULTS

Eight studies employing 1,813 respondents examined gender differences in the use of *persuasion* in managerial influence attempts. Results of the meta-analysis revealed that the average correlation was not statistically significant across studies ($r = -.001$). Chi-square analysis confirmed that the amount of variation is statistically insignificant ($X^2 = 5.31$, $df = 7$, $p > .05$; see Table 7.2.) Thus, Hypothesis 1 was supported.

Nine studies employing 2,019 respondents investigated gender differences in the use of *threats/punishments* in managerial influence attempts. Meta-analytic results revealed that males reported using these tactics significantly more often than did females. The average correlation was significant across studies ($r = .038$). Chi-square analysis confirmed that the amount of variation in these cases is statistically significant ($X^2 = 15.61$, $df = 8$, $p < .05$; see Table 7.2.).

Six studies including 920 respondents examined gender differences in the use of *altruism* in managers' influence attempts. Results revealed that the average correlation was not statistically significant across studies ($r = -.066$). Chi-square analysis confirmed that the amount of variation is statistically insignificant ($X^2 = 9.12$, $df = 5$, $p > .05$). Hypothesis 2 was not supported.

Six investigations including 1,143 respondents examined the relationship between gender and the use of *rewards* in managerial influence attempts. Meta-analytic results revealed that male managers reported using these tactics with employees signficantly more often than did females ($r = .048$). Chi-square analysis confirmed that the amount of variation is statistically significant ($X^2 = 11.03$, $df = 5$, $p < .05$; see Table 7.2.)

Table 7.2
Average Effect Sizes for the Relationship between Gender and Tactic Choice

	r	*N*	*K*	X^2
Persuasion	−0.001	1813	8	5.31
Threats/Punishments	0.038	2019	9	15.61*
Altruism	−0.066	920	6	9.12
Rewards	0.048	1143	6	11.03*

NOTES:

r = Average correlation. **A positive correlation indicates that males use the tactic more often; negative correlation indicates that females use the tactic more often.**
N = combined sample size.
K = number of studies.
* $p < .05$

DISCUSSION

While the statistical differences are small, there is still some variability in managerial influence attempts that can be predicted by biological sex. Male and female managers mainly are similar in their use of rational persuasion and altruism, but are somewhat different in their use of rewards and coercive tactics with employees. That men reported a greater inclination to use both rewards and punishment in their downward influence attempts may reflect a gender-socialized difference in how male and female managers use their power in organizations. It appears the use of some influence tactics for male managers in organizations may be conditioned by stereotypical gender socialization—in particular, the use of harsher tactics such as threats and punishment. That this pattern of results appears and partially mirrors those found in a meta-analysis of gender differences in the selection of conflict management strategies (Gayle, Preiss, & Allen, 1991) lends additional support for the inclusion of gender in the development of theoretical explanations for strategic message behavior. The more frequent use of reward tactics among male managers is not necessarily consistent with gender-stereotypical predictions. It is possible male managers have access to (or perceive they have access to) more resources to use as rewards in their influence attempts, and thus rely on them more often. The use of rewards also draws attention to the status inequality between reward-giver and reward-receiver. It involves an explicit use of authority that male managers may feel more comfortable with due to gender socialization or organizational socialization processes. It may be that male managers are more comfortable with their perceived right to use their authority explicitly, and in some cases, more harshly.

Organizational socialization processes could be conditioning similarities in the extent to which male and female managers use rational persuasion in their compliance-gaining attempts with their employees. The symbolic importance of behaving, acting, and communicating rationally in organizations (Feldman & March, 1981) may be "ambient" socialization knowledge, equally available to all organizational members. Given the importance of communicating rationally or appearing to communicate rationally, practices such as backing up requests with logical explanations occur more frequently and publicly and thus are more likely to be subjected to reinforcement through ongoing organizational socialization forces.

That both similarities and differences persist between male and female managerial compliance-gaining choices reveals that neither gender-stereotypical nor organizational socialization processes are uniform and complete. Instead, the research patterns illustrate that both gender and socialization processes occur together in organizational settings. The use of certain types of managerial compliance-gaining tactics (i.e., those related to the use of coercion for males) may depend at least to some extent on gender-stereotypical socialization. The widely reported use of rational persuasion in both female and male managerial influence attempts may be one consequence of organizational socialization processes that evenly penetrates the communicative repertoires of all organizational members.

To some extent, this study was limited by the relatively narrow range of influence tactics that we were able to code for. While some of the studies assessed a broad range of tactics, many assessed just a few. Consequently, in developing our coding scheme, specific tactics related to processes such as "negotiation" had to be subsumed within broader categories, and some tactics such as "coalition formation" or "appeals to higher authorities" had to be ignored altogether.

Second, we suspect that there are structural explanations for gender similarities and differences in managers' influence tactic choices, but due to an insufficient number of studies, we were unable to test for the possible moderating effects of positional power. According to this view, men and women who occupy identical structural positions of power learn to attempt influence in ways that are appropriate and effective for anyone who occupies these roles. Thus, what appear to be gender differences in organizational communication are really differences due to the power associated with one's position. Once structural position is controlled for, gender differences should disappear (Kanter, 1977). Indeed, some research reveals that when male and female managers occupy positions with identical levels of formal power, they select similar types of influence tactics. Students who role-played managers (presumably with equal levels of power) revealed similarities only in their selection of tactic choices (Riccillo & Trenholm, 1983). Similarly, when male and female managers were assigned to equally powerful and powerless conditions, no significant gender differences in compliance-gaining choices were reported (Hirokawa et al., 1990). However, additional evidence suggests that male managers perceived that they had significantly more power than did female managers (Schlueter et al., 1990). Thus, it cannot always be assumed simply because men and women occupy similar hierarchical positions in organizations that they possess—or perceive that they possess—equal levels of power.

Additional studies report gender differences in tactic choice, even among male and female managers who supposedly occupy similar structural positions in organizations. For instance, while both men and women in high dependency (i.e., low power) jobs acquiesced more than men and women in low dependency jobs (i.e., high power), low power women acquiesced to a *greater extent* than did low power men (Mainiero, 1986). In addition, in obligatory work situations (where managers presumably had the "right" to correct an errant employee), men and women appeared to use their power differently. While both groups used rationality tactics similarly, men also relied more on punishment-based strategies than did women (Harper & Hirokawa, 1988). Women, on the other hand, relied more on altruism in obligatory situations than did men (Harper & Hirokawa, 1988; Schlueter et al., 1990). Relatedly, one study reported situational confidence as a significant predictor of influence tactic choice. Specifically, while women used more coercion that did men, much of this difference could be attributed to lower levels of situational confidence reported among the women (Instone et al., 1983).

To summarize, while we lacked a sufficient number of studies to test for their effects in the meta-analysis, results from individual studies suggest that situational confidence, structural location in the organization, and self-perceptions of organizational power may combine with gender to affect managers' tactic choices. Future research should continue to consider possible relationships between various forms of power and influence tactic choices in organizations. Many researchers have measured level in the hierarchy or attempted to control for power by assigning men and women to experimental conditions of equal power. Available research suggests that such "objective" measures of power alone may be inadequate to assess actual levels of organizational power, since men and women may experience and use their power differently. It also is necessary to assess female and male managers' self-perceptions of power, even when they appear to occupy identical structural positions in the organization.

Third, while no studies were found that examined gender and sequences of managerial influence attempts, it is possible that gender-based similarities and differences in tactic choice will depend to some extent on when the influence attempt occurs in an ongoing stream of interaction. Conflict management research indicates that women and men both report using harsher tactics, but that women opt to use these tactics later in the confrontation (Conrad, 1991).

Finally, as increasing numbers of women advance to positions of authority in organizations, it may be necessary to reconsider what it means to be influential. Preestablished measures of organizational influence may not successfully capture, and instead underrepresent, uniquely feminine ways of being influential in organizations (see Ferguson, 1984; and Kolb, 1992). The possibility that women could be reconstructing what it means to enact power in organizations should not be overlooked in our research.

REFERENCES

Conrad, C. (1991). Communication in conflict: Style-strategy relationships. *Communication Monographs, 58,* 135-155.

Cooper, H. M., & Rosenthal, R. (1980). Statistical versus traditional procedures for summarizing research findings. *Psychological Bulletin, 87,* 442-449.

Eagly, A. H., & Johnson, B. T. (1990). Gender and leadership style: A meta-analysis. *Psychological Bulletin, 108,* 233-256.

Feldman, M. S., & March, J. G. (1981). Information as sign and symbol. *Administrative Science Quarterly, 36,* 171-186.

Ferguson, K. E. (1984). *The feminist case against bureaucracy.* Philadelphia: Temple University Press.

Gayle, B. M., Preiss, R. W., & Allen, M. (1991). Sex differences in conflict management selection: A meta-analytic review. Paper presented at the annual meeting of the International Communication Association, Chicago.

Harper, N. L., & Hirokawa, R. Y. (1988). A comparison of persuasive strategies used by female and male managers I: An examination of downward influence. *Communication Quarterly, 36,* 157-168.

Hedges, L., & Olkin, I. (1985). *Statistical methods for meta-analysis.* Orlando, FL: Academic Press.

Hirokawa, R. Y., Kodama, R. A., & Harper, N. L. (1990). Impact of managerial power on persuasive strategy selection by female and male managers. *Management Communication Quarterly, 4,* 30-50.

Instone, D., Major, B., & Bunker, B. B. (1983). Gender, self-confidence, and social influence strategies: An organizational simulation. *Journal of Personality and Social Psychology, 44,* 322-333.

Kanter, R. M. (1977). *Men and women of the corporation.* New York: Basic Books. Kipnis, D., Schmidt, S. M., & Wilkinson, I. (1980). Intraorganizational influence tactics: Explorations in getting one's way. *Journal of Applied Psychology, 65,* 440-452.

Kolb, D. M. (1992). Women's work: Peacemaking in organizations. In D. M. Kolb & J. M. Bartunek (Eds.), *Hidden conflict in organizations: Uncovering behind-the-scenes disputes* (pp. 63-91). Newbury Park, CA: Sage Publications.

Krone, K. J. (1992). A comparison of organizational, structural and relationship effects on subordinates' upward influence choices. *Communication Quarterly, 40,* 1-15.

Krone, K. J., & Ludlum, J. (1990). An organizational perspective on interpersonal influence. In J. P. Dillard (Ed.), *Seeking compliance: The production of interpersonal influence messages* (pp. 123-142). Scottsdale, AZ: Gorsuch Scarisbrick Publishers.

Ludlum, J. T., & Krone, K. J. (1990). Towards a competency-based perspective on compliance gaining in organizational settings. Paper presented at the annual meeting of the Speech Communication Association, Chicago.

Mainiero, L. A. (1986). Coping with powerlessness: The relationship of gender and job dependency to empowerment-strategy usage. *Administrative Science Quarterly, 31,* 633-653.

Neuliep, J. (1985). The influence of theory X and theory Y management styles on the selection of compliance-gaining strategies. *Communication Research Reports, 4,* 14-19.

Offerman, L. R., & Schrier, P. E. (1985). Social influence strategies: The impact of sex, role, and attitudes toward power. *Personality and Social Psychology Bulletin, 11,* 286-300.

Riccillo, S. C., & Trenholm, S. (1983). Predicting managers' choice of influence mode: The effects of interpersonal trust and worker attributions on managerial tactics in a simulated organizational setting. *Western Journal of Speech Communication, 47,* 323-339.

Rizzo, A., & Mendez, C. (1988). Making things happen in organizations: Does gender make a difference? *Public Personnel Management, 17,* 9-20.

Rosen, B., & Jerdee, T. (1973). The influence of sex-role stereotypes on evaluations of male and female supervisory behavior. *Journal of Applied Psychology, 57,* 44-48.

Schlueter, D. W., Barge, J. K., & Blankenship, D. (1990). A comparative analysis of influence strategies used by upper- and lower-level male and female managers. *Western Journal of Speech Communication, 54,* 42-65.

Seibold, D. R., Cantrill, J. G., & Meyers, R. A. (1985). Communication and interpersonal influence: In M. L. Knapp & G. R. Miller (Eds.), *Handbook of interpersonal communication* (pp. 551-611). Newbury Park, CA: Sage.

Turner, L. H., & Henzl, S. A. (1987). Influence attempts in organizational conflict: The effects of biological sex, psychological gender, and power position. *Management Communication Quarterly, 1,* 32-57.

Wilkins, B. M., & Andersen, P. A. (1991). Gender differences and similarities in management communication: A meta-analysis. *Management Communication Quarterly, 5,* 6-35.

8

Sex, Schemata, and Social Status: TV Character Identification and Occupational Aspirations among Adolescents

Robert J. Griffin, Shaikat Sen, and Rhonda Plotkin

Female characters on television are being presented more frequently in what traditionally had been male occupations (Dambrot, Reep, & Bell, 1988). Since television viewing has been found to contribute to adolescents' attitudes toward gender roles (Morgan, 1987), this trend in television content offers new opportunities to examine the relationship between television character identification and occupational aspirations among male and, particularly, female adolescents.

During their high school years, adolescents realistically explore their vocational choices and become aware of opportunities and constraints (Raskin, 1985). Television can expose these adolescents to a wider array of occupational alternatives than they will encounter in their daily lives (Faber, Brown, & McLeod, 1978).

Recent trends in mass communication research would suggest, however, that televised depictions of occupations as related to gender might not affect all adolescents in the same way. Mass-mediated information seems to offer a base from which viewers differentially construct some of their concepts of the world, based on their preexisting experiences, knowledge, aspirations, expectancies, needs, and values (Mendelsohn, 1990). "To a very important degree," Mendelsohn observes, "we are slowly returning to a rather fundamental principle: Humans act according to what they know and understand (or misunderstand) and not necessarily according to what they simply see or hear" (p. 38).

For example, any media influence on occupational aspirations will probably be mitigated by various personal experiences adolescents have with different careers. According to Faber et al. (1978), "a viewer who has had little personal experience with a range of occupations . . . may more readily accept the television portrayal of various occupations, while a viewer who has had personal experience with persons in the occupation will compare the television portrayal with his or her prior understanding of the occupation" (p. 217). Both gender and social status could affect an adolescent's personal exposure to persons in various occupations and thereby temper any television effect.

STATUS AND GENDER

Press (1989) proposes that examining both gender and social class may be "crucially important for the study of media audiences" (p. 250). Our study will examine the relationship between televised occupational depictions and adolescent occupational aspirations in the context of gender and social status differences.

Experiential exposure to potential occupations can be a by-product of social class. Parental modeling of occupational and domestic roles can be a significant influence on adolescents developing adult expectations (Katz, 1987). Parents in lower status homes, as well as their adult relatives and friends, are quite likely to display traditional occupations for males and particularly females. And research indicates that adolescents from lower socioeconomic levels do tend to manifest more traditional gender stereotypes and behaviors than middle-class adolescents (Katz, 1987).

Adolescents from lower social class backgrounds also tend to watch more television than those from higher social strata, and tend to perceive television as more "real" than do adolescents from higher status families (Faber et al., 1978). This would suggest that adolescents from lower social strata could be affected more than others by traditional depictions of occupational gender roles on television, and possibly by changes in those depictions if they represent new occupational opportunities outside the realm of their usual experiences.[1]

Gender differences can also affect occupational experiences and aspirations. Females tend to participate in fewer types of jobs than do males, and males are more likely to come to occupy higher status, professional positions (England, 1992). A number of authors (e.g., Danziger, 1983; Geis, Brown, Jennings, & Corrado-Taylor, 1984) even maintain that gender is associated with status, since the social ranking of females has traditionally been lower than that of males. Danziger (1983) proposes that being female could interact with social class to affect career aspirations, although academic achievement can mitigate the effects of gender and status. She observes that the higher the social status of females, the more their aspirations resemble males'.

The combination of gender and status differences suggests that lower status female adolescents, as compared to male and higher status female adolescents, probably have much less experiential exposure to a range of occupations, especially those not traditionally held by females, and therefore may be more likely to be affected by television portrayals of female occupations. The portrayal might at least affect the awareness lower status females have of other occupational opportunities, and possibly their aspirations. This may be especially true if adolescents perceive these characters as role models, as people they would like to be like in the future. Our study will concentrate on the relationship of such character identification with occupational aspirations among adolescents, divided along the dimensions of gender and social status.

MEDIA AND OCCUPATIONAL STEREOTYPES

By and large, depictions of male and female roles on television have been very traditional (Signorielli, 1991) and would seem to reinforce the stereotypes that adolescents from lower social strata tend to hold. Female characters have been cast in traditional roles and depicted as having limited employment possibilities (Signorielli, 1985). As of the mid-1980s, however, there were changes in the depictions of women such that more than half of the programs showed women in occupations. About half of these depictions portrayed women in nontraditional occupations and about half in traditional (Calvert & Huston, 1987). There is no equivalent attempt, however, to show men in nontraditional roles (Williams, Baron, Phillips, Travis, & Jackson, 1986).

Various studies (e.g., Miller & Reeves, 1976; Signorielli & Lears, 1992) have indicated that gender-stereotyped television portrayals may play a role in shaping children's gender role-perceptions, attitudes, or behaviors. Some studies have found a relationship between the career aspirations of children and adolescents and the kinds of television content to which they are exposed, in particular the kinds of gender-role stereotypes portrayed (e.g., Beuf, 1974; Jennings-Walstedt, Geis, & Brown, 1980). Experimental evidence suggests that counter-stereotypical presentations can influence occupational aspirations at least among preteens (Williams, LaRose, & Frost, 1981; Johnston & Ettema, 1982). Wroblewski and Huston (1987) found that television serves as a source of occupational information for 10-to-13-year-olds, and that girls expressed considerable interest in the nontraditional occupations portrayed. Boys, however, showed more traditional attitudes toward male occupations portrayed. The authors suggest that television can indeed affect the gender schemata of early adolescents. Our study examines this relationship among high school age adolescents.

MEDIA AND GENDER SCHEMATA

Schemata represent organized knowledge held in long-term human memory about a given concept or type of stimulus (Fiske & Taylor, 1984). Based on cumulative experience, schemata provide people with expectations that guide their perceptions and their processing and storage of information in memory (Bem, 1981). Therefore, schemata help people anticipate the future, set goals, and choose the appropriate behaviors to reach those goals. Gender schemata, specifically, include self-defining characteristics such as descriptions of physical, psychological, and role expectations (Liben & Signorella, 1987).

Schemata help people comprehend television and other media content. For example, when information is lacking or ambiguous, people can use schemata to generate inferences and interpretations. Similarly, schemata allow people to create and use generalizations to take the place of specific examples (Calvert & Huston, 1987). Thus, television depictions of specific characters could be stored in viewers' memories as general cases, representing broader types. For example, a female television character depicted in a specific occupation not traditionally held by many women (e.g., a construction worker) could represent to viewers the broader group of females in a variety of nontraditional occupations for women.

Children tend to select programs, and develop schemata, "appropriate" to their genders (Calvert & Huston, 1987). Boys and girls tend to choose same-sex role models from those available to them, although girls are more likely than boys to identify with characters of the opposite sex (Eisenstock, 1984).[2] The realism of the televised portrayal will also play a role in determining whether the adolescent considers the depictions relevant to his or her task of determining various occupational opportunities (Faber et al., 1978). In general, adolescent viewers may use and reconstruct gender-related occupational information from television according to their informational needs, mental schemata, and related perceptions of reality.

RESEARCH QUESTIONS AND HYPOTHESES

To help us understand and validate the patterns of gender and status constraints within which the students are developing their career plans, our first research question is: what differences will be found between higher and lower status male and female adolescents in terms of their educational and occupational plans? Based on our review of the literature, we propose that:

H1: Status and gender will interact such that higher status adolescent females will prefer occupations that are more nontraditional (i.e., more similar to those of males) than the occupations preferred by lower status females.

Our second research question is: what is the relationship of television exposure and the perceived realism of shows adolescents watch to their identification with television characters in occupational roles? In particular, since adolescents who perceive television occupational depictions as real would be more likely to consider those depictions relevant to their career decisions, we propose:

H2: There will be a positive relationship between the perceived reality of television shows that adolescents watch and the likelihood that they will identify with characters in occupational roles on those shows.

Our third research question is: what differences will be found in adolescents' identification with occupational television characters based on the viewers' gender and social status differences? Based on prior research, we expect that adolescents would generally identify with same-sex characters, and that girls would be more likely than boys to identify with characters of the opposite sex. In regard to status and gender, we hypothesize:

H3: Higher status girls will be more likely than lower status girls to identify with female characters in less traditionally female roles.

Our fourth research question is: what is the relationship between the female traditionality of occupations to which adolescents aspire and the female traditionality of the occupations of television characters with which they identify? Given that lower status females are expected to have comparatively less experiential exposure to a wide variety of female occupations, we propose that:

H4: There will be a positive relationship between the female traditionality of the characters with which lower status females identify and the female traditionality of their own preferred occupation.

We do not expect to find similar relationships between these variables among higher status girls, or among higher or lower status boys.

METHOD

A survey of a probability sample of students ($N = 542$) from eight randomly chosen public high schools in the Chicago suburbs was conducted in the spring of 1988. Schools were in the more affluent suburbs as well as in areas of lower-middle income.

Each student indicated his or her preferred occupation in an open-ended question that asked, "What would you like your occupation to be 20 years from now?" Responses were coded along two dimensions: the Duncan (1961) socioeconomic status scale, and "female traditionality"--the proportion of those in that occupation who are females, according to census data. Responses of "homemaker" or equivalent were coded as 99% female. This coding system for female traditionality of occupations produced a useful, richly coded, continuous scale.

To measure identification with television characters, students were given a list of nine male and eleven female main characters who were depicted in occupational roles in various primetime television shows on the air in the spring of 1988, grouped according to the shows on which they appear. Students were told to "take a look at the characters listed under the shows you watch. Are there any that you would very much like to be like in the future?" If so, they were to check-mark the character. They were told that they could name as many or as few (or even none) as they need. Students could also write in the names of other characters they would like to be like in the future.[3]

A measure of the female traditionality of each job portrayed by a character was derived by using the census data to rate each job according to the percentage of real-world job holders who are female in that occupation. Each student who identified with at least one female character received a score representing the traditionality (or average traditionality, if more than one character was selected) of the occupation that character is portrayed as holding on television. The same was done in regard to the male occupational characters with which each student identified. (Both scales are calibrated as percent female.)

Students were also asked to rate each show they watch according to how "real" the show seems to them, "in other words, how much does the show represent the way things are in everyday life?" Television exposure was measured as the number of hours the student said he or she watches television between 4 P.M. and midnight on weekdays.

Other items in the questionnaire were used to measure parents' social status, the student's gender, and the amount of education he or she plans to complete.

Basic control variables included measures of the student's age, race, and high school grade point average (GPA). Various analyses also employed, when appropriate, controls for television exposure, perceived realism, traditionality of each parent's occupation, and the frequency that the student talks with parents, teachers, guidance counselors, and friends about his or her future career, based on student responses to questionnaire items.

RESULTS

Education, Occupation

The first research question asked what differences would be found between higher and lower status male and female adolescents in terms of their educational and occupational plans. (See Table 8.1, on the following pages.) Controlling for the effects of high school GPA, age, and race, lower status students tend to be planning less further education than their higher status counterparts. Concomitantly, higher status students aspire to somewhat higher status occupations than do their lower status peers. As might also be expected, academic success in high school, in terms of GPA, is associated positively with desires for further education and the status of occupations the students would like to have.

The career aspirations of boys are toward jobs which are more traditionally male than the careers to which the girls, on the average, aspire. The hypothesized interaction between status and gender (H1) is supported, since Table 8.1 indicates that higher status girls desire careers that are comparatively less traditional for females than those desired by their lower status counterparts. On the average, higher status girls aspire to careers in which males are traditionally the majority.

The negative relationship between high school GPA and traditionality of preferred occupations (*beta* = <.17, p = .001, in Table 8.1) is stronger among girls (partial r = <.26, p = .001) than among boys (partial r = <.02, *ns*), indicating that academic success relates to high school girls' aspirations for less traditionally female occupations regardless of age, race, and social status. The relationship of race to traditionality of preferred occupations (*beta* = .13, p = .01, in Table 8.1) similarly is stronger among girls (partial r = .21, p = .001) than among boys (partial r = <.05, *ns*), indicating that white girls are somewhat more likely than nonwhite girls to want traditionally female occupations, controlling for age, status, and GPA.

Television Exposure, Realism

The second research question concerned the relationship of television exposure and the perceived realism of shows adolescents watch to their identification with television characters in occupational roles. Exposure relates positively to the number of characters the students identify with (partial $r = .24$, $p = .001$, with control for gender, status, race, age, GPA, and perceived realism of shows). Hypothesis H2 is supported, since there is a positive, albeit small, relationship between the perceived realism of the television shows the adolescents watch and the likelihood that they will identify with characters on those shows (partial $r = .16$, $p = .001$, with control for gender, status, race, age, GPA, and exposure). The relationships of exposure and perceived realism, used as covariates, to students' identification with male and female characters are also shown in Table 8.1. There are no statistically significant differences in television exposure or in perceived realism of shows across gender and social status groups.

Gender, Status, Identification

The third research question asked what differences would be found in adolescents' identification with occupational television characters based on gender and social status differences. Table 8.1 indicates that there are marked differences across gender in regard to the gender of characters with which the students identify. There are no differences by status. Traditional distinctions are apparent. As expected, girls tend to identify with the female characters more than boys do and boys tend to identify with male characters more than girls do. And girls are more likely than boys to identify with characters of the opposite gender.

Patterns are also found when analyzing the female traditionality of the job role of the characters with which students identify. Among those who identify with male characters, girls are more likely than boys of the same status level to identify with male characters in less traditionally male roles. In support of H3, higher status girls are more likely than lower status girls to identify with female characters in less traditionally female roles, as the interaction in Table 8.1 indicates. Higher status girls are even more likely than higher status boys to identify with female characters in more traditionally male roles. On the average, higher status girls who identify with female characters tend to choose those depicted in occupations that are quite non-traditional for women (83% male).

Identification, Aspiration

The fourth research question concerned the relationship between the female traditionality of occupations to which adolescents aspire and the female traditionality of the occupations of television characters with which they identify.

Among lower status girls there is indeed a statistically significant, positive relationship between the female traditionality of their desired occupations and the

Table 8.1
Education, Occupation, and Television Character Identification by Gender and Social Status (Adjusted Means)

Independent Variables		Females		Males		Significance			
		Lower Status (a)	Higher Status (b)	Lower Status (c)	Higher Status (d)	Main Effects: Status	Sex	Interaction	Significant covariates
Education Planned	M =	4.8bd	5.2ac	4.8bd	5.1ac	$F_{(1,430)} = 14.31$, $p = .001$			GPA, .41***
	n =	106	126	106	99				
Status of Preferred Occupation	M =	60.8bd	69.0ac	62.0bd	66.7ac	$F_{(1,389)} = 10.51$, $p = .001$			GPA, .32***
	n =	105	112	90	93				
Female Traditionality of Preferred Occupation	M =	51.6bcd	43.8acd	19.3ab	25.4ab		$F_{(1,389)} = 119.98$, $p = .001$	$F_{(1,393)} = 9.45$, $p = .002$	GPA, -.17*** Race, .13**
	n =	105	112	87	92				
TV Occupational Characters Identified With: *Male*	M =	0.5cd	0.5cd	1.3ab	1.3ab		$F_{(1,469)} = 72.20$, $p = .001$		Exposure, .20*** Perceived Realism, .11*
	n =	120	133	115	110				

Female	M =	.07cd	0.8cd	0.2ab	0.3ab	$F(1,469) =$ 31.52, $p = .001$	Exposure, .18*** Perceived Realism,.12**
	n =	120	133	115	110		
Cross-sex	M =	0.5cd	0.5cd	0.2ab	0.3ab	$F(1,469) =$ 7.25, $p = .005$	Exposure, .14** Perceived Realism, 08*
	n =	120	133	115	110		
Female Traditionality of Occupations of Characters Identified With:							
Male	M =	42.4cd	37.4d	29.6a	27.5ab	$F(1,172) =$ 14.31, $p = .001$	
	n =	30	32	59	60		
Female	M =	30.1b	17.0ad	19.5	35.6b		$F(1,147) =$ 8.08, $p = .005$
	n =	53	66	16	21		

SCALES: **Education Planned:** 1 = some high school; 2 = finished high school; 3 = trade school; 4 = some college or junior college; 5 = college degree; 6 = graduate or professional degree. **Status of Preferred Occupation:** Duncan Scale (higher values = higher status).
NOTE: Covariates of age, high school grade point average (GPA), and race (0 = nonwhite, 1 = white) were used in all the analyses above. Weekday evening television exposure and perceived realism of shows watched were also used as control variables for analyses of television character identification variables. Covariate coefficients are betas. The significance key is as follows: * $p = .05$; ** $p = .01$; *** $p = .001$. Comparisons among means were conducted using Scheffé procedure, after a significant main effect or interaction was found. In any given row, an initial (a through d) for each value of M indicate that the mean is significantly different (.05 level) from the mean in the column with that initial. For example, "b" indicates that the mean is significantly different from the mean for higher status females.

female traditionality of the occupation of the characters they identify with (partial r = .37, p = .026, taking into account controls for race, age, GPA, television exposure, perceived realism of shows watched, discussions with others about future careers, and occupational traditionality of parents). There are no other statistically significant relationships between traditionality of occupational desires and traditionality of occupations of characters identified with in any of the other three gender-by-status groups. Therefore, there is support for H4.

From the standpoint of schema theory, it is important to note that overall only 8.2% of students who identify with a character aspire to the same occupation as that character in the future. Low status girls are not any more or less likely than the other groups to name the same preferred occupation as the character has (ϵ = 4.9%, X^2 = 1.74, df = 3, ns). Given the correlations between character identification and aspirations found among lower status girls, it is likely that they engaged mentally in some form of abstraction from the character's occupation to a broader class of occupations with similar levels of female traditionality.

DISCUSSION

Gender and social status differences in the processes that relate to occupational choice were very apparent in this study. Some constraints on the occupational aspirations of lower status girls in particular are evident. It does appear, however, that academic success in high school could inspire these girls to pursue more education and careers that are higher in status and less traditionally female. Given that their experiential exposure to these alternative careers was expected to be somewhat limited, however, we explored the relationship that media depictions of careers, including those showing women in nontraditional occupational roles, might have with the occupational aspirations of lower status females in particular. It was in this group of lower status females that we found a relationship between the traditionality of the occupations they would like and the traditionality of the occupational television characters they identified with. From the standpoint of possible media effects, this result suggests that television character depictions might affect the awareness that lower status females have of alternative careers for themselves, and perhaps their desires for such careers.

The identification that male and female adolescents made with characters generally followed the traditional same-gender pattern indicative of processes of socialization to gender roles. Although girls were more likely than boys to identify with characters of the opposite gender, girls who identified with male characters tended to choose those in occupational roles that are less traditionally male than the characters chosen by boys of the same status level. Therefore, cross-gender identification for girls is still sensitive to the gender traditionality of the role played by the character. These results are consistent with Eisenstock's (1984) observation that some children imitate behavior they see which is appropriate for their own gender or gender-role preference, regardless of whether the person performing the behavior is male or female.

It is likely that cognitive processes guided by schema formation account for part of the relationship that media occupational depictions had with occupational desires. To some adolescents in this study, television characters shown in occupations seem to represent not just the character's job role but a broader class of occupations (e.g., professions that are not traditional for women). Therefore, these teen viewers must be cognitively adjusting (e.g., abstracting and customizing) the televised information in the process of storing it in memory. For example, some adolescents might feel that they like the kind of social role or power that goes along with being the doctor or lawyer they identify with on television, yet realize that real-world constraints would make it difficult for them to get into that occupation. They might strive instead toward a career that provides at least some of the same attributes that are important to them, but that might be more attainable. Accordingly, it is noteworthy that only among lower status girls did we find relationships between traditionality of character occupation and traditionality of desired careers. Therefore, that kind of gender-related occupational information was probably more relevant to their career aspirations than it was to the career desires of the others. The others may have identified with various characters for reasons not related to occupational traditionality, or had greater, experientially based information that regulated the impact of televised depictions on their career aspirations.

The relationship of perceived realism of shows to identification with characters on those shows indicates that adolescents probably take some care in selecting such role models and potential sources of occupational and gender-role information.

CONCLUSION

In general, the more recent television depictions of female characters in nontraditional occupational roles for women seem to have some indirect relationship with occupational aspirations among those female adolescents whose social status provides few alternative, real-world role models for such occupational roles. The television depictions generally appear to work, not by providing direct occupational role models, but by stimulating schematic processes in long-term memory that abstract the character's specific occupation to that of a broader class of occupations with similar attributes, in this case, the female traditionality of the occupation. The value of the occupational information to lower status girls in our study probably motivated their use of the information-processing steps involved to draw occupational inferences.

NOTES

1. Social class may well influence students' occupational aspirations by affecting the opportunities they perceive themselves as having, but states Danziger (1983), there are other variables as well: status can also affect students' occupational desires by affecting their mental and educational performance, by influencing indirectly their estimates of their own abilities, and by affecting their parents' ability and sometimes

willingness to pay for education. Thus, there are various constraints on aspirations among lower status students that experiential and television exposure to a wider array of occupations might not overcome.

2. Wroblewski and Huston (1987) argue that girls would be more likely than boys to be motivated to develop cross-sex schemata, given the value society has traditionally placed on the male role. Therefore, they might be more likely than boys to identify with television characters of the opposite gender.

3. Characters were chosen for presentation after a pretest at another high school in the Milwaukee area the previous fall. In the pretest, students were asked which of a larger set of characters they identify with, and nominated other characters in an open-ended measure. In the final study, characters presented to students represented a mixture of male and female characters depicted in traditional and non-traditional occupational roles for their gender.

REFERENCES

Bem, S. (1981). Gender schema theory: A cognitive account of sex typing. *Psychological Review, 88* (4), 354-364.

Beuf, A. (1974). Doctor, lawyer, household drudge. *Journal of Communication, 24* (2), 142-145.

Calvert, S., & Huston, A. (1987). Television and children's gender schemata. In L. Liben & M. Signorella (Eds.), *Children's gender schemata* (pp. 75-89). New Directions for Child Development, 38 (Winter). San Francisco: Jossey-Bass.

Dambrot, F. H., Reep, D. C & Bell, D. (1988). Television sex roles in the 1980s: Do viewers' sex and sex role orientation change the picture? *Sex Roles, 19* (5/6), 387-401.

Danziger, N. (1983). Sex-related differences in the aspirations of high school students. *Sex Roles, 9* (6), 683-695.

Duncan, O. D. (1961). A socioeconomic index for all occupations. In A. J. Reiss, Jr. (Ed.), *Occupations and social status* (pp. 263-275). New York: Free Press

Eisenstock, B. (1984). Sex-role differences in children's identification with counterstereotypical televised portrayals. *Sex Roles, 10* (5/6), 417-430.

England, P. (1992). From status attainment to segregation and devaluation. *Contemporary Sociology, 21* (5), 643-647.

Faber, R., Brown, J., & McLeod, J. (1978). Coming of age in the global village: Television and adolescence. In E. Wartella (Ed.), *Children communicating: Media and the development of thought, speech, understanding* (pp. 215-249). Sage Annual Reviews of Communication Research (Vol. 7). Beverly Hills, CA: Sage.

Fiske, S., & Taylor, S. (1984). *Social cognition.* Reading, MA.: Addison-Wesley.

Geis, F., Brown, V., Jennings, J., & Corrado-Taylor, D. (1984). Sex vs. status in sex-associated stereotypes. *Sex Roles, 11* (9/10), 771-785.

Jennings-Walstedt, J., Geis, F., & Brown, V. (1980). Influence of television commercials on women's self-confidence and independent judgment. *Journal of Personality and Social Psychology, 38,* 203-210.

Johnston, J., & Ettema, J. (1982). *Positive images: Breaking stereotypes with children's television.* Beverly Hills, CA: Sage.

Katz, P. (1987). Variations in family constellation: Effects on gender schemata. In L. Liben & M. Signorella (Eds.), *Children's gender schemata* (pp. 39-56). New Directions in Child Development, 38. San Francisco: Jossey-Bass.

Liben, L., & Signorella, M. (Eds.) (1987). *Children's gender schemata.* New Directions in Child Development, 38. San Francisco: Jossey-Bass.

Mendelsohn, H. (1990). Mind, affect, and action: Construction theory and the media effects dialectic. In S. Kraus (Ed.), *Mass communication and political information processing* (pp. 37-45). Hillsdale, NJ: Erlbaum.

Miller, M. M., & Reeves, B. (1976). Dramatic TV content and children's sex-role stereotypes. *Journal of Broadcasting, 20* (1), 35-50.

Morgan, M. (1987). Television, sex-role attitudes, and sex-role behavior. *Journal of Early Adolescence, 7,* 269-282.

Press, A. (1989). Class and gender in the hegemonic process: Class differences in women's perceptions of television realism and identification with television characters. *Media, Culture and Society, 11,* 229-251.

Raskin, P. M. (1985). Identity and vocational development. In A. S. Waterman (Ed.), *Identity in adolescence: Processes and contents* (pp. 25-42). New Directions for Child Development, 30. San Francisco: Jossey-Bass.

Signorielli, N. (1985). *Role portrayal and stereotyping on television.* Westport, CT: Greenwood.

Signorielli, N. (1991). *A sourcebook on children and television.* Westport, CT: Greenwood.

Signorielli, N., & Lears, M. (1992). Children, television, and conceptions about chores: Attitudes and behaviors. *Sex Roles, 27* (3/4), 157-170.

Williams, F., LaRose, R., & Frost, F. (1981) *Children, television, and sex-role stereotyping.* New York: Praeger.

Williams, T. M., Baron, D., Phillips, S., Travis, L., & Jackson, D. (1986). The portrayal of sex roles on Canadian and U.S. television. Paper presented to the International Association for Mass Communication Research, New Delhi, India.

Wroblewski, R., & Huston, A. (1987). Televised occupational stereotypes and their effects on early adolescents: Are they changing? *Journal of Early Adolescence, 7* (3), 283-297.

9

Interruptions and the Construction of Reality

Sara Hayden

Numerous scholars have claimed that when women talk with women, the style of conversation is cooperative and interactional (Coates, 1986; Maltz & Borker, 1982; Sheldon, 1992). The goal of the participants is not to dominate, but to show affection and concern. Yet it has also been suggested that when women talk with other women, interruptions are frequent (Edelsky, 1981; Maltz & Borker, 1982; Tannen, 1990). This is counterintuitive, in light of how interruptions are commonly understood.

In "Interruptions in Cross-Sex Conversations," Candace West and Don Zimmerman (1983) define interruptions as incursions that "have the potential to disrupt turns at talk, disorganize the ongoing construction of conversational topics, and violate the current speaker's right to be engaged in speaking" (p. 105). Moreover, they assert that an interruption is "a device for exercising control in conversation" (p. 103). Clearly one would not expect to find frequent use of a device for gaining dominance in a conversation that is interactional, cooperative, and supportive. How, then, is one to understand interruptions in women's conversations? (See Table 9.1.)

Deborah Tannen (1989) suggests that "simultaneous speech can be 'cooperative overlapping'—that is, supportive rather than obstructive, evidence not of dominance but of participation, not power, but the paradoxically related dimension, solidarity" (p. 7). This interpretation of interruptions better explains how interruptions might work in women-to-women talk; however, I believe it can be taken one step further. In *Talking and Listening from Women's Standpoint*, Marjorie L. DeVault (1986) suggests that many of the speech patterns common in the talk of women are the products of women using language to give voice to issues about which it is difficult to speak. Thus, she suggests that the researcher listen to such speech patterns as clues to experiences that are inadequately coded in our language.

In this essay I analyze a conversation that took place among six women in which there are many interruptions. Following the work of DeVault, I argue that the interruptions are not signs of dominance, and although they can be interpreted as evidence of solidarity and support, this is not their sole function. Instead, I argue that they are some of the tools the women use to help one another put words to experiences they have difficulty voicing.

Table 9.1
Conversation Transcription Key
Modeled on the technique described by West and Zimmerman

Mary: I ⌈**don't know**⌉ **John:** ⌊**You don't**⌋	Brackets indicate that portions of utterances are simultaneous. The left-hand bracket marks the onset of of simultaneity, the right-hand bracket its resolution.
CAPS or <u>underscore</u>	Both capitalization or underscoring are used to represent heavier emphasis (in speaker's pitch).
(1.3)	Numbers in parentheses show the seconds and tenths of seconds ensuing between speaker turns. They can also indicate the duration of pauses internal to a speaker's turn.
((softly))	Double parentheses enclose "descriptions," not transcribed utterances.
A: I (x) I did	An "x" in parentheses indicates a hitch or a stutter on the part of the speaker.
( )	Empty parentheses signify untimed pauses.
A: I know... **B:** ...what you mean.	Ellipses indicate either a sentence left unfinished, a sentence finished after an interruption, or a sentence finished by another speaker.
A: angry .. it's a real	Two dots in the middle of a speaker's sentence indicate a change of topic without finishing the sentence and without pause.

METHOD

Data for this study were gathered during a session of a weekly support group for chronically ill women. The meeting lasted approximately two hours. An audiotape was made of the meeting. During the session there were six women in the room—myself, two facilitators, and three patients. Gerry,[1] the main facilitator, is a social worker and nurse practitioner. She has suffered from colon cancer and is chronically ill. Mary, the other facilitator, is a licensed practical nurse with a background in psychiatric nursing. Barry, a new member in the group, was diagnosed as having Lupus. Jane is suffering from Lyme disease and depression. Linda is undiagnosed.

Although I am not living with chronic illness, the role I took during the session was that of a participant/observer. The participants were made aware of my position, interests, and research goals, and verbally consented to the audiotaping of, and my participation in, the group meeting. To prepare for participation in the session, I spent a number of hours discussing the group philosophy with the facilitators. During this time I also was briefed on the condition of each of the patients.

To analyze the data for this essay, I listened to the audiotape I had made of the session many times, and then transcribed those sections of the tape that displayed the most interruptions. In the essay I provide close textual analysis of one of those segments. I established representational validity for these findings by discussing the results reported here with the facilitators of the group and other women living with chronic illness.[2]

ANALYSIS

In the conversation I examine, Gerry has just brought up the issue of mortality. At first, the women appear to be hesitant to talk about this topic and the conversation is slow. Eventually, Barry begins to speak about an uneasiness she experienced around people who were joking about death. The other patients in the group quickly begin to support her in her talk through the use of minimal responses and through the sharing of similar experiences in their own lives. In the following section Barry discusses her inability to confront her husband with her uneasiness.

31 B: ...But I mean it was like I couldn't even .. the whole thing was so terrifying to me that I couldn't even make myself say "I'm afraid to hear that." I was afraid to say THAT even.

32 G: I .. what?

33 B: I couldn't even TELL him that I was afraid of hearing those things. Just the thought of talking about it. Just to say that much was too scary.

34 ?: Hmm (2)

35 G: You you had something to say that was scary...

36 B: ummhmm

37 G: ...and you couldn't tell him that?

38 B: It frightened me to say I was frightened if that makes any sense?

39 ?:   mmmhmm.[3]

With this section begins one of the most interesting segments of the conversation. Prior to this point, the conversation had followed "typical" patterns of women's talk. Each participant had been cooperative and supportive; there had been a clear effort to make each speaker know she was being understood. However, at line 32 Gerry breaks this pattern. Barry has acknowledged an inability to verbalize her experience. Rather than simply accepting what Barry has said and encouraging her to continue, Gerry pushes her on this point and asks Barry to clarify her statement.

At line 33 Barry again attempts to describe her experience; however, Gerry continues to violate expected norms and rather than accepting what Barry has to say, Gerry says nothing for two seconds, and then follows with a question (35 and 37) continuing to push Barry to clarify her point. For the third time, Barry attempts to explain herself (38). She ends her explanation asking whether what she has said "makes any sense?" Still, Gerry does not respond.

This segment of the conversation has taken place solely between Gerry and Barry. Next, the other women in the room jump in. They attempt to come to Barry's aid, giving her words to help her say what she wants to say. At this point, the interruptions begin.

```
38  B:  It frightened me to say I was frightened if that makes any sense?
39  ?:                  mmmhmm
40  L:  To like to like acknowledge it...
41  B:  ...Yeah!  And it wasn't telling him so much as it was...
42  L:  ...just saying that ⌈ it was like...                        ⌉
43  B:                     ⌊        ...saying it to myself...       ⌋
44  J:  ...Mmmhmm...
45  B:  No cause he's really easy to tell things to and
        he's very ⌈ sensitive to...                                ⌉
46  G:            ⌊              ...Were you hav⌋ing trouble admitting it was scaring you?
47  B:  Yeah.
48  L:  To herself...
49  B:  ...Yeah...
50  J:  ...yeah...
51  B:  ...yeah... For me ⌈ to say that...                ⌉
52  G:                    ⌊  ...to say it to him⌋ you first had to say it to ⌈ yourself... ⌉
53  B:                                                                       ⌊ Yeah       ⌋
54  G:  Is that what you're saying?
55  B:  Yeah, there you go.
56  G:  If you had said it to him would he have .. what would he hear?
57  B:  Oh he would have heard it right away.  I didn't want to hear it.
58  G:  You didn't want to hear ⟋ yourself...           ⌉
59  B:                          ⟋Are you making⌋ this difficult or am I?  (Laughter)
60  G:  No, I am.
```

The first interruption occurs at line 42. Linda was attempting to help Barry describe her experience. She ties into Barry's difficulty of saying something was frightening her; Barry breaks in to emphasize that her difficulty lay with "saying it to herself." This is clearly an interruption. Tannen (1989) identifies Zimmerman and West's operational definition of interruptions as violations in the turn-exchange system. They distinguish interruptions from overlaps:

> If a second speaker begins speaking at what could be a transition-relevance place, it is counted as an overlap. The assumption is that the speaker mistook the potential transition-relevance place for an actual one. If a second speaker begins speaking at

what could not be a transition-relevance place, it is counted as an interruption. (p. 3)

Linda had not finished her sentence and she had not paused. Clearly, Barry could not have believed that Linda was at a transition-relevance place; she interrupted her. On the other hand, she does not seem to be "disrupting the talk" or attempting to "control the conversation." Instead, this interruption occurred as the two women worked together as they tried to verbalize what Barry had been having difficulty saying.

A second set of interruptions occurs between Gerry and Barry. At line 45 Barry begins to discuss her husband's ability to hear what she is saying. At line 46 Gerry breaks in. She attempts to direct the conversation away from Barry's husband's ability to hear Barry and toward Barry's inability to express her reality. Once again this interruption clearly does not occur at a transition-relevance point. At line 51 Barry begins again; however Gerry does not let her finish. Instead she interrupts Barry and finishes her point. Barry acknowledges that Gerry's verbalization is correct. The affirmation of this point continues for a number of turns until at line 57 Barry clearly states that *she* did not want to hear (or, one can infer, to verbalize) her situation.

The interruptions that occur between Barry and Gerry are different in tone than the interruptions between Barry and Linda. In the first set of interruptions discussed, Linda had been indicating that she understood what Barry was trying to say and Linda was attempting to help Barry find the words to express her meaning. On the other hand, when Gerry interrupts Barry she does so in the role of the facilitator. She is attempting to focus the discussion; she appears to want to emphasize Barry's inability to verbalize something to herself. Nonetheless, the function of all of the interruptions remains the same. The women are working together to enable Barry to speak her reality.

At line 59 Barry breaks the tension by laughingly asking Gerry "Are you making this difficult or am I?" Gerry's answer of "I am" brings on yet another attempt by Barry and the other women in the room to express Barry's point:

61 J: I think I ⎡understand what you are saying.⎤
62 M: ⎣Because of the possibility that ⎦ this might actually be happening and
        you don't want to deal with that part of it.
63 B: Yeah, it wasn't, it wasn't, it didn't actually have anything to do with telling⁄him...⎤
64 M: ⁄right... ⎦
65 B: ...it had to do with my⎡ own... ⎤
66 M: ⎣...saying⎦⎡ I might be ⎤ dying...
67 B: ⎣...willingness...⎦
68 M: ...or I might be...
69 B: ...right
70 M: ⎡...and I ⟍don't⎡ want⎤ to ⎡hear⟍ that ⎡ yet, ⟍I ⎡can't ⟍accept that..
71 B & J⎣ ... Yeah⟍ ⎣.. ummhmm⎦⎣.. right⟍ ⎣.. yeah.⟍ ⎣ right...⟍
72 B: It had nothing to do with being able to tell him it was (x) to tell anybody. I don't
        think I could have wrote it on a piece of⁄paper⟍and put it down the toilet.
73 J: ⁄ummhmm⟍
74 L: 'Cause it made it seem real...?
75 B: Yup

76 J: ...umm umm
77 B: You know, don't wish for something you might get it.
78 L: Yeah that's almost like...
                    (2) and umms
79 G: I needed to know if (x) you're having trouble saying it to yourself or saying it to somebody.
80 B: No saying it to MYSELF. If I had to say it out loud to somebody else I first would...
81 L: ...have to say it ⌈ to yourself...   ⌉
82 B: ⌊   ...have to say it to myself⌋
83 J: ...ummhmm..
84 B: I just, (x) I mean I couldn't. I would go into a panic attack just hearing other people talk about it. (7) I mean if I went to bed at night feeling awful and my last thought was, I wonder, you know, if I'm going to be here when the radio comes on in the morning and then to have Herb get up and drink a cup of coffee and say "This gets the old ticker started," uhhahh (4) I mean it would just be enough to just make me roll over. (9)
85 B: Don't try to understand me [Gerry]...
                    Laughter
86 G: I understand you, I understand you. I'm not the only one who can talk.
        (Laughter, (2))

At line 61, Jane verbally gives her support; she is interrupted by Mary, the other facilitator, who expresses Barry's situation from yet another angle. In lines 63 through 69 Barry and Mary continuously interrupt each other; both are pursuing different but parallel thoughts. Yet neither woman finishes her sentence. Instead, they work together to construct a meaning. Importantly, at line 66 the issue that is at the core of this discussion is first verbalized. Mary says the word "dying." As Mary verbalizes this, both Barry and Jane enthusiastically indicate their agreement through minimal response statements. For Barry, verbalizing her fear granted it reality. To say she might be dying "made it seem real."

At this point, it is clear that the three patients and Mary, the cofacilitator, understand Barry's point. Gerry, however, has not voiced anything during this segment of the interchange. At line 79, after a two-second pause, she explains her previous action. In her role as a facilitator, she had been working to get Barry to distinguish between an inability to say something to herself and an inability to say something to someone else.

In response, Barry reiterates that her difficulty had to do with saying it to herself. Significantly, at this point the other women do not interrupt her. Barry is still struggling to say what she wants to say. Her style of speaking is not literal but instead is metaphorical, yet her meaning is clear. In the past she had been afraid to speak about dying. Now, through the help of the other women in the room, she has been able to say what before had been unsayable. At line 86 Gerry affirms both that she understands the reality Barry had difficulty expressing as well as what has been accomplished. By working together, the women have helped Barry to find her voice. Gerry is not the only one who can talk.

CONCLUSION

The interruptions in this conversation are not attempts to gain dominance nor do they signal a desire to control the conversation. Further, although they show solidarity and support, this is not their only function. Barry had been experiencing a fear of death, and this fear was so strong that she had been unable to articulate her feelings, even to herself. In response, the women in this group drew on the resources of "women's talk" and worked with Barry to enable her to express her reality.

Of course, the fear of death is not something only women face. Certainly, many men experience the same kind of fears, and for some men, like Barry, these fears are so strong they too are rendered silent. Thus, gender is not an issue in terms of the topic being discussed, but it is an issue when it comes to the style within which the discussion occurs. Recognizing Barry's difficulty, the women in the group draw on patterns of conversation typical to women so that Barry can give voice to her experiences. Through the use of interruptions in this conversation, Barry is given both the support and the tools she needs to express a reality she had not been able to express before.

In the past, the style of speaking identified as "women's talk" has been denigrated. Indeed, Robin Lakoff (1975), the first theorist to identify a category of speech particular to women, asserted that the use of women's language is a means through which a speaker can remain passive and thus avoid responsibility for her words. Others have argued that women's styles of speaking are powerless (O'Barr & Atkins, 1980; Sayers, 1988). Recently, there has been a move to revalue women's styles and women's words (Coates, 1986; DeVault, 1986; Sheldon, 1992; Tannen, 1990). I offer this essay as further support in that endeavor. Following DeVault, I argue that the women involved in the conversation analyzed in this essay used elements of "women's language" in an effort to enable one woman to give voice to an issue about which it was difficult for her to speak.

NOTES

1. The names of the participants have been changed.

2. It should be noted that in this conversation there are many elements of language that could be referred to and analyzed as being representative of "women's talk." However, in this essay I have chosen to focus on interruptions only.

3. See Table 9.1 for transcribing conventions.

REFERENCES

Coates, J. (1986). *Women, men and language.* UK: Longman Group.

DeVault, M. L. (1986, August). *Talking and listening from women's standpoint: Feminist strategies for analyzing interview data.* Paper presented at the annual meeting of the Society for the Study of Symbolic Interaction, New York, NY.

Edelsky, C. (1981). Who's got the floor? *Language in Society, 10,* 383-421.

Lakoff, R. (1975). Women's language. *Language and Style: An International Journal, 10, 4,* 222-247.

Maltz, D., & Borker, R. (1982). A cultural approach to male/female miscommunication. In J. J. Gumperz (Ed.), *Language and Social Identity.* (pp. 196-215). New York: Cambridge University Press.

O'Barr, W. M., & Atkins, B. K. (1980). "Women's language" or "Powerless language"? In S. McConnell-Ginet, R. Borker, & N. Furman (Eds.), *Women and language in literature and society* (pp. 93-110). New York: Praeger.

Sayers, F. (1988). Sex, sex-role and conversation: Review of the literature and rationale. In C. Valentine & N. Hoar (Eds.), *Women and communicative power: Theory, research and practice* (pp. 19-33). Annandale, VA: Speech Communication Association.

Sheldon, A. (1992). Conflict talk: Sociolinguistic challenges to self-assertion and how young girls meet them. *Merrill-Palmer Quarterly, 38, 1,* 95-117.

Tannen, D. (1989, April). *Interpreting interruption in conversation.* Paper presented at the annual meeting of the Chicago Linguistics Society, Chicago, Illinois.

Tannen, D. (1990). *You just don't understand: Women and men in conversation.* New York: Ballantine Books.

West, C., & Zimmerman, D. H. (1983). Small insults: A study of interruptions in cross-sex conversations between unacquainted persons. In B. Thorne et al. (Eds.), *Language, gender and society* (pp. 103-118). New York: Newbury House Publishers.

Part II

EVALUATING GENDER RELATIONS

In this section, the essays move away from contrasting men's and women's communication and the frameworks that explain the differences among critical analyses of how women have been represented, and have represented themselves, in language, the media, and popular culture. These analyses discuss how language and speech affect women's and men's attitudes toward life and the world.

Essays 10 and 11 explore issues in two popular culture sites where aspects of women's gender are constructed: children's literature representing stepmothers, and contemporary women's magazines. In her survey of children's books (1980-1991) portraying stepfamilies and stepmothers, Pamela Cooper found that stepmothers were shown as either wicked or incompetent (sometimes both). Since she understands that children's books often function as a kind of therapy, Cooper finds this portrayal troubling. Instead of offering models which could help children and stepmothers to see themselves as able to integrate in a new blended family, these books hamper integration. Bren Murphy makes a similar observation about women's magazines. In a widely ranging survey, Murphy discovers that magazines omit contemporary feminism—they present images of women worthy of the prefeminist consciousness of the 1950s (meaning that their identity is found in their good looks) and assume postfeminist times (where all the feminist battles are won, women are equal in every arena to men, and women are all-powerful). As with any assumption, this one, too, is shown to have serious flaws.

In Chapter 12, Sean Gilmore presents the seamier side of undergraduate men. Conducting extensive interviews at a midwestern university, Gilmore finds men there have symbolically constructed sex as sport by developing a language in which men are the players and women are the points (highest points are scored for what these men consider as less desirable women, i.e., overweight, older, non-Caucasian, disabled). Chapter 13 follows on the heels of 12, extending its implications, to show how grown men constructed a symbolic environment for women employees at a steel company, an environment in which the men were the predators and women the sexual prey. On a regular basis, women there were called sluts, bitches, cunts, and whores. Case's interview with the boss finds him claiming such language "motivates" women.

In welcome relief, Chapters 14 and 15 put forth images of women controlling their own language environment, at least to an extent. Hardman's analysis of linguistic markers of gender in the South American cluster of Jaqi languages show how that culture represents women as autonomous beings, landowners, who belong to themselves (not to men). In contrast to this, as Western "developers" entered the culture, they renamed the women as wives of husbands and ignored the women's ownership of land. Hardman graphically shows what a culture, and especially its women, can lose when Western constructions of gender relations distort existing relations. Finally, in Chapter 15, Kathryn Remlinger presents the example of Indian women attending an American university. Adept at their own language, which has a public (male-identified) and a private (familial- and mother-identified) face, and at English, able to use both formal and idiomatic forms, these women consciously exert control over their language usage to accommodate interpersonal status and relationships.

10

The Image of Stepmothers in Children's Literature, 1980–1991

Pamela J. Cooper

From earliest times, the image of the stepmother has been negative—hard, hateful, wicked, ugly, cruel. The very concept of "step" implies loss. If one has a stepmother, she/he has a "mother-loss," total or partial, in terms of the ideal we hold for an ever-present mother (Smith, 1990). Given this, enacting the role of stepmother is not easy. Indeed, stress is a major characteristic for all members of a stepfamily (Whitsett & Land, 1992), an ever-increasing family form (Flick, 1989). However, stepfamily researchers generally agree that the most stressful stepfamily relationship is that of stepmother/stepdaughter (Visher & Visher, 1985).

All children have an image of a stepmother. This image derives, primarily, from children's literature. Folktales are among the first literature to which children are exposed. The oldest and best-loved tales such as "Cinderella," "Snow White," and "Hansel and Gretel" feature stepmothers who are, without exception, cruel. In addition, folktales and all children's literature have important social and cultural influences. They educate children to hold approved values and attitudes.

In recent years, several books have been published for children to help them cope with difficult childhood experiences. Using books to help children resolve personal problems is included in the concept of bibliotherapy, which encompasses everything from using literature to counsel prisoners to sharing a picture book about a new baby with a preschooler. Several books have been published in recent years to help children cope with becoming a member of a stepfamily.

Theoretically, the process of bibliotherapy is threefold. First, readers/listeners identify with the story's character. Next, the character encounters a difficult situation that is resolved. Finally, readers/listeners, who vicariously have shared in the character's situation, reflect upon their own situations and internalize some of the character's coping strategies depicted in the story. It is hoped that readers/listeners will utilize these strategies when dealing with similar personal problems. Obviously, the more realistic and "healthy" the coping behaviors depicted in the literature a child reads, the more helpful these behaviors will be when the child utilizes them to solve problems.

This chapter examines images of stepmothers in children's literature. If literature is to help children cope with the problems and frustrations of living in a stepfamily, it should depict realistic and "healthy" images of stepmothers. In order to determine whether or not the literature does indeed depict accurate, healthy images, this chapter (1) reviews existing literature on stepfamilies to determine what researchers indicate about the image of the stepmother and the effects of this image on the stepfamily; (2) analyzes available children's literature on stepfamilies to determine the image of stepmothers portrayed; and (3) analyzes, from the perspective of bibliotherapy, whether or not the images from the review and analyses "mesh," and the effects of the "meshing" or the lack of it.

METHOD

In recent years, several books (both fiction and nonfiction) have been published to help children cope with both a parent's remarriage and the child's own adjustment to a stepfamily. For this study, I was interested not in all the books published dealing with stepmothers, but in the books to which children were most likely to be exposed. In other words, a book that is published but is not readily accessible to children has little "therapeutic" value. I examined the card files of three large public libraries in the Chicago metropolitan area and found 51 books (42 fiction; 9 nonfiction) that dealt with stepmothers published between 1980 and 1991. (See Table 10.1.) Only books listed as dealing with the stepmother/stepdaughter relationship were analyzed. Interestingly, few books that deal specifically with stepmothers and stepdaugthers have been published since 1991. Those that have been were not available in the libraries utilized for this research.

I compared the role of the stepmothers portrayed to the "ideal" role discussed in adult stepfamily literature (for example, Savage & Adams, 1988; Einstein & Albert, 1986; Prilik, 1988; Smith, 1992). Although a wide range of roles is possible, from Super Stepmom (who rushes in trying to make the relationship work by insisting on family togetherness, assuming a peacemaker role, striving to be perfect, insisting she loves her stepchildren) to the Reluctant Stepmom (who avoids building a relationship with stepchildren and becomes resentful of feeling "left-out" of the biological parent/child relationship), stepmothers who define their role as friend are usually the most satisfied and successful (Savage & Adams, 1988).

RESULTS

In analyzing the books, three categories related to the "ideal" stepmother role were used: (1) "competent" (the stepmother was a friend), (2) "incompetent" (the stepmother chose a different role), and (3) "wicked" (stepmother portrayed as cruel). These categories were generated based on those found in the thereapeutic literature on stepfamilies (Clubb, 1991; Savage & Adams, 1988).

Nine nonfiction books were analyzed. The majority of these presented a positive image of the stepmother. Of the nine nonfiction books, five presented the stepmother as a possible friend (Bradley, 1982; Burt & Burt, 1983; Craven, 1982; Evans, 1986; and Rosenberg, 1990). Children are told stepparents will not replace the noncustodial parent, but can be an addition, another adult who cares about them.

Four of the nonfiction books portray a less positive image. Hyde (1981) portrays the stepmother as a disciplinarian. Berman (1982) suggests primarily negative aspects of being in a stepfamily. The two positive aspects, getting lots of birthday cards and getting to know more people, would do little to enhance a child's image of stepfamily living. Gardner (1982) suggests, "A stepparent does not necessarily have to be mean and cruel" (p. 177). However, the underlying assumption seems to be that stepmothers will be wicked. One who is not is the exception rather than the rule. Of the seven images of stepmothers presented in Getzoff and McClenahan's (1984) book, only one is positive and fits the "friend" role.

Thus, nonfiction books tend to portray the stepmother in a positive light. However, in those books that present a negative image, this image is extremely negative. In other words, very little of the positive nature is discussed.

Forty-two fiction books were analyzed. Of those, 15 portrayed "competent" stepmothers, 16 portrayed "incompetent" stepmothers, and 11 portrayed stepmothers as "wicked." A total of 27 books portrayed negative images, with only 15 offering a positive image.

"Competent" stepmothers chose the friend role. For example, in *The Not-So-Wicked Stepmother* (Boyd, 1987), Molly, the stepmother, does not "rush in" and try to be a loving mother to Hessie. Rather, she allows Hessie time and space to adjust to her as a friend. The stepmothers in *No One is Going to Nashville* (Jukes, 1983), *If You Need Me* (Adler, 1988), and *Maggie Forevermore* (Nixon, 1987) are "competent" because, among other things, they do not interfere until their stepchildren ask them to do so. They are supportive always, but do not "jump in" to solve problems until they are asked. For example, Kiki, the stepmother in *Maggie Forevermore* (1987) patiently waits for her stepdaughter, Maggie, to approach her for advice on how Maggie can help a friend who is being cheated by her agent. Kiki and Maggie devise and execute a plan together.

Even when stepmothers are portrayed as "competent" in terms of being a friend, stepchildren may still perceive them as a problem. For example, in *She's Not My Real Mother* (Vigna, 1980) and *Daddy's New Baby* (Vigna, 1982), the stepmother is portrayed in a very positive light—she is kind, considerate, patient, and loving. Yet the stepchild never really accepts her and continues to express her feelings as, "But she's not my real mother."

Several of the books that portray "competent" stepmothers depict the long struggle in developing a friendship relationship (Benjamin, 1982; Senn, 1985; Wolkoff, 1982; Zalben, 1982). Even when this relationship begins positively, children worry that the stepmother will turn wicked (see, for example, Wolkoff, 1982). Thus, stepmothers never seem to be really trusted. The wicked stepmother image is always present.

Stepmothers who are incompetent are depicted in three major ways: "Super Stepmother," incompetent women, and immature/self-centered.

Often, "incompetent" stepmothers fall into the "Super Stepmother" role. They simply try too hard (Hahn, 1986; Okimoto, 1980; Park, 1989; Snyder, 1984; and Wittman, 1990). They try to counteract the wicked stepmother image by becoming "Super Stepmother"—doing whatever the child wants. By so doing, these "Super Stepmothers" hope to win the stepchild's love and respect. In general, disaster follows as the stepchild demands more, and the stepmother becomes more frustrated that no matter what she does, it is never enough.

Incompetent stepmothers are portrayed as incompetent women. They are nice people, but inept (Colman, 1985; O'Neal, 1982; York, 1980). For example, Dori in *A Formal Feeling* (O'Neal, 1982) is depicted as a sweet, petite lady who doesn't understand her intellectual husband, hates housework, and breaks dishes.

Stepmothers who are immature and self-centered (Coontz, 1983; Gerber, 1981; Klein, 1980) or inhospitable (Colman, 1984; Hopper, 1987; Mahy, 1985; Pevsner, 1987; and Rabe, 1980) are likewise unworthy of friendship. Stepchildren perceive little reason to be friends with stepmothers portrayed in these ways. Thus, the stepmothers are unable to fulfill the "competent" stepmother role—that of a friend.

Stepmothers may be portrayed as wicked rather than simply incompetent. Eleven fiction books portray the stepmother as "wicked." Three are classic Cinderella-type fairy tales (Cooney, 1982; Farjeon, 1984; Lewis, 1987). Rachel, in *Rachel Vellers How Could You?* (Fisher, 1984) is depicted as a neglected, poor, suffering modern day Cinderella. In Adler's *In Our House Scott is My Brother* (1980), Jodi's stepmother, Donna, is an alcoholic. She tries to change everything about Jodi and Jodi's father. Eventually, Jodi's (and most stepchildren's) dream is fulfilled: the stepmother leaves. Jodi's father is completely powerless to stop Donna's behavior. He, like the father in classic fairy tales, lets Donna do whatever she desires—even if it hurts Jodi.

Millicent (Amoss, 1989) forces her husband to make his daughter, Lindy, live with the woman next door. Katie, in *Gimme an H, Gimme an E, Gimme an L, Gimme a P* (Bonham, 1980), is suicidal because her stepmother is cruel and favors her own child. Sylvia's stepmother (Klass, 1983) makes her have a nose-job. The stepmother in *Goodbye Glamour Girl* (Tamar, 1984) is portrayed as a whore who sleeps with every available man while her husband is away at war.

Finally, two books go so far as to portray stepmothers as murderers. In *The Case of the Frightened Friend* (Newman, 1984) the stepmother is suspected of wrongdoing in the death of her husband. In *Locked in Time* (Duncan, 1985), the stepmother tries to kill her stepchild and her husband.

Fiction books tend to depict stepmothers in a negative way—either as incompetent (as a stepmother, woman, or both) or as wicked. Such images, seen from a bibliotherapy perspective, do little to help a child deal effectively with a stepmother.

CONCLUSION

Stepmothers are sometimes "in-step" with their role and sometimes "out-of-step." Becoming a stepmother is like learning a new dance. You believe you will be able to learn it. You work very hard to learn it. You stumble over your own feet and that of your partner's as well. Just when you think you've learned the dance, someone changes the tempo of the music or changes the steps to the dance. Stepmothers are neither wicked nor saintly, simply human beings with all that entails. The real gift to stepmothers (and children) would be to be portrayed in children's literature as human beings with strengths and weakensses.

Of the 51 books reviewed, only 20 portrayed the stepmother in a positive, competent role. Twenty portrayed the stepmother as incompetent and 11 portrayed her as wicked. Thus, only 39% of the stepmothers were portrayed in a positive, competent role. Reading this literature provides little support for the idea that a healthy, positive relationship is possible between children and stepmothers.

One might wonder why the negative image of stepmothers persists. This question is even more puzzling when one realizes that the majority of authors of these books are female (35 female; 9 male). Why aren't women being more sensitive to the needs of their own gender? Is it because (1) the wicked stepmother is easier to create than a more realistic version, (2) the wicked stepmother is more interesting, more exciting from a literary perspective than the more human, true-to-life version, or (3) are these writers unaware of the dynamics of stepfamily living and so are unaware that their portrayal is unrealistic, even harmful? Perpetuating these stereotypes of stepmothers is a disservice to stepmothers, to their stepchildren, to their own children, to their spouses. No one wins when literature portrays such a negative image of stepmothers.

Literature makes a difference. The image portrayed time and again in literature is the image children will believe. The wicked stepmother image continues to be the predominant one. To argue that the wicked and incompetent stepmother images discussed in this chapter are irrelevant and make no difference is, quite simply, wrong.

Consider the fact that the stepfamily is the fastest growing family form (each day, 1300 new ones are formed [Savage & Adams]). Stepmothers play a pivotal role in contemporary society. Given their numbers and their importance, it would seem logical that stepmothers could find realistic, empathic treatment in literature directed at their children; and yet the opposite is true.

The stepmother nearly always is portrayed as wicked, or at the very least, incompetent. Most stepmothers are neither. And yet, the images discussed here result in their disadvantage. And, as Santrock, Warshak, and Elliott (1982) suggest, stepmothers have difficulty in escaping the psychological effects of the "wicked stepmother" image. Cultural images (in this case, as they appear in children's literature) reflect society's attitudes and greatly influence a stepmother's lot.

From the perspective of biliotherapy, children need literature that depicts stepmothers in positive ways—as children's friends. They need to see children in literature exhibit positive coping strategies when dealing with stepmothers, so that they can use these strategies when relating with their own stepmothers. As long as negative stepmother images and negative coping strategies are depicted in children's literature, stepfamilies will lack healthy models and, perhaps, play out the dysfunctional relations given privilege in this literature.

BOOKS ANALYZED

Adler, C. S. (1980). *In our house Scott is my brother.* New York: Macmillan.

Adler, C. S. (1988). *If you need me.* New York: Macmillan.

Amoss, B. (1989). *The mockingbird song.* San Francisco: Harper and Row.

Benjamin, C. L. (1982). *The wicked stepdog.* New York: Crowell Junior Books.

Berman, C. (1981). *What am I doing in a stepfamily?* Secaucus, NJ: Lyle Stuart.

Bonham, F. (1980). *Gimme an H, gimme an E, gimmee an L, gimme me a P.* New York: Scribner.

Boyd, L. (1987). *The not-so-wicked stepmother.* New York: Penquin Books.

Boyd, L. (1990). *Sam is my half brother.* New York: Penquin Books.

Bradley, B. (1982). *Where do I belong? A kids' guide to stepfamilies.* Reading, MA: Addison, Wesley.

Burt, M., & Burt, B. B. (1983). *What's special about our stepfamily?* New York: Doubleday.

Colman, H. (1984). *Just the two of us.* New York: Scholastic, Inc.

Colman, H. (1985). *Week-end sisters.* New York: William Morrow.

Connty, O. (1983). *Isle of the shape-shifters.* Boston: Houghton-Mifflin.

Cooney, B. (1982). *Little brother and little sister.* Garden City, NY: Doubleday.

Craven, L. (1982). *Stepfamilies: New patterns of harmony.* New York: Julian Messner.

Duncan, L. (1985). *Locked in time.* Boston: Little, Brown.

Evans, M. D. (1986). *This is me and my two families.* New York: Magination Press.

Farjeon, E. (1984). *The glass slipper.* Philadelphia: Lippincott.

Fisher, L. (1984). *Rachel Vellers, how could you?* New York: Dodd, Mead.

Gardner, R. (1982). *The boys and girls book about stepfamilies.* New York: Bantam Books.

Gerker, J. (1981). *Please don't kiss me now.* New York: Dial.

Getzoff, A., & McClenahan, C. (1984). *Stepkids: A survival guide for teenagers in stepfamilies.* New York: Walker and Co.

Hahn, M. D. (1986). *Wait til Helen comes.* New York: Clarion Books.

Hopper, N. (1987). *Carrie's games.* New York: Dutton.

Hyde, M. O. (1981). *My friend has four parents.* New York: McGraw-Hill

Jukes, M. (1983). *No one is going to Nashville.* New York: Alfred Knopf.

Klein, N. (1980). *Breaking-up.* New York: Pantheon.

Kloss, S. (1981). *To see my mother dance.* New York: Scribner.
Kloss, S. (1983). *Alive and starting over.* New York: Scribner.
Lewis, N. (1987). *The stepsister.* New York: Dial Books.
MacLacklan, P. (1986). *Sarah, plain and tall.* New York: Harper and Row.
Mahy, M. (1985). *Aliens in the family.* New York: Scholastic.
Newman, R. (1984). *The case of the frightened friend.* New York: Atheneum.
Nixon, J. L. (1987). *Maggie forevermore.* San Diego: Harcourt Brace Jovanovich.
Okimoto, J. O. (1980). *It's just too much.* New York: G. P. Putnam's Sons.
O'Neal, S. (1982). *A formal feeling.* New York: Viking Press.
Park, B. (1989). *My mother got married (and other atrocities).* New York: Alfred A. Knopf.
Pevsner, S. (1987). *Sister of the quints.* New York: Clarion.
Rake, B. (1980). *Who's afraid?* New York: Dutton.
Rasley, G. (1981). *Nothing stays the same.* New York: Crown.
Rosenberg, M. (1980). *Talking about stepfamilies.* New York: Macmillan.
Senn, S. (1985). *In the castle of the bear.* New York: Atheneum.
Snyder, S. K. (1984). *Blair's nightmare.* New York: Atheneum.
Tamar, E. (1984). *Good-bye glamour girl.* Philadelphia: Lippincott.
Vigna, J. (1980). *She's not my real mother.* Chicago: Albert Whitman.
Vigna, J. (1982). *Daddy's new baby.* Niles, IL: Albert Whitman.
Wittman, S. (1990). *Stepbrother sabotage.* New York: Harper and Row.
Wolkoff, J. (1982). *Happily ever after—almost.* Scarsdale, NY: Bradley.
Wright, B. R. (1981). *My new mom and me.* Milwaukee, WI: Raintree.
York, C. B. (1980). *Remember me when I am dead.* New York: Elsevier/Nelson.
Zalken, J. (1982). *Maybe it will rain tomorrow.* New York: Farrar, Straus Giroux.

REFERENCES

Clubb, A. (1991). *Love in the blended family.* Deerfield, FL: Health Communication.
Einstein, E. & Albert, L. (1986). *Strengthening your stepfamily.* Circle Pines, MN: American Guidance Service.
Galvin, K. & Cooper, P. (1991). *Development of involuntary relationships: The stepparent-stepchild relationship.* Paper presented at the International Communication Association Convention, Chicago, Illinois.
Glick, P. C. (1989). Remarried families, stepfamilies, and stepchildren: A brief demographic profile. *Family Relations, 38,* 24-27.
Prilik, P. (1988). *Stepmothering: Another kind of love.* Los Angeles: Forman.
Santrock, J. W., Warshak, R. A., & Elliott, G. L. (1982). Social development

and parent-child interaction in father-custody and stepmother families. In M. E. Lamb (Ed.), *Nontraditional families: Parenting and child development* (pp. 289-314). Hillsdale, N.J.: Lawrence Erlbaum Associates.

Savage, K. & Adams, P. (1988). *The good stepmother: A survival guide.* New York: Avon.

Smith, D. (1990). *Stepmothering.* New York: St. Martin's Press.

Visher, E. B. and Visher, J. S. (1985). Stepfamilies are different. *Journal of Family Therapy. 7,* 9-18.

Whitsett, D. & Land, H. (1992). The development of a role strain index for stepparents. *Families in Society: The Journal of Contemporary Human Services, 73,* 14-22.

11

Women's Magazines: Confusing Differences

Bren Ortega Murphy

Since the mid-1980s, U.S. newspapers and women's magazines have ostensibly addressed the contemporary women's dilemma of "having it all." That they even have acknowledged the problem indicates a significant difference from the days when Betty Freidan (1963) criticized women's magazines for the "finite pattern of femininity" they offered their readers. These days it is rare to find an article that overtly argues that women are, by definition, only suited for domesticity. Nor do glib descriptions of "super women" (the textual equivalents of airbrushed photographs) abound. Instead, journalists seem to have identified balance and options as key concerns and fill pages on what to do about the problems that arise in our multifaceted society.

Despite all this "help," many women counselors have observed that their clients often complain about feelings of low self-esteem (Merrill, 1991). Consultants working with corporations on gender issues in the workplace have found that women identified many more sources of stress than male counterparts in achieving professional and personal goals (Murphy, 1992-4). Moreover, sociologist Ruth Seidel (1990) reports that an increasing number of women either feel alienated from each other or fail to assess their life choices realistically.

One explanation for these findings is that popular discourse, especially as conducted in women's magazines, provides insufficient and confusing consideration of the complex issues many women confront on a day-to-day basis. These issues are rooted in assumptions about the sociopolitical responsibilities of women in such various domains as the domestic, economic, artistic, spiritual, and civic spheres of contemporary society. They involve such basic questions as: what does a woman need to know in order to function appropriately in these spheres? What does she have to contribute? How do the structures within the spheres shape her contributions? How does being a woman in these spheres differ from being a man? These assumptions even involve such seemingly trivial questions as: What are a woman's obligations regarding private decor? How much time and money should a woman devote to the physical beauty of her home? her children? herself? Although these questions are rarely raised directly in women's magazines, implied answers abound in the topics these publications choose to cover, the products they choose to advertise, and the images they chose to display.

In the United States, throughout the nineteenth and first half of the twentieth century, what were known as "women's magazines" played a key role in this discourse, because many women looked to them as a primary source of information. Indeed, some assumed that all other periodicals must be "men's," although magazines such as *Harper's* were not so labeled (Franzwa, 1975: Geise, 1979; Hoekstra, 1972; Mather, 1977). Although this assumption changed significantly after the 1950s, several scholars have observed that magazines aimed expressly at women continue to have an impact, offering guidelines and standards that purport to encompass a woman's (everywoman's?) world (Cagan, 1978; Seidel, 1990; Shevelow, 1989; White, 1970; Wolfe, 1991). Through images as well as text, women's periodicals report on what it means to be a woman, a wife, a mother.

Although several new magazines were founded in the wake of the women's liberation movement, the most traditional women's magazines (e.g., *Ladies' Home Journal, Good Housekeeping*) continued to dominate distribution into the early 1990s. After experiencing circulation dips in the 1970s, editors adapted to demographic shifts and regained readership. Thus, they remain the most widely distributed, with subscriptions well over five million (compared to *Ms.* at approximately 500,000 in 1991). Even women who do not subscribe encounter the worldview of these magazines in checkout lines, waiting rooms, and other public places. One does not have to sit down and read these periodicals word for word in order to get their most obvious messages. One of those messages is that they continue to speak to all American women, setting norms and reflecting reality. The newer magazines proclaim, at least in title and editorial statement, that it is really they who address the "new woman."

What, if any, is the difference between these types of periodicals? Despite the changes, do any construct messages that could *make a difference* in the discourse about the nature and value of the roles contemporary American women play? This essay "takes a snapshot" of traditional and innovative women's magazines published in 1991, in order to respond to these questions. It examines patterns of words and visual images in order to identify the predominant messages sent about the "proper" areas of women's concerns and the standards to which women's efforts in these areas should be held. A related purpose is to analyze these messages in terms of the possible role they play in the public and private discourse regarding the nature and effects of contemporary women's life choices.

METHODOLOGY

Nine issues of women's magazines were considered, all from October 1991. Five (*Woman's Day, Good Housekeeping, Family Circle, Ladies Home Journal,* and *McCall's*) are considered general interest and enjoy circulation ranging from five to over six million. In title and/or mission statement they purport to address a wider variety of issues for a wider variety of people than age-restricted publications such as

Seventeen or topic-specific publications such as *Glamour.* Four other magazines (*New Woman, Working Woman, Lear's,* and *Ms.*) were considered because, in one way or another, they present themselves as responses to women's liberated status. Although their circulation is much lower than that of the general interest magazines just cited, they were considered significant to this study because they purport to "make a difference." In title and/or mission statement, each positions itself as distinct from traditional women's magazines. Thus, these are periodicals, both individually and collectively, that adult women skim, peruse, or even read intently for a vision of the world that goes beyond fashion and food.

A standard content analysis was done on four aspects of the magazines: cover (photographs and article titles), ads (photographs and product categories), nonfiction (articles and regular departments), and fiction. There were no close analyses of narrative text. Instead the emphasis was on obvious topic categories (usually indicated in the table of contents: e.g., food, fashion), in the belief that most of the magazines considered in this study are read casually. Pages are often skimmed for the main idea, images are registered but not consciously critiqued. Indeed, their very format—with page after page dominated by photographs, headlines, and captions—signals that articles are not the true focus. As Goldman (1992) illustrates, images, particularly those used in ads, are encoded to elicit strong responses but not conscious analysis. In fact, they can disrupt the kind of sustained thought usually needed for careful reading.

Although the narrative texts were not closely analyzed for particular arguments, some notice was paid to article length and the types of issues considered, on the premise that these factors signaled the importance and complexity of those issues, at least in the world created by the magazine. Topics presented only through anecdote and/or without any sociopolitical context were contrasted to analyses that attempted to make connections between the topic at hand and other aspects of the readers' world.

ANALYSIS: A CONFUSING
SNAPSHOT OF THE NINETIES WOMAN

The General Interest Magazine

There were no significant differences among the five magazines labeled general interest. As such periodicals have done in the past (Ferguson, 1983; Shevelow, 1989), the October issues of *Family Circle, Good Housekeeping, Ladies' Home Journal, McCall's,* and *Woman's Day* presented self-contained, self-absorbed worlds that revolved around white middle-class women's responsibilities as homemakers, consumers, and sexual partners. Although each magazine made some attempt to "branch out" into other areas with articles on such topics as political candidates, battered women, crime, and various health concerns, discussion of these topics was greatly curtailed both by article format and context. In the first place, these articles were usually short (1-2 pages, often interrupted by human interest sorts of photographs). Second, they were surrounded by pages and pages of ads and articles that made very different kinds of observations and arguments (the themes of which will be considered shortly). Finally, because discussions of the "serious issues" were invariably constructed as relatively simple problem/solution scenarios or personal reflections, there was no acknowledgment of the contradiction, confusion, or even relationship that might have existed between any given issue and the dominant themes.

What were the dominant themes? One was that the "normal" world is white and middle/upper-middle class. In the five October 1991 issues considered, 99.5% of the people visually depicted in articles and ads seemed to be Anglo-American. In *McCall's,* the only pictures larger than one inch of African-American women are in a story about battered women imprisoned for killing their abusive husbands. Latina and Asian women were seldom represented. With the exception of a very few articles (the average was one per issue), the lifestyle assumed throughout is free from serious economic pressures and related problems such as hunger, crime-ridden neighborhoods, chronically poor schools, substandard housing, and inadequate health care. Upper-class women are presented as appropriate role models. The three issues with "cover girls" (is there such a term as "cover woman?") featured four wealthy celebrities.

Another theme was that women are domestic. They are properly concerned with—and almost solely responsible for—cooking, cleaning, decorating, sewing, and nurturing. Forty to 58% of the major ads (one-half to full page) in these issues concerned food, household items, child care products, and decorating materials. None show the products being used by a man. Granted, these magazines are targeted at women. But ads for health care and clothing did not evidence such exclusivity (in health care ads, all doctors depicted were male). Several articles were also devoted to an apparently all-female domesticity. Although most recipe articles focus on food rather than the sex of the cook, there is little to suggest that cooking is a shared activity. Neither are sewing Halloween costumes, putting a party together, or decorating. Occasionally, parenting is acknowledged as a joint effort (ironic, since the problems of actual single-parent households were not discussed in these issues). Moreover, the implied standards for all of these activities are relatively high. Homes are beautiful; not to mention immaculately neat and clean. Wholesome, complete meals are made from scratch (except those used in ads to promote ready-made products such as canned cheese sauce). Children are impeccably groomed and outfitted.

A minor subplot of this theme has to do with health. In varying degrees, each of the magazines examined addressed issues such as diagnosis, home treatment, medical procedures, and prevention. *Family Circle* ran a fairly extensive article on how to "take charge" in spite of the medical establishment. *Good Housekeeping* devoted seven pages to women and heart disease. The cover story for the *Ladies' Home Journal* was celebrity triumph over breast cancer. Even severe critics of such women's magazines have acknowledged that this medium has done much to raise the level of general awareness regarding important issues such as the ones mentioned here. However, I did not designate it as a dominant theme in its own right for two reasons. First, unlike the others, it was not widely reinforced by other aspects of the text, thus making questionable its role as an integral aspect of womanhood. Second, the woman's role in these articles whether patient, survivor, or the family's nurturing caretaker, continued to make her primary sphere of activity that of private domesticity. She is rarely the doctor, the professional health advocate, or the legislator.

A third, obvious theme was that women are expected to be beautiful according to very particular criteria and that they needed to *do something* in order to meet those criteria (in keeping with the "Steel Magnolias'" dictum that there is no such thing as natural beauty). Wolf's *The Beauty Myth* (1991) explicates this "third shift" and points to the role that women's magazines play in maintaining it.

> When the restless, isolated, bored and insecure housewife fled the Feminine Mystique for the workplace, [magazine] advertisers faced the loss of their primary consumer. How to make sure that the busy, stimulated working women would keep consuming . . . somehow, somewhere, someone must have figured out that they will buy more things if they are kept in the self-hating, ever-failing, hungry and sexually insecure state of being aspiring 'beauties.' (p. 66)

Wolf acknowledges that mainstream women's magazines such as the five examined here as well as those even more explicitly devoted to glamour, have published articles critical of artificial standards and the effort it takes to pursue them. But she argues these relatively self-contained perspectives are severely undermined by the relentless and more seductively constructed advertising and editorial messages surrounding the few such articles that do appear.

In the "snapshot" of women's lives presented by these five issues, the view was even more skewed. Of the over 130 major articles printed, not one challenged "the beauty myth." There were articles on why to color your hair, taking years off your looks, girdles that feel good, hairstyles, plaid fashions, perfect skin, diet danger zones, transforming your body, and the ubiquitous makeover; 16 in all. Factor in the ads, dominated by airbrushed images of women who comprise a very narrow range of physical type, and the real message is clear—a real woman, a good woman, an enterprising woman should try to conform to these images—very thin, carefully coifed, fashionably dressed, with cosmetically enhanced, Western European facial features.

The percentage of ads for beauty/fashion products *per se* ranged from 12% to 29% per issue. But these figures do not take into account that ads for other types of products sell a narrowly proscribed beauty as well. A Kotex ad talks about "being a woman . . . being curved" and shows a young, thin blonde model leaning suggestively into a mirror as she puts on lipstick. Virginia Slims cigarette ads, with their familiar boast about women's progress, depict these "new women" as invariably slim (what else?!), young, and beautiful. Even Moisture Drops features Debbie Reynolds—not so young, but definitely trying to radiate glamour.

A fourth and final dominant theme identified in this study is consumerism, defined here as a belief that buying is a valuable, necessary, and constant part of the readers' lives. In each of these five issues, a reader was much more likely to find consecutive pages of full-length ads than consecutive pages of solid text. Even articles functioned as ads. *McCall's* attempt to tell "the truth about six beauty myths" contains numerous product endorsements. And, of course, almost every fashion article centered around things to buy; usually things to buy for no other reason than because they were "in" (corollary: what the reader bought before is "out"). Makeovers of rooms as well as people implied that what the reader has now can be improved through effort and some sort of purchase.

Perhaps the most blatant articulation of the theme of consumerism came in the ads for collectibles; things to have just to have. There were numerous plates never intended to hold food, and dolls (all white) that were never intended for play. The $495 "collector" Monopoly game could be played but, presumably, no differently than the $15 version. Even "functional" items such as statues and Christmas ornaments were presented as only one of a "must have" series.

Based on this analysis of mass-distributed, general interest periodicals, the model contemporary woman is white and middle class (though she is not adverse to taking cues from higher socioeconomic classes). She is intensely interested in cooking, decorating, child care, and other aspects of creating a wonderful home. After all, that is her responsibility. She is concerned with health. She is somewhat aware of sociopolitical issues, especially on a "human interest" basis. She looks young, is very thin and proscriptively beautiful—though there is always more she could do to improve her appearance. She loves shopping, especially for new items. As Gloria Steinem observed, she tends to be "upbeat," with an "institutional smile" (1991, p. 12-13).

Four "Alternatives"

New Woman, Working Woman, and *Ms.* announced in their titles that they were directed at women who lead different lives than Friedan's frustrated housewives of the 1950s. As was also the case with *Lear's,* this perspective was made explicit in editorial statements and certain table of contents categories as well. The October 1991 editorial in *New Woman* decried the fact that the word "feminist" has acquired negative connotations for many and affirmed its own position as a feminist publication. *Lear's* October 1991 "Table of Contents" revealed such established topics as finance, automobiles, and interviews with prominent thinkers, artists, and activists conducted by Frances Lear, the white-haired editor-in-chief and outspoken advocate for women "over forty." *Working Woman* featured departments such as "Management Advice" and "Career Strategies." The October 1991 issue of *Ms.* began with an editorial that discussed ecofeminism, followed by a table of contents that featured political news and analysis (both global and national) alongside arts commentary, health and environmental reports.

What of the dominant themes identified in the general interest magazines: normality as white and middle class, women as primarily domestic, beauty as necessity, consumerism as a way of life? When the reader got past the titles, was there really much of a difference?

Certainly there was, in domesticity. The women addressed by these issues' articles and ads had careers, traveled, paid attention to grooming, saw films, got involved in politics, went to school, read books, exercised, and had romantic relationships. But they did not, as a rule, have children; nor did they cook, clean, or even decorate their homes. Approximately 10% of all articles dealt with familial relations in any respect. *New Woman* gave them the most attention with features on the "myth of quality time," being the daughter of an alcoholic, and memories of a grandfather. At the other end of this short spectrum, *Working Woman* eschewed food, home care, and children altogether. All four issues did address topics of health care; none, though, from the perspective of the woman as caregiver. Thus, the self-styled alternative magazines did present alternatives to one of the dominant themes established by traditional women's magazines.

However, examination of the alternative issues' texts and visual images with regard to the three remaining themes revealed some interesting "differences among the differences."

With the notable exception of *Ms.*, the world of these "new women" is still predominantly white. *Lear's* did feature Chinese novelist Ching Bezine, lowering the visual quotient of Anglo-American women to 98%. The only woman of color in *New Woman* was an African-American model selling Virginia Slims. Needless to say, there was no article addressing the charge that cigarette companies had begun to target minority, working-class and poor communities. Indeed, the world of *Lear's, New Woman,* and *Working Woman* was upscale with a vengeance. These women needed investment advice, entrepreneurial tips, and buying guides.

This raises the theme of consumerism. Not surprisingly, the three magazines that promoted upper-middle-class aspirations did so, in large part, by promoting expensive products through advertising (an average of 54 ads per issue) and even feature articles. Although there was not the emphasis on "collectibles" found in traditional women's magazines, there was the assumption that one could (must?) buy her way into "new womanhood."

And one of the most important aspects of purchased womanhood was beauty. As was the case in the traditional issues, the vast majority of ads (51-67%) were for beauty/fashion products. Moreover, ads for other items often featured a singular type of beautiful, fashionable woman. So did feature articles on topics such as dating, professional role models, clothing, and staff management. As mentioned earlier, these women were almost always Caucasian. Like their sisters in general interest magazines, they looked expensively dressed, thin, and young. Although *New Woman* touted an interview with Betty Freidan on its cover, it did not use her picture, opting instead for a standard model shot. *Lear's* puts women "over forty" on its cover, but only if they look "under forty" (this issue, it was Twiggy.) *Working Woman* ran the famous Nike ad that trades heavily on a woman's need to find self-esteem from within (give or take an exercise shoe or two) only to follow it with 14 pages of advertising promoting self-esteem through make-up and clothing.

As with the ethnic theme, only *Ms.* consistently broke the mold of consumerism and manufactured beauty as essential parts of a women's identity. The absence of advertising was striking, not only because it seemed to encourage more diverse visual depictions of women, but also because, as Steinem (1990) predicted, it allowed much more room for sociopolitical analysis. *Ms.* was free in this issue to examine various environmental topics, interview breast cancer survivors, explore cultural etiquette with regard to race, profile a collective, critique Spike Lee, and look at college campus life without worry that its analysis offended or even excluded product manufacturers, its investors, or advertising agencies. The world of women that *Ms.* assumed was by no means all-inclusive. It did not claim to be. But it did send very distinctive messages about the legitimate spheres of women's interests, activities, and worth.

CONCLUSION

Are there differences among "women's magazines" and, if so, can they make a difference in the lives of women in the 1990s? This analysis suggests that, despite minor nods to selected social issues, traditional general interest magazines reinforce traditional female roles of domestic caretaker, manufactured sexual object, and consumer. Moreover, the norms in each of these areas include being white and middle/upper-middle class. The new women's magazines examined in this study offered some alternatives, especially with regard to domestic duties, but three out of four seemed to send conflicting messages with regard to women's interests and self-esteem. It may now be acceptable to be independent, politically involved, sexually active, committed to a career; even to be over forty. But it's only acceptable if you look right and have the necessary accoutrements.

As observed earlier, mainstream journalism has pulled away from overt adulation of "super women." According to this analysis, however, direct advocacy has been replaced by an often confusing array of concerns, role models, and standards with little guidance as to how to critique, choose, or balance them.

No wonder women find themselves in boardrooms and at dinner parties, therapists' offices and P.T.A. meetings aware that something is wrong with the picture but unable and/or unwilling to articulate it. Why has "having it all" become only a woman's problem: a matter of individual will or choice that could also be addressed by at least discussing the depth and breadth of standards held up for them? Women's magazines may not be the clear cut villains in this scenario, but they are definitely voices in the ongoing construction of gender and, as such, bear careful examination.

REFERENCES

Banner, L. (1984). *American beauty.* Chicago: University of Chicago Press.

Brownmiller, S. (1984). *Femininity.* New York: Linden Press.

Cagan, E. (1978). The selling of the women's movement. *Social Policy, 9,* 4-12.

Ferguson, M. (1983). *Forever feminine: Women's magazine and the cult of femininity.* London: Heinemann.

Franzwa, H. H. (1975). Female roles in women's magazine fiction, 1940-1970. In R.

K. Unger & F. L. Denmark (Eds.), *Woman: Dependant or independant variable?* (pp. 42-53). New York; Psychological Dimensions.

Friedan, B. (1963, 1974). *The feminine mystique*. New York: Norton.

Geise, A. L. (1979). The female role in middle-class women's magazines from 1955 to 1976: A content analysis of nonfiction selections. *Sex Roles, 5,* 51-62.

Goldman, R. (1992). *Reading ads socially*. New York: Routledge.

Hoekstra, E. (1972). The pedestal myth reinforced: Women's magazine fiction, 1900-1920. In R. B. Nye (Ed.), *New dimensions in popular culture* (pp. 43-58). Bowling Green, OH: Bowling Green University Popular Press.

Johnston, W. (1987) *Workforce 2000*. Indianapolis: Hudson Institute.

Merrill, N. Private interview, March 10, 1991.

Murphy, B. O. (1992-4). Unpublished data collected in workshop series. Men and women as colleagues. Arthur Andersen and Co., S. C.

Seidel, R. (1990). *On her own: Growing up in the shadow of the American dream*. New York: Viking.

Shevelow, K. (1989) *Women and print culture: The construction of femininity in the early periodical*. New York: Routledge.

Steinem, G. (1990). Sex, lies and advertising. *Ms., 1,* 12-13.

White, C. (1970). *Women's magazines: 1693-1968*. London: Michael Joseph.

Williamson, J. (1981). *Decoding advertisements: Ideology and meaning in advertising*. Boston: Marion Boyars.

Wolfe, N. (1991). *The beauty myth*. New York: William Morrow.

12

Sport Sex: Toward a Theory of Sexual Aggression

Sean Michael Gilmore

During a workshop discussion on ways language can objectify people, talk turned to how women can be named as sex objects. After the workshop, two of the men asked to speak privately with me. We found a vacant classroom and closed the door. Once they were sure no one could hear us talking, they began explaining a game called "hogging." I later learned that this game is also called "pigsticking," "houndhunting," "slumming," "no pride," and "whaling." In this game, young men purposely sought out and engaged in sexual activity, "from kissing to intercourse," with women who were perceived to be unattractive. The man who "makes it" with the woman judged to be the most unattractive wins the game. I was shocked, and wondered how pervasive this type of behavior was and how it was manifested in their communication about women and sex.

A group in California called the "Spur Posse" gained national media attention with their sex game. Twenty to thirty men played a game in which they earned one point each time they "scored" with a different female (Smolowe, 1993). While the media touched upon the manner in which members of the Spur Posse talked about sex as a game, there have been few empirical studies of how male-only groups talk about women and sex. Timothy Beneke (1982), however, describes men's metaphors for sex, including sex as achievement, as conquest, as performance, as instruction, as a game, as a commodity, and discusses how these metaphors were linked with status, hostility, control, and dominance. While he mentions the issue of sex as a game, he does not address the complexity of that metaphor.

In *Coming of Age in New Jersey: College and American Culture,* Moffatt (1989) describes the sex life of college students. He mentions that about one out of three men talk about sex in terms of conquest, but he describes neither their actual sex talk nor the type of sexual conquests enacted by men. In fact, the author quickly skims over this topic. Warshaw (1988) also briefly discusses some of the labels fraternity men have been recorded as using when referring to sex and women. Women new to the school are referred to as "new meat." "Landsharking" refers to the act of fraternity brothers biting a woman on the rear end. A group rape is called a "gang bang." The two pages Warshaw allots to this subject are an interesting introduction to the topic, but do not suffice as a complete analysis of young male sex talk. Therefore, I became involved in a research team, advised by Norm Denzin, an expert in qualitative methods (1989), examining how young men and women talk about relationships and sex.

This essay reports some of the findings of this research project. Specifically, this essay explores how young males encourage each other to view women as points to be scored in sexual games. The focus in this essay is on how young males, rather than females, talk about sex because it is male discourse concerning sexuality that was found to be extremely problematic. In this essay, I will explain several male sex games that the research team discovered through open-ended interviews and anonymous surveys. I will also discuss how the discourse of male sex "games" creates and reinforces a culture where sexual intercourse is viewed as sport.

METHODS

The research team consisted of four women and four men, all under age 30. Interviews were conducted with 61 males and females between the ages of 18 and 22. All subjects interviewed were white, middle class, and lived in the midwest. Women were interviewed by women and men were interviewed by men. Of the 31 females interviewed, 16 attended college and 15 did not. Thirty males were also interviewed: 15 attended college and 15 did not. In addition, five workshops provided 116 anonymous, open-ended survey responses on men's and women's talk about sex. Sixty-four of these were written by men, of whom 29 attended college and 35 did not. Fifty-two women also turned in survey responses; 27 attended college and 25 did not. There was no overlap between subjects interviewed and anonymous surveys.

The interview format was open-ended. Following the methods of Norm Denzin (1989), interviews were conducted much like a friendly conversation, with discussion dependent upon the initiatives of both the interviewee and interviewer. The interviews ranged from sixteen minutes in length to three hours and nineteen minutes. All were audio taped and transcribed.

The analyses reported here were derived from the interview transcripts and survey responses. The inductive system of methodology proposed by Glaser and Strauss (1967) was employed. Themes and categories were abstracted and constructed from the actual data; then, the relationships among these themes were analyzed.

FINDINGS

There was no significant difference in talk about sex between the college population and the non-college population. On the other hand, gender did influence the degree to which subjects talked about sex as a game. Two important differences were the double standard of sexual promiscuity (promiscuity was presented as positive for men and negative for women) and that men talked about sex as a game far more than women did.

Stud Mythology

The male informants referred to men who have had multiple sex partners as "studs," studs received centrality, the attention and envy of their friends. Women who have had multiple sex partners were often referred to as "sluts," "sleazes," "whores," and "tramps" by both men and women. Clearly, this is not new. The familiar double standard concerning sexual promiscuity is common in the discourse of young women and men. One male informant stated, "There is a pressure to sow your oats among guys. It's good for you and becomes a way of proving manliness."

The mythology of the stud is constructed through the discourse of "scoring"; that is, men bragging about the number of women they sexually conquered. There exist multiple competitive, discursive practices that males engage in concerning sexuality, and the key element within these discourses is numbers. To be a member of the "virgin killer club," a male must score (have sexual intercourse) with three virgins; and to have "done the rainbow," a male must have scored with one female from each of at least three ethnic backgrounds, that is, African-American, Caucasian-American, and Latino. In addition, men constantly bragged about multiple positions, multiple locations, scoring women of different hair color, scoring women of different sizes, and the number of women scored, et cetera. The key terms within these discursive practices were multiple and different. Having sex did not legitimate a man as a stud. To be a stud required having sex with multiple women in various shapes and colors in unusual places and positions.

In addition to peer pressure to have sex with multiple partners, in multiple places and positions, in "stud culture" there is pressure for males to avoid monogamous relationships. One example of this pressure was apparent in descriptions of male/female interaction which other males can overhear. When ending conversations on the telephone, men often state they feel intimidated by other men not to respond "I love you" to the woman at the other end of the telephone. They often respond with "ditto" or else whisper so the other men do not "razz" them about being married. The men indicated they felt pressure not to disclose any information that would reveal or signify their position as being in a committed relationship, (e.g., "I miss you," "I'll see you real soon," or "I'll be over later").

Other examples of commitment as reserved for women included lavaliering and pinning among fraternity men. When a man gives a woman his lavaliere (a charm, usually of his fraternity insignia), she is lavaliered, or labelled as sexually belonging to him. Since she wears a sign that she is the property of a specific man, other men are warned away from sexual activity with her. Yet the man does not wear any signifier of the relationship.

Although this sexual practice is common, where men claim ownership of women, it is in opposition to the stud mythology. Men who lavaliered or pinned women were perceived as making a mistake that must be punished. Men who quit playing the field were symbolically stripped of their manhood by their peer group, and often this ritual was physically enacted. The traitors who lavaliered were sometimes stripped naked by their fraternity brothers, who then shaved their pubic hair, or applied BenGay to their testicles, or conducted some other symbolic removal of their manhood. Most commonly, however, fraternity members who lavaliered were stripped naked and tied to an object outside the sorority house. As one such brother stated, "We tied him up to a tree right outside of the girls' house. We had stripped him naked and everything. No one has lavaliered since then." Whether the drama was enacted physically or not, men who lavaliered always were punished by their peers.

The language that accompanied these events positioned the man as woman, a person who has lost his manliness and is now like the opponent, the woman. These men were called "pussies" and were told that they should "join the sororities." They have lost their position of dominance and now were under the control of the other, the female. They were "pussy-whipped" or "whipped." As one respondent stated,

> Whipped—I can tell you about this form of razzing. I found this chick that was the best fuck I ever had in my life. You know, she was like this sex toy I could do anything with. I started seeing her a lot and my friends started razzing me that I was married and shit like that and the tension caused me to break up with her. I haven't found a female that fucks as good as her yet.

In the above situation, a young man had sex, the "best fuck" of his life. A woman was labelled a "sex toy" who he talks of as if he owns, and yet he feels pressured into breaking up with her. Within this age population it was often not discussed as acceptable for men to have sex with a woman continuously, even if they treated her as a sex object. In fact, men who did so were often verbally and sometimes physically abused by their peers. Men were described as committed only to playing the field, which entailed "scoring" multiple women in order to be on the starting lineup of the men's team.

Sex Games and Contests

One male informant made the parallel between playing the field and "extra curricular activities." Upon an in-depth interview with this subject, I learned exactly what he meant by "extra curricular activities." He and his friends played a game referred to as "the point game." One point was awarded a male for engaging in sexual intercourse; two points were earned by a male having intercourse with an overweight female; three points were given to a player who allowed his peers to watch the score in action; and players received four points when two or more males scored the same female, simultaneously or consecutively.

Women were described as points to be scored in various sexual games, and most importantly, as one male respondent claimed, "repeat performances don't count." Another male responded concerning women, "You know how it is. You find them, feel them, fuck them, and forget them." In the interviews, six different versions of the above phrase were given. All of these statements ended with "forget them." Many males also expressed a desire to have sex with two or more women, at different times, during a single night. For example, one male interviewee stated with enthusiasm, "The ultimate score is to fuck a chick, leave her, and then find another one the same night, and fuck her too."

Through their language, men in this midwestern city have produced and reproduced a competitive sexual reality. In this discursive reality, they competed among each other for the title of "most valuable player," and women became points in their sex games. As one male respondent stated, "We call women points. You know, I scored a point." The most popular game was "scoring babes," having sex with the greatest number of attractive women. But it appears once sex was viewed as a game, and women were viewed as points, it became easy to change the rules of the game. For example, instead of finding the most attractive female, some of the men often competed for the perceived least attractive female—often called "hogging." As one subject explained, "Sometimes we get tired of trying to score good looking girls and so we change the rules and try to have sex with, well, ugly fat girls. It's kind of a funny contest."

Other examples of sex games included the "virgin killer club" and "doing the rainbow," discussed above, and "gross out," which entails saying sexually disgusting things to a woman while on a date with her. One group of men played a game called "golfing" or "nine holes." The first man who placed his hand down the pants of nine different women won the game. Having sex with women from different sororities was called "doing the sorority circle." Having sex with women in each branch of the military was called "doing the branches."

Different groups of men played different games and many of the men interviewed never labelled their competitive sexual practices. Rather, they participated in informal bragging stories concerning their sexual achievements. One male stated, "We say things like 'I got some pussy last night. I have gotten more pussy than you have had this year.'"

Many men interviewed believed that women played the same or similar games. This is not accurate. The women interviewed did not identify men as sex objects to be scored. Women respondents did not say "I got some dick last night. As a matter of fact, I've gotten more dick than you have this year." In fact, women who did have sex with multiple partners were often referred to in negative terms, by both women and men. As one woman stated, "Women don't compete for sex. So many guys are looking for sex, it's easy to get. And if you get too much sex or with too many guys, you are called a slut." The women interviewed did not go "hogging," play "gross out," or go "golfing"; the women respondents in this study did not play any such sexual games. In their discussions, sex typically was framed as part of the development of a relationship, not as a once only phenomenon.

DISCUSSION

Language defines and constructs what is and is not real. To label an object is to construct what it is and what it is not. For example, to call an object a "chair" is to position the object as something useful that people can sit on, but that same object can be labeled a "piece of junk," defining it as useless, something to be discarded. Language and labels suggest how actors understand and value their experiences. This research shows how a group of young males created a discursive reality in which women were not just sex objects, but points in sexual contests.

One of the best known theories concerning the objectification of women as sexual things was proposed by MacKinnon (1989). She explains that the dominant heterosexual ideology is: "Man fucks woman—subject, verb, object." This ideology positions man as the aggressor, the hunter, the conqueror. Women are to be submissive, the hunted, and the conquered. Men "get" sex; women "give up" sex. Men attack; women get attacked. Men fuck; women get fucked. Her theory of male sexual dominance is not limited to the bedroom. For men to be sexy, they are supposed to dominant, assertive, and aggressive. Conversely, for women to be sexy, they are supposed to be submissive, compliant, and passive.

MacKinnon's ideas concerning sexual dominance and conquest add insight and direction to the examination of the sexual discourse produced by these young men. But a slight adaptation of her theory is needed to fit this particular subculture. Her theory of "Man fucks Woman" manifested itself within this population as "players score points in sexual games." These young men compared each other's track records and competed with each other to see who scored the most points in the various sexual games. Their discourse concerning sexuality was marked by competitiveness. I label this competitive discourse "sport sex." It is a discourse that positions males as "players," sex as "games," and females as "points."

MacKinnon claims that females, in our society, are positioned as things that are to be owned and dominated by males. She labels this ideology "thingification." My research on male sexual discourse supports her argument. In the talk and ideology of these young men, women were figured as a very specific category of things—points in men's sexual contests. In the stud mythology and sport sex, women have no other value. As one male informant crudely stated, "What is the difference between a beer and a woman? Once you have a beer, the bottle is worth a dime."

CONCLUSION

As long as there exists positive symbolic reward for males who have sex with multiple partners, and simultaneously negative symbolic punishment for young men who demonstrate signs of commitment toward a woman, many young men will be socialized into competing with each other for studhood. When competing for studhood, sex becomes a game and women become points, objectified as something to score. Young men never say, "I got some human being last night. As a matter of fact, I've gotten more human being than you have this year." Men must objectify women, strip them of their dignity and respect, dehumanize them, in order to play these sex games. By playing these sex games, young men create a reality in which the objectification and exploitation of women becomes the accepted and encouraged norm. For too long, young men have been bragging about sex games and competitions behind closed doors. When we expose the true nature of their sexual discourse and the negative position it creates for women, then action can be taken to rectify the situation.

REFERENCES

Beneke, T. (1982). *Men on rape: What they have to say about sexual violence.* New York: St. Martin's Press.

Denzin, N. K. (1989). *The research act: A theoretical introduction to sociological methods.* Englewood Cliffs, NJ: Prentice Hall.

Glaser, B. G. & Strauss, A. (1967). *The discovery of grounded theory.* Chicago: Aldine.

Koss, M., Gidycz, C. A., & Wisniewski, N. (1987). "The scope of rape: Incidence and prevalence of sexual aggression and victimization in a national sample of higher education students." *Journal of Consulting and Clinical psychology, 55,* 162-170.

Mackinnon, C. A. (1989). *Toward a feminist theory of the state.* Cambridge: Harvard University Press.

Smolowe, J. (1993, April 4). Sex with a scorecard. *Time,* 41.

Moffatt, M. (1989). *Coming of age in New Jersey: College and American culture.* New Brunswick, NJ: Rutgers University Press.

Warshaw, R. (1988). *I never called it rape.* New York: Harper and Row.

13

Courtroom Uses of Linguistic Analysis to Demonstrate a Hostile Work Environment for Women

Susan Schick Case

An analysis of the language environment of a major steel company was conducted to determine whether or not there was evidence of a hostile work environment for women at that company, as charged in a discrimination suit. The analysis formed the basis of expert testimony presented to the court on behalf of the 26-year-old female plaintiff. It included careful examination of legal depositions of the plaintiff and two of the company's principal executives, as well as all correspondence concerning charges of harassment between the plaintiff and company management.

As part of expert testimony, the quality of human relationships in the steel plant, as indicated in the language of these documents, was examined. This analysis led to the conclusion that an organizational culture existed that was characterized by asymmetrical communication patterns involving gender-specific language as well as nonverbal communication messages. The court found that this organizational culture constituted a substantially discriminatory, hostile work environment for women employees in general, even when the particular nature of the "rough" work setting was taken into account. In this environment, sexual comments and overtures were acceptable and even expected, causing both tangible and intangible job detriment.

In this essay, we present the results of this exercise in linguistic analysis of courtroom evidence. After a brief discussion of the origins of a hostile work environment, five communication areas are examined to show the salient characteristics of the environment in which women employees were required to work.

These areas include: (1) language and symbols as indicators of underlying values; (2) defensive communication patterns; (3) degrading talk, including nonequivalent use of derogatory terms for women and asymmetry of both joke telling and swearing; (4) disciplinary language; and (5) nonverbal aspects of social control. The final section discusses the effects of a hostile environment, again interweaving the role of language in the discussion.

ORIGINS OF A HOSTILE WORK ENVIRONMENT

Everyday conversations at work reflect and transmit important aspects of an organization's culture. An organization's culture is invisible but extremely powerful in governing worker behavior. A hostile, negative culture can reduce commitment among employees and divide the workforce, so that some are seen as "better" or more "valuable" than others, not on the basis of performance, but on characteristics such as sex, race, age, or religion. Even in reasonable work situations there will be an occasional insensitivity to a group, confined to particular people or situations. However, in a hostile environment, the pattern of hostility, degradation, and abuse of power is consistent, recurring, and has debilitating effects on a group of people that transcend any individual worker who may have experienced its hostility and filed a complaint.

For example, sexual harassment is not an event or conversation that happens between just two people. The norms, rules, and constraints set by top management and the hierarchical nature of work organizations affect the way people in these organizations behave (Daft, 1989; Garvin, 1991; Paludi & Brickman, 1991). Aspects of organizational culture can either encourage or discourage sexual overtures or sexual hostility. When management tolerates or condones sexual harassment of employees by allowing sexual remarks to be made, by not investigating allegations of harassment and then applying sanctions against harassment in any form, the practice of acceptance reverberates throughout the organization (Gutek, 1985). Employers are now being held liable for offensive environments created by supervisors (Sperry, 1990).

Surveys of women in the workplace estimate the rate of sexual harassment to be between 25 and 53% (Sandruff, 1992), but find it even higher among women in male-dominated companies. Riger (1991) concluded in her review of the literature that women with low power and status, whether due to being young, single, or divorced, or in a marginal or token position in an organization, are more likely to be harassed.

Occupational segregation of the sexes is perhaps the most visible structural phenomenon associated with the creation of sexually hostile work environments. Gutek (1985) found that male-dominated environments tend to be sexualized, while female- dominated work environments tend to be asexual. Konrad and Gutek (1986) also found that in gender-integrated environments where men and women work together in equal numbers on the same jobs, there are virtually no social-sexual problems, since men consider sexual behavior inappropriate to the workplace. In contrast, men in gender-segregated jobs do not.

Skewed sex-ratios affect communication in daily organizational life (Popovich & Licata, 1987). Harassment is more prevalent in work environments with skewed sex-ratios where there is heightened power differential between groups of workers, and women are in traditional work roles such as secretary, where they are treated as women first, and work-role occupants second. Harassment is more likely to occur in such work contexts because our culture has socialized people to communicate in predominantly male/female role-bound ways which then "spill over" to work contexts (Booth-Butterfield, 1989; Case, 1993; Gutek, 1985; Gutek & Cohen, 1987; Nieva &

Gutek, 1981; Popovich & Licata, 1987).

The maintaining of dominance and power is easily recognized through the language used by organizational members. When there is greater equality between people, language is linguistically parallel with forms used being symmetrical between conversational partners. The greater the inequality between people, the greater is the use of nonreciprocal linguistic behaviors (Case, 1992; Poynton, 1985). Two ways men maintain their dominance and sustain a sexualized work environment are through the use of sexual humor and swearing (Case, 1992). When men joke at work, women often are the subjects and objects (Duncan, Smeltzer, & Leap, 1990). Swearing is not only an indicator of male solidarity, but a mechanism of "doing power" (Case, 1988). It functions to exclude women, facilitating group ties with men, reinforcing their masculinity (Padovic, 1991).

The use of derogatory terms for women is one way an in-group (men) stereotypes an out-group (women). Language is "carefully guarded by the superior people because it is one of the means through which they conserve their supremacy" (Rowbotham, 1973, p. 32). Words charged with negative emotion, publicly taboo and distasteful words, not only reflect the culture that uses them, but teach and perpetuate the attitudes that create them. Such anti-woman language has the two basic ingredients of prejudice: denigration and gross overgeneralization (Allport, 1954, p. 34).

METHOD

The case described involves a young woman who worked as a secretary in a steel plant where there was a clear division of labor between male supervisory staff and female clerical workers: men in high-status, high-paying jobs involving salary with bonuses and commissions; women in low-status, poorly paid hourly wage, or low-salary jobs. In the context of a case study, a framework is presented to show how certain conversational patterns point to a harassing organizational culture. The purpose is to expand the identification of this construct through quotations and examples from a legal case, since forms of verbal abuse are viewed as less offensive than physical harassment (Zalucki, 1989).

The analysis in this paper is based on examination of documents used in the filing of a successful sexual discrimination suit. These included legal depositions of the plaintiff and two executives, and all correspondence concerning charges of harassment between the plaintiff and management of the company. Within these documents, competing views of several incidents are described, including the plaintiff's writing of a letter requesting a stop to what she felt was sexual harassment at the plant.

As an expert witness on behalf of the plaintiff, the first author examined the quality of relationships in the steel plant, indicated in the language of these documents, to determine whether or not there was evidence of a hostile environment for women as charged in the discrimination suit. After an initial reading of the general manager's deposition, a content analysis was done to understand the work environment for women employees, and whether the environment could be considered hostile. Two independent coders examined more than 1,300 pages of transcript for language patterns that might have contributed to a discriminatory and hostile culture for women in this organization. Reliability of at least 82% was obtained on each of fourteen specific indicators for five identified categories .

LANGUAGE, SYMBOLS, AND
UNDERLYING VALUES IN ORGANIZATIONS

The first of five communication areas examined was the managers' role in perpetuating the values of the organization through language and symbols. Explicit and implicit messages filtered down through the organization by what the managers paid attention to, how they reacted to critical incidents, and how they allocated rewards, status, and punishments.

At this plant, managers paid attention to the sexuality of the female workforce. An attractive appearance and personality were essential for women to get ahead. The work environment was characterized by sex-role spillover; where the work role of women was deemphasized, and their sex role was exaggerated. Men frequently socialized with subordinates who were attractive, personable, and held low-paying, low-prestige clerical jobs. This seemed natural and normal to people there, indicating the power of sex roles to shape their view of the world. Many women believed that women who slept with their male superiors were given more favorable work assignments than women who did not. The sexually charged atmosphere gave women the message that they were sexual objects rather than competent and respected workers, trivializing their accomplishments; and it gave men the message that they were superior to women. Thus it was "acceptable" for the men to use harassing language, jokes, and expect sexual behavior to be reciprocated.

Managers' attention to the sexuality of their female workforce was also reflected in daily conversations that helped maintain women's secondary status. The general manager described his use of "unique language" to motivate his workers. He claimed that "calling them sleazy sluts, sleazy bitches, and cunts gets them moving on the job." He further stated that "Women loved being told that they had 'nice tits' or a 'great ass.'" Sometimes he'd tell them "their hooters were too small" to "get them riled up to work harder."

As the general manager stated, "I intended to use my unique language to upset, move, and motivate my women. The girls loved it." He seemed aware of its potential problems saying it was both "upsetting to some women and endearing to others." He also stated that "the language and behavior were used with all female staff and were therefore not discriminatory, although whether or not it would be viewed as derogatory depended on who the recipient was and what they thought." He said, "Language is a sensitive thing to certain people and under certain circumstances. I'm a sensitive man. I know who likes this stuff."

It was assumed, within the management of the company, that unless women complained, such behavior was "perfectly acceptable." The general manager argued that "no one had ever been offended or had ever complained about his behavior or language in the past until the plaintiff sent a letter to upper management, in which she talked of unwelcome sexual advances that she found offensive."

Women at this plant did not frequently complain of sexual advances, but many indicated that such advances were totally unwanted, that there was sexual pressure by men, including lunch-break trysts, and that many men in the company were frequent touchers. Women remained at the lowest level of jobs in the organization. They faced embarrassment and humiliation, describing internalized anger because senior staff encouraged a sexually exploitative environment. " I kept quiet for so long, but I was so angry. No one questioned the display of naked women hanging on managers' office walls. No one cared about the rubbing, kissing, and pawing by men, of female staff. It is so hard to raise objections. I'll either be crazy or I'll get fired." At this company there was no policy about harassment. As a result, it was clear to all employees that harassment was not taken seriously. Yet, management categorically denied that any harassment existed, and contested—and lost—the court case.

But just as important as what the managers paid attention to in this company was what was ignored or tolerated. For example, in the general manager's testimony, he indicated that he did not pay attention to women employees being told that their "hooters were too small," their breasts referred to as "tits," and their buttocks as "asses." He did not pay attention to male employees' discussions of their sex lives at work. He did not pay attention to verbal complaints, "It's just letting off steam." The company did not even pay enough attention to the sexual harassment letter of complaint by the plaintiff to document its findings in a report. They said, "We categorically deny that any harassment exists." Yet, the general manager also indicated that the complaints were treated as "serious."

Even with a formal complaint, no attention was paid to alleged discriminatory behavior in this workplace. The way the top managers responded to the crisis sent an important message to employees working there about what would happen if they were to raise a complaint. The plaintiff complained in writing, and within a short period of time was fired after her personnel file became newly documented with work-problem statements that had never previously appeared. These statements were issued only after the initial complaint letter about harassment was filed, and not retracted. The response to the plaintiff's complaint letter was indicative of the underlying values of this company. When the complaint letter was received, it was described as "wholly and absolutely false," rather than being given the benefit of any doubt or warranting a fair and impartial investigation before judgments were formed. The acceptability of sexual behavior was so commonplace that the vice president to whom it was sent immediately saw it "as the retaliation of an angry woman" and "as the character assassination of a good family man." This male breadwinner norm is a central aspect of gender identity in steelworkers' shop floor cultures, which are bastions of traditional, working-class masculinity (Livingstone & Luxton, 1989).

A meager attempt at an investigation was conducted by the plaintiff's superiors, including the accused. No independent, disinterested staff were involved. In this situation, status and power issues became confused with the investigation of impropriety. The investigators had difficulty accepting the allegations. The complainant felt "intimidated and unwilling to continue to disclose full information" to her boss. If a complainant's charges were not substantiated by an impartial investigator, it would appear that she was a troublemaker; if the charges were substantiated, she would appear disloyal.

The sexual nature of the verbal and physical conduct that no one in the company had paid attention to created a hostile, offensive, and discriminatory work environment. It poisoned the atmosphere of employment for all women. The plant management's overall attitude was "if a woman wished to venture into the men's world of work, then she should expect overtures from men and be able to handle them." These examples indicated to the women at this plant that they were low-value, sexual commodities. Managers who initiated, condoned, and participated in such activities served as role models to those further down the hierarchy, giving the impression that "this is what successful people in this organization do." Such managers gave no encouragement to women to perform their jobs well, to take initiative, or to rise in the organization. The company sent a clear message to its women employees that accusations of sexual harassment would not be taken seriously and would not lead to serious punishment. The message they gave was that not only were such situations acceptable, but that such accusations might result in bodily harm to the complainant, which occurred in this case when the plaintiff refused to retract her complaint.

Critical comments and reports were added to the plaintiff's personnel file after she sent her complaint letter to senior management. Those reports were later used to assist in her removal from the organization. Their use to fire a nonconforming employee told other women who might have wished to complain that it was potentially dangerous to do so. "If you complain, you attract attention to yourself, which means that anything bad you do receives far greater notice; as a result, your job may be at risk." The plaintiff was told by her supervisor, prior to the insertion of negative evaluation comments, that "he would make it his business to be in the Purchasing Department every day to raise the flag on her job performance." When a complaint becomes tied to the content of one's personnel file, there is strong disincentive to make a complaint.

DEFENSIVE PATTERNS OF COMMUNICATION

The second language area examined was defensive communication patterns used in the organization. Such patterns generally occur when people feel under threat. In defensive communication, only the dominant party is allowed full voice. The communications female employees received at this plant were evaluative, controlling, manipulative, communicating superiority of management, with aims to win and remain one-up at all cost. There were many instances of such communications that triggered defensiveness at this company. For example, comments made to the women were frequently, and intentionally, evaluative, usually derogatory, and sexually explicit. Women were not just told that their work performance was not good; their moral worth was questioned with use of such terms as "lazy sleazy slut" and "sleazy bitch." This is one of the most extreme forms of evaluation possible, since it occurs in the context of a punitive environment, one in which a plaintiff's harassment complaint was defensively viewed as "absolutely false . . . an overreaction."

The plaintiff had put her harassment experience in a letter requesting that she be allowed to do her job: "I come to work each day to do my job. No more; no less . . . and all I ask is the sexual harassment wrought upon me be put to a halt." In response, her experiences were first denied, then declared "false" without an investigation. She was viewed as "overreacting," then chastised and berated for writing the letter charging sexual harassment, threatened "with consequences unless she wrote a letter of retraction," and ultimately, upon refusal to retract her statement, was grabbed, wrestled with, and thrown to the ground in front of witnesses, with enough force to seek hospital treatment. Soon, she was fired, mostly because as the general manager said, "she was not a proper woman who knew her place."

The symbolic stratification of speech that was important in maintaining sexual dominance and reinforcing authority over women in this plant compounded the plaintiff's problems because of her so-called gender-inappropriate assertiveness in speaking out. The rules about appropriate ways to behave were not the same for the two sexes. Blatant assertiveness or aggression was prohibited for women, but not for men. When anger was expressed by women, they ran the risk that it would elicit counter-anger and retaliation by men. In this organization, when women protested male gestures that they felt had gone too far, they were either ignored or answered with a personal attack.

Another example of defensive communication involved an exchange between the plaintiff and a manager in the company concerning her picking up a stranded employee whose car broke down on his way to work. The plaintiff was planning to pick him up since she got the phone call, and often had done this as part of her job. The manager to whom she said, "I'm leaving to pick up Bob," yelled: "Don't you pick him up. I'm telling you not to pick him up. Don't you pick him up! Don't do it! Don't!" The manager appeared more concerned with controlling the plaintiff's behavior than solving the problem of whether a stranded employee should be picked up, and by whom. His intervention was aimed at provoking, not problem solving. His language was controlling, dogmatic, and stubborn, not investigative. He ignored her position on the issue and that Bob was waiting for her to pick him up.

Messages sent to female employees at this company were also manipulative. When the general manager used "unique language" to greet, motivate, or evaluate his employees he ignored them as competent workers. Repetition took out the shock value of the words, eventually resulting in the "girls" believing that they were inferior. "We were made to believe we were inferior. We expected to be called 'cunts.' Everyone did it. We had no option but to tolerate it." This form of address, and its corresponding touching behavior, was expected, accepted, and tolerated. The general manager said in contrast, "The women didn't complain. They took it like a compliment. They smiled and laughed at being touched and cuddled. They loved it." The harassment had become invisible.

It was not at all surprising that most of the women in this company did not complain about their conditions. They were more concerned with keeping their jobs, so they appeared to be satisfied and happy to avoid personal attack. They apparently accepted the "unique language" used by supervisors to upset, move, and motivate them. Their only option appeared to be to tolerate this "unique language," "taking it like a compliment," to smile, and even to laugh at being repeatedly touched and cuddled, but not to complain. This is a central part of avoidance, submission, and learned helplessness. It also is indicative of fear. If everyone else accepts such behavior around them, it is likely to be a very brave person who does not.

DEGRADING TALK

A third communication area examined was degrading talk. We looked at the use of sexist derogatory terms for women, asymmetry of joke telling by men at the expense of women, and swearing, analyzing the nonequivalent use of language. Language use reflects how we think, causing us to behave in certain ways. Thus, the use of sexist derogatory language, accompanied by denigrating touching behavior, had serious implications for the women at this plant. In this company the language of domination involved swearing, joke telling, endearments commonly used publicly to women, and sexist derogatory terms that ranged from addressing physical appearance ("sexy legs"), body parts ("tits"), to referring to women as sexual objects ("slut," "whore"), or merely as sexual organs ("cunts").

The general manager argued that whether or not an action was derogatory depended on whether the initiator "means it," although he also recognized that "employees have rights, and should not be denied dignity, and that there are limits to the use of rough language." He said, " I find 'nigger' an acceptable word, but not 'nigger bitch'. The rest of my language I don't see as offensive."

Asymmetry was also present when men made jokes at the expense of women, who often laughed hard. "Men made jokes at our expense. We laughed hard. What else could you do?" Status in this case was signaled by the so-called witticism, and subordination by laughing. A lack of parallelism in language use creates problems. This lack of parallelism was particularly clear in how men used swearing in the plant (Poynton, 1985). Since women also swore at the steel company, language examination had to demonstrate nonequivalence of swearing, stating that there was a difference between the type of sexually gendered language like "cunt," which applied to women only, and phrases like "fuck" and "screw," which all employees used. All employees commonly said, "I got screwed," or "My boss fucked me over." Although this language is vulgar in some contexts, it reflects the informal language used in society by both sexes.

There is a difference between the type of sexually gendered language that only applies to women and phrases like "fuck" or "screw," which were used frequently by many employees across gender lines. In organizations such as this, there is a frequent use of synonyms for copulation in blaming, just as there is use of scatological language such as "shit," "piss," and "asshole." We analyzed various slang uses in the steel company of "screw" and "fuck" to mean betray, cheat, wrong, take advantage of, deceive, attack, or destroy. For example, the plaintiff felt she "got screwed" when she was suspended without pay, because she was betrayed by her boss. She also felt that she worked very hard when her employer needed her, only to be fired when she complained of harassment: "my boss screwed me"; "I got fucked over." Women and men in this company often cried out, "Screw you!" or "Fuck you!", when denouncing another. These words were used by both men and women differently than the gendered sexual terms ("slut," "bitch," "cunt," "whore"), which were only used for women and were negative, aggressive, and hurtful. In English, there are no equivalent terms for men that carry the same negative connotations.

EMPLOYEE DISCIPLINE AND COMMUNICATION

The fourth communication area examined, employee discipline and communication, focused on language indicators of fear and distrust; supervisory communication emphasizing negative feedback, errors, and defects; a "we-them" adversarial distinction between employees and management; and supervisor-to-employee language in which employees were treated more in a parent-child, abusive way than in an adult-to-adult, cooperative manner. All of these can lead to employees feeling unfairly and unjustly treated and may contribute to discriminatory practices and a hostile work environment.

Within the steel company charged, there were indicators of fear and distrust. For example, the plaintiff felt the need to use a hidden tape recorder during an interview with her manager concerning her harassment complaint. This indicated a lack of trust. Furthermore, the letter that she initially wrote to top management, complaining of sexual harassment, was written while on forced leave without pay, further indicating fear: She indicated "I was only able to complain when I was away from the organization, and then only in writing."

The second indicator, negative feedback, was present in general comments and evaluations of female staff at the steel company. These comments and evaluations emphasized errors and defects rather than providing constructive performance appraisals. Only negative evaluations and incidents were ever recorded in the plaintiff's file, and all occurred after her letter about harassment was sent to top management. As mentioned earlier, the general manager used negative feedback to motivate female employees. This included derogatory, gender-specific expressions which he asserted were part of his "unique language."

The way in which disciplinary actions were allocated at the plant gave a strong indication that there was a "we-them" atmosphere within this organization, adding to perceptions of unfairness and injustice often felt by employees in hostile work environments. Differential priorities were attached to who got what punishment depending on the status of the offender, rather than on the type of digression. The punishment allocated to the manager, charged with criminal assault of the plaintiff who received hospital treatment, was three days' leave with full pay. This type of punishment was token in nature. It could almost be regarded as a reward rather than a punishment, a three-day paid vacation; compared with the week of unpaid leave that the plaintiff received because she was not properly compliant. The general manager stated, "It is completely unacceptable for an employee not to be compliant. She was an insubordinate, headstrong bitch."

This distinction sent important messages to other staff in the organization about injustices in their work environment. It also told them what was, and was not, tolerable or accepted behavior to management, and what would happen to them if their behavior was perceived as unacceptable. The message transmitted was that it was acceptable for a manager to throw an employee to the ground causing injury after she refused to retract a harassment complaint, but it was completely unacceptable for a female employee to challenge a male manager's order.

Clear examples of parent-child relationships between superiors and subordinates at this company added to the hostility. Women working there were frequently referred to as "girls" and patted or kissed on the head, as children or pets might be patted or fondled. This is paternalistic, and it lessens feelings of competence, weakening one's self-image. Women had no choice but to go along with it. The manner in which the manager dealt with the plaintiff's reason for picking up a stranded employee with car trouble bore a strong similarity to the way a dominating parent might deal with a disobedient child: "Don't you pick him up. I'm telling you not to pick him up. Don't you pick him up. Don't do it. Don't." The coercive nature of such interactions is characteristic of a hostile environment.

SOCIAL CONTROL ASPECTS
OF NONVERBAL BEHAVIOR

The fifth communication area examined was nonverbal behavior as an avenue for social control on a large scale and interpersonal dominance on a smaller scale, including patterns of asymmetric exchange in relation to women around space, eye contact, smiling, and touching. Nonverbal communication can be subtly used to control women and maintain the power structure because of women's socialization to docility and passivity and their frequent interaction with those in power. The nonverbal message overpowers the verbal one carrying 4.3 times the weight (Argyle, Llajee, & Cook, 1968) and more than 65% of its meaning (Birdwhistle, 1970).

The use of dominant nonverbal behavior was prevalent in this company. There were frequent examples of touching, patting, hugging, kissing, cuddling, ogling, and leering of the female staff. "There was wholesale touching of us. We were community property." They "touched, rubbed, kissed my head." They "ogled and leered at me. I looked away." "They gazed at my body . . . looked me up and down." "I smiled to cover my uncomfortableness." It was argued by management that such behavior was liked by the women ("She smiled because she liked it.") and, as with the "unique language," was "non-discriminatory and non-derogatory because it was applied to all the women workers." There were repeated violations of personal space with nonreciprocal touch used for control. Men "hovered over the women." They "sat on their desks while they worked."

Jourard and Rubin (1968) take the view that "touching is equated with sexual intent, either consciously or at a less conscious level " (p. 47), whereas Lewis (1972) writes: "In general for men in our culture touching is restricted to the opposite sex and its function is primarily sexual in nature" (p. 237). Touch is one of the most powerful of communication channels and the most carefully guarded and regulated. It is a primary means for not only expressing affection and intimacy, but control (Thayer, 1988). The touching behavior used in this plant was a clear sign of dominance. The smiling, laughing, and apparent acceptance was a clear sign of submission. Such behavior was an "acceptable" part of the corporate culture here, where women were too fearful to challenge the male power hierarchy.

EFFECTS OF A HOSTILE ENVIRONMENT

In this plant, women were sent signals to be passive, tolerant, and accepting of discriminatory behavior. In our expert witness report and testimony, we made a case through an analysis of the linguistic environment. A case was made that there were adversarial employee relations, defensive communications, inappropriate managerial behavior, sexually degrading language, and nonverbal dominance cues contributing to a hostile work environment for female employees at this company, leading to sexual harassment and other kinds of sexual behaviors.

In general, women are hurt by sex in the workplace, since it affects not only their dignity, but their physical health and productivity, whereas, men are not, since it is irrelevant to their work performance, health, or self-image. Research has shown a large gender gap in attitudes toward sex in the workplace, with 85% of men consistently saying they are flattered by sexual overtures by women. In contrast, 84% of women are insulted by sexual overtures (Gutek, 1985). There are clear "gender differences in the construction of social reality" (Paludi & Brickman, 1991), with conduct many men consider unobjectionable, being offensive to women (Simon, 1991).

An environment that encourages sexual harassment discourages optimum productivity. The longer harassment is ignored, the more it demoralizes employees, disrupts work, and reduces job satisfaction, leading to lower productivity and increased absenteeism. The steel company in question encouraged sexual overtures and hostility by its general laxness about maintaining a professional atmosphere at work. Women were often asked to do tasks unrelated to work, were treated disrespectfully, and were subjected to a work environment where swearing and sexual joking was common and where gender was a factor in how they were treated and hired. In such a setting, women are not viewed as serious professional workers, and their accomplishments are invisible. The repeated assertion of an employee's sexual identity over her identity as worker is a manifestation of harassment in the workplace.

Given the prevalence of harassment and its detrimental effects on the women involved, it is reasonable to ask why there are not pervasive complaints of its existence. The absence of complaints does not mean that there is no harassment. Direct confrontation in the form of a complaint is only one possible response to the experience of sexual harassment (Gruber, 1989; Terpstra & Baker, 1989). The vast majority of harassed women do not make formal complaints because they are afraid to speak up. They are concerned about their own futures, they believe that management "just won't get it," and in some cases are concerned with the career of the harasser (Hill v. Thomas [Crenshaw, 1992]).

The one who complains is not a fluke. She is not being overly sensitive. She is not crazy; imagining the whole thing. She does not have severe emotional problems. To protest to the point of court action requires a quality of inner resolve that is both reckless and serene, a sense of "This I won't take" that is both desperate and principled. It also reflects an absolute lack of any other choice at a point at which others with equally few choices do nothing (MacKinnon, 1979). A more rational view of a formal complaint like the one filed in this case is to see it as the "tip of the iceberg"—an indication of problems in the workplace, not an indication of a problem woman.

REFERENCES

Allport, G. W. (1954). *The nature of prejudice.* Cambridge, MA: Addison, Wesley.

Argyle, M., Llajee, M. & Cook, M. (1968). The effects of visibility on interaction in a dyad. *Human Relations, 21,* 3-17.

Birdwhistle, R. L. (1970). *Kinesics and context.* Philadelphia: University of Pennsylvania Press.

Booth-Butterfield, M. (1989). Perceptions of harassing communication as a function of locus of control, work force participation, and gender stratification. *Social Problems, 29,* 236-275.

Case, S. S. (1993). The collaborative advantage: The usefulness of women's language to contemporary business problems. *Business and the Contemporary World,* Summer, *5,* 81-105.

Case, S. S. (1988). Cultural differences, not deficiencies: An analysis of managerial women's language. In L. Larwood & S. Rose, *Women's careers: Pathways and pitfalls* (pp. 40-63). New York: Praeger.

Case, S. S. (1992). Organizational inequity in a steel plant: A language model. In M. Bucholtz, K. Hall & B. Moonwoman (Eds.), *Locating Power: Procedings of the 1992 Berkeley Women and Language Conference, Vol. 1* (pp.36-48). Berkeley, CA: Berkeley Women and Language Group.

Crenshaw, K. (1992). Race, gender, and sexual harassment. *Southern California Law Review, 65,* 1467-1476.

Daft, R. L. (1989). *Organizational theory and design* (3rd. ed.) St. Paul, MN: West Publishing Co.

Duncan, W. J., Smeltzer, L. R. & Leap, T. L. (1990). Humor and work: Applications of joking behavior to management. *Journal of Management, 16,*

2, 255-278.

Garvin, S. (1991). Employee liability for sexual harassment. *HR Magazine, 36,* 101-107.

Gruber, J. E. (1989). How women handle sexual harassment: A literature review. *Sociology and Social Research, 74,* 3-7.

Gutek, B. A. (1985). *Sex and the workplace.* San Francisco, CA: Jossey-Bass, Inc.

Gutek, B. A., & Cohen, A. G. (1987) Sex ratios, sex role spillover, and sex at work: A comparison of men's and women's experiences. *Human Relations, 40,* 2, 97-115.

Jourard, S. M., & Rubin, J. E. (1968). Self-disclosure and touching. *Journal of Humanistic Psychology, 8,* 39-48.

Konrad, A., & Gutek, B. (1986). Impact of work experiences on attitudes toward sexual harassment. *Administrative Science Quarterly, 31,* 422-438.

Lewis, M. (1972). Parents and children: Sex-role development. *School Review, 80,* 229-40.

Livingstone, D. W., & Luxton, M. (1989). Gender consciousness at work: Modification of the male breadwinner norm among steelworkers and their spouses. *Canadian Review of Sociology and Anthropology, 26,* 2, 240-275.

MacKinnon, C. A. (1979). *Sexual harassment of working women.* New Haven, CT.: Yale University Press.

Nieva, V. F., & Gutek, B. A. (1981). *Women and work: A psychological perspective.* New York: Praeger.

Padovic, I. (1991). The re-creation of gender in a male workplace. *Symbolic Interaction, 14,* 279-294.

Paludi, M. & Brickman, R. (1991). *Academic and workplace sexual harassment.* Albany, NY: SUNY Albany.

Popovich, P. M., & Licata, B. J. (1987). A role model approach to sexual harassment. *Journal of Managment, 13,* 149-161.

Poynton, C. (1985). *Language and gender: Making the difference.* Victoria, BC: Deakin University Press.

Riger, S. (1991). Gender dilemmas in sexual harassment policies and procedures, *American Psychologist, 46,* 497-505.

Rowbotham, S. (1973). *Woman's consciousness: Man's world.* Baltimore: Penguin Books.

Sandruff, R. (1992). Sexual harassment: The inside story. *Working Woman,* June, 47-51, 78.

Simon, H. A. (1991). *Ellison v. Brady.* A "reasonable woman" standard for sexual harassment. *Employee Relations Law Journal, 17,* 71-80.

Sperry, M. (1990). Hostile environment, sexual harassment and the imposition of liability without notice: A progressive approach to traditional gender roles and power based relationships. *New England Law Review, 24,* 917-952.

Terpstra D. E. & Baker, D. D. (1989). The identification and classification of reactions to sexual harassment. *Journal of Organizational Behavior, 10,* 1-14.

Thayer, S. (1988). Close encounters. *Psychology Today, 22,* 3, 30-36.

Zalucki, B. L. (1989). Discrimination law: Defining the hostile work environment claim of sexual harassment under Title VII. *Western New England Law Journal, 11,* 143-177.

14

"And If We Lose Our Name, Then What About Our Land?" Or, What Price Development?

M. J. Hardman

Ak markanqa warmiq warmjamchaqa, karmaps karmajjamchaqa.
(Here in Tupe women are as women themselves and men are also as men themselves.)
—TUPE SAYING

On the high, wind-swept plateaus and in the rugged, steep valleys of the Andes, Andean civilizations flourished for centuries, maybe millennia. From what remains and from what can be reconstructed, we know the cultures in existence a little over 500 years ago were thriving cultures with intimate and specific knowledge of the rugged environment that allowed not only survival but prosperity. The steep, terraced hillsides were richly productive in agriculture, everyone had enough to eat, an extensive, well-maintained road system allowed exchanges for a rich diversity in food and other products.[1]

Cultural norms were of equality between women and men with complementary, sometimes overlapping roles, with a balance of power between the sexes, both believed to be equally necessary to a viable human community. The languages, in consonance with the cultures, had no structures for the denigration of women; rather, the grammatical structures affirmed humanness. The major grammatical divisions are not sex-based but rather human-based, with a separate set of pronouns for human beings and another for all else, including animals. The major inflectional category is not number, but data source, that is, sentences are marked as to the source of the material being presented, whether personal experience, knowledge-through-language, or some nonpersonal source. The languages grammaticalized the simile and have no easy way of ranking comparatively. The language and culture were deeply rooted in community and cooperation, not in ranking and competition.

Five hundred years ago, out of Europe, a conquest swept over the Americas devastating the existing cultures and leaving in its wake the European version of sexism with its own particular characteristics deeply rooted in the structure of the IndoEuropean family of languages (Miller 1977). The specific grammatical structures that so lowered the status of women in the Andes, as elsewhere, are sex-based gender with the feminine as a derivation of the masculine, number with plural derived from the singular, and the pervasive ranking comparative/absolute. I call the interplay of these three structures "derivational thinking."

Sex-based gender marking in the world's languages is not necessarily rare, although the way in which grammars have been written by members of the conquering European societies gives us a biased idea of frequency and typology. The language structures brought by these conquerors involved not only the obligatory marking of sex-based gender, but a derivation of the feminine from the masculine, the result of a tradition at least 5,000 years old, in a constant feedback loop between women's place in these European societies and in their languages.

Part of the realization of this derivation is in the naming practices imposed on all conquered populations, patronymics that labeled all people, and by implication all goods, as belonging to men. The power to name implies much of the power of creation. Our patronymics give the power to name people exclusively to men; without a father the child "has no name"; ancestry and family are identified through father's name; mother loses her name and identity at marriage. Our old property rights exactly echoed these practices: old Anglo law allowed no property to a woman; what was her father's became her husband's at marriage and her son's on his death. Recent times have modified these practices, but the underlying attitudes remain, particularly as "development" is practiced on "third world" countries. The devastation of the conquest was compounded for women as these practices were imposed by law, denying them the name, property, and identity rights that they had never had any reason to think were not theirs by birthright.

Current efforts at "development" threaten to destroy what little language and culture has survived the original European conquerors. The affected women lose status, position and, often, their very means of livelihood. Women's resistance to schooling, for example, is frequently a recognition of the loss such implies for them (Stein, ms.). At the same time, the rest of us may be losing models for what nonsexist societies might look like, a chance to imagine ourselves as living and growing in such societies. I argue this is a loss to the women and men of the affected societies and also to ourselves as participants in the European-derived societies. In the languages of the conquerors, other women are invisible to us.

The Jaqi family of languages has been the focus of my research. As an anthropological linguist, my primary training enables discovery of the grammar of a language previously undescribed. This involves, in so far as possible, seeing a language within its context in order to discover the meaning and function of grammatical particles. Necessarily, one must understand the sentences, discourses, and cultural contexts in which these are used if one is to account for the distribution.[2] Part of the methodology is the collection of "texts" for analysis. These texts include narrations which include, among other things, stories, autobiographies, biographies, histories, myths, descriptions, and also the recording of such ongoing events as conversations, speeches, celebrations, and ceremonies. For accurate language analysis, these texts must be collected without a translation interface, that is, in the context of the language being studied, not of a dominant prestige group. A language needs to be studied where it is spoken.

Jaqaru is a member of the Jaqi family of languages, which also includes Aymara, a major language of Bolivia, of southern Perú and of northern Chile. There are today some three and a half million speakers of Jaqi languages, the remnant of an empire that, before the time of the Incas, stretched from Ecuador to Argentina. The homeland of the Jaqaru speakers is a steep valley heavily terraced on both sides. The plaza is a little over 9,000 feet above sea level. Although under Spanish rule for 500 years, they have been able to maintain many of their own cultural constructs. This they have done by internal community cohesion, by the use of the language, and by reconstructing much of what they have been given to better fit their own worldview.

I, personally, have gained much from observing the women in Tupe. I first went there in the 1950s, when women's choices in the United States were far more circumscribed than they are today. I watched women working, not in the home and with no notion of the role of "housewife." I listened to and worked with a language that carried no deprecations of women and with texts from strong, self-possessed women who could not understand subservience. I remember one incident: my husband and I were living a long-distance marriage for professional reasons, which meant that he was not with the children. I was complaining of this to a Jaqaru friend. Utterly baffled as to why I had a problem, her solution was, "Well, you just tell him where he should live." For myself, as a young woman in the 1950s, this possibility had not occurred to me.

About fifteen years ago I invited my children's godparents to visit with us in Tupe, where Jaqaru is spoken. The godparents are very tall, fair *gringos* (the usual word in Perú, often said with affection, for European-looking foreigners). Because Tupe is a two-day trip from Lima, the second day on foot for some twenty-five kilometers and with a climb of some 5,000 feet, foreign visitors were, and are, exceedingly rare. One evening, after my *compadres* had recovered from their climb, I introduced them to a group assembled for tea and conversation in the home of one of my Tupe friends. The godparents' English name was very difficult for the people of Tupe to pronounce. For the godfather they finally got it right: *Erdmann*. Then they all braced for the god-mother's name. I will never forget the look on the Tupinos' faces when her name turned out to be the same!

The only possible explanation for the two sharing a name that would have occurred to any of the Jaqaru people was that they were blood kin, therefore: incest. The godmother asked me to explain as, for this situation, her Spanish was failing her. I explained how in the United States a woman took her husband's name at marriage, losing hers, resulting in their having the same name. So that was why the names of my *comadre* and my *compadre* were the same. A young woman farmer, married to the man schoolteacher, looked quite perplexed and said to me: "But what, then, of inheritance, what of our land?" Yes, a good question indeed. The name attached to the land is also the name of the owner of the land. If a woman would have no name of her own, then how could she have land of her own? European practices had certainly long reflected that. At the time this conversation took place, it had only been legal for about a year for a woman to buy property in Florida without a male relative's signature.

EUROPEAN LANGUAGE
AND EMBEDDED SEXISM

As part of the European conquest, the European system of patronymics was introduced. From early baptismal records found in Andean churches (Collins, 1983, and personal communication) the practice was apparently resisted. Today, children throughout the Andes follow the law in taking both the mother's and the father's patronyms. However, women do not take the husband's name, not even in Andean newspapers. One does find the name change practice, in almost Anglo style, among the upper classes with heavy international contacts. These are also the women who find our style of feminism most congenial and, by their names, are an example themselves of one of the ways in which importation of our traditions may be detrimental to other women. That this loss is serious was recognized by the woman quoted in the title of the paper, from the anecdote above. Her motive was to prevent loss, but even she did not know how much was already gone.

Most detrimental is the notion, based in the grammatical structure of derivational thinking, that, if one has in hand the masculine (in most cases for social sciences this means the men's point of view), then one has everything and all else can be derived therefrom. This, together with the singular and the ranking comparative/absolute, I call "derivational thinking." Derivational thinking has given us, in all the sciences, studies of and by men that have purported to be studies of us all. This is also the case in the fields of linguistics and anthropology. For example, in anthropology, the ethnographies have been written of half a culture and then labeled as though the ethnography were valid for the whole. In linguistics not only do we have the problem in grammars, as mentioned above, but, as an example, the defining work for sociolinguistics, Labov's work on New York dialects, was exclusively of men and boys (Labov, 1966). Women are, by the view fostered through this grammatical structure, grammatically unnecessary for physical reproduction of the species, or for language or cultural reproduction.

Some of the societies affected by the conquest may or may not have had a sexism of their own, though the Jaqi clearly did not. In any event, whatever sexism did exist was of a different structure, both in language and in culture, from that which the conquerors would impose. In some cases, the impact of the imported sexism has been so heavy that by now we can no longer know the nature of the original social structure. Florence Babb (1980) discusses the imposition of sexism as she details the devastating effect on women of the Vicos project, held up by many as a model of proper third world development, run by Cornell anthropologists in Perú. Vicos is located in the northern Andes of Perú; the people speak one of the Quechua languages, the largest family of languages extant in the Andes, Jaqi being the second. She states that there was a mild form of sexism already in place. The people involved were by then into at least the tenth generation of serfdom on an *hacienda* (plantation). To what degree the in-place sexism was original and to what degree imposed by the overlords is difficult to know. She discusses the reaction of the women to the loss of land being imposed on them by the male anthropologists from the United States, together with the loss of the Quechua language (Stein, ms.), and how the introduction of European values and economics also included the teaching of violence toward wives.

Another example of historical loss reclaimed is found in the work of Maria Rostworowski (1983)on Inca society at the time of the conquest. She has sharply challenged the notion of a single male leader, suggesting, rather, that the power of appointment was in the hands of the sisterhoods (*pana*, "sister," clearly an important political concept within the Inca structure, but baffling to European men scholars) and that at all times there were two male executive secretaries, or administrators, appointed by the sisterhoods. These men, assumed by Europeans to be dictatorial monarchs, were, according to this study, subject to recall. This means that at the very point of conquest the original gender roles all but disappeared, as the Spanish elevated these administrators to all powerful "Incas" and furthermore assumed them to be singular.

The success of the imposition of sexism by colonial powers is widely documented. In fact, it has been so complete that the assumption is voiced frequently that all women in all times and places have been oppressed in the same way. To the contrary, at least in some cases, the strength of the nonsexist native culture has been able, in part, to maintain the balance of women's and men's positions within the realm of the culture itself. A brief description of Jaqi women, what they have and what they have lost, what they seek and how they are currently placed within their own culture, the national culture, and on the world stage may be of value to perceive the possibilities for alternate constructions of social structure.

WOMEN AND LANGUAGE
IN JAQI CULTURE

The Jaqi women of the Andes are primarily farmers and merchants, with some number talented also in weaving and other trades. They have been the primary movers behind the education of their children, wishing the best for their children and believing that education will give them a better life. Sometimes the impact of education is not what they had hoped for; in the case of their daughters it is almost always a deep disappointment. What is sad to see is strong, self-possessed grandmothers, making great sacrifices to go to the coast or to the cities in order to further the education of their children and themselves struggling to learn some Spanish, then coming down hard on their daughters whom they perceive as failures. The grandmothers, coming from a native culture of equality between the sexes, perceive school as equal opportunity. When the girls do not achieve as the boys nor are offered jobs equal to those of the boys, the old women perceive this to be the fault of the girls, rather than of the culture into which they have been thrown. Sometimes this leads to the decision of families not to educate their daughters, and sometimes one finds the granddaughters turning to European-based feminism to undo the damage done to their mothers.

What is even sadder is that these young women are sometimes blinded by the coastal culture and by the rhetoric of the imported European feminism to all that their grandmothers had and have lost, in spite of the few voices that have recently been raised to the contrary (Alderete, 1992; Mita & Montecinos, 1992). They learn to see their grandmothers as illiterate, ignorant peasants with no culture at all and, in the process, lose their own history.

The Jaqi languages themselves function to structure perceptions of women by both women and men such that the European version appears "uncivilized," or irrational. The Jaqi languages themselves have no gender marking of any kind. The pronoun sets distinguish human as contrasted to nonhuman, and inclusiveness or not of addressee; they do not distinguish sex.[3] For example, the human pronouns are: *naya* (I, we but not you), *juma* (you), *jupa* (she, he, they), *jiwasa* (you and I, with or without others). The non-human pronouns are: *aka uka k"aya*. These are usually translated as "this," "that," "yonder X," that is, as demonstrative pronouns, which obscures their function as nonhuman pronouns and leads to unfortunate translations. There are specific vocabulary items that refer to people such as *Jaqi* (people) or *Wawa* (child, baby); to women and men, such as *Warmi* (woman, wife), *Awila* (grandmother, old woman), and *Chacha* (man, husband), *Achachila* (grandfather, old man); to girls and boys, such as *Imilla* (girl child), *Tawaqu* (teenage girl, young unmarried woman) and *Yuqalla* (boy child), *Wayna* (teenage boy, young unmarried man) and so on. These are all roots, none derived from another, unlike European languages, as in English *woman* is perceived as being derived from *man*. The terms with sex meaning are applicable when appropriate but there is no need to refer to sex when it is irrelevant to the conversation. Words for animals are different from those for humans, also as different roots, for example: *uywa* (domestic animal) *qachu* (female animal) and *urqu* (male animal). Use of these terms for people is equivalent to our own type of insults whereby men are insulted with terms for women. On the other hand, the highest praise for anyone, and the goal for children, is to be *Jaqi*, "human."

EUROPEAN-IMPORTED SYMBOLIC SEXISM IN THE JAQI CULTURE

In all of the sayings and jokes that I have collected within the language, I have found no deprecations of women in general. There is nothing like, for example, our class of "woman driver" or "dumb blonde" jokes. There are other classes of jokes, for example, the "idiot" jokes. Regarding men, a sort of running comment is that they are lazy. In fact one word in Jaqaru, *Aymara*, means "lazy," although, because this somehow became the name of the sister language, its use is now in rapid decline. When the men shift into Spanish, one does find antiwoman jokes and sayings. With loss of the native language comes the loss of the native perspective; women become objects of ridicule.

The denigration of women and of women's work and the difficulty of perceiving women and women's work as autonomous, following the European language structure, shows up in any and all aspects of social interaction. For ourselves, that women's work be less valued is not a surprise. Among the Jaqi, it directly reflects where the conquerors have been successful. For example, the impact of the importation of sexism from the conquerors can be seen in the tax structure. Within the community, where the tax is based on labor, a woman's day is exactly equal to a man's day, that is, it is a human labor day. These activities are primarily dealt with in Jaqaru. When cash money, an introduction from Europe, is used, as in cash wages, a woman day is worth exactly half a man's day. These latter activities are mostly dealt with in Spanish.

Women who remain farmers and who sell, for example, cheese, on the open market or who, for example, run restaurants during fair/market days, can do very well indeed. Women, in fact, are major business entrepreneurs within the Andes, though ignored by international development concerns. For example, when I needed a truck to move my household goods from Bolivia to Perú it was done by an Aymara woman who owned a fleet of trucks for international commerce; she hired a man to drive the truck to Perú for me. Given the European belief in the name/property tie and the man/name tie, economic development is aimed at men only, including in the Andes commerce; but in the Andes, women are the merchants and the money handlers. No international small business loans or development materials ever go in their direction.

Another example of how the sexism is imposed and what is does to women's status is how the school system, held universally to be a "good" and to be a way to improve oneself, acts differentially on the girls and the boys, not because of the native culture but because of the imposition of the behaviors associated with derivational thinking from the dominant society. If a woman goes to school, then her possibilities become circumscribed by the Hispanic norms, which in the Andes are less severe than Anglo norms, but are nevertheless far more restrictive than the comparable status in the native cultures or for men in the European-derived sectors.

With the conquest, the imposed loss of name, and the loss of land came also the threat, and the reality, of violence, specifically in the form of rape. Rape was apparently unknown in the Jaqi societies; there is no easy linguistic way even of speaking of it, no name for it. Even today, in this aspect, there has not been a great deal of impact within village life. However, in language terms, a whole new genre of oral literature has developed to warn young women of this danger from Spanish speakers. Even in these stories the danger is depicted as seduction and betrayal, not as the violence with which we are so familiar. This new genre is one of the creative ways in which the Jaqi people have tried to cope with the new dangers specific to women. Translating or understanding structured violence toward women is difficult for people coming from a different sexual reality.

In texts I have recorded from Jaqi women, it is often what they do not say that is very telling. Their stories focus on themselves, not on their husbands, on their own land, not on the land of their husbands. Land is held personally; I have not yet met any Andean woman willing to pass the title of her land to her husband. This is a major issue in land reform, at least to the women involved, whether coming from revolution or internal politics or imposed by foreign institutions (BID, USAID, etc.) in the name of development. Florence Babb (1976; 1980) cites a particularly appalling example of development depriving women of land rights. In Vicos, men were given formal title, although under the old system women also had had land use rights. One woman came to the meeting to protest the loss of her land. Her husband was ordered by the anthropologists to throw her out. He did nothing; according to the local culture he had no such right over her—so the anthropologists bodily threw her out in a demonstration of the modern, developed way to treat women.

Many of the land reforms have worked in this way, especially since the World War II when norms from the United States have had hegemony. I have known of some women in good marriages who decided not to fight the law. They have come to regret their acquiescence because they cannot then bestow the land to inheritors as they wish. They do indeed lose, sometimes the land itself, and thus their livelihood, if for any reason the marriage ends. Others have gone to great lengths in attempts to keep land, sometimes involving Byzantine paperwork and creative use of the Andean custom of multiple homes.

Grammatical number is an important component of the patterns of perception described here. By our naming patterns, the "family" becomes "one," by the name of the "man," which makes it grammatically easy to handle as a singular, which we also equate with "good." Land reforms have attempted to place one "man" (i.e. family) in one house on one plot of land. For people who farm widely separated plots of land in as many ecological zones as possible, and who have several houses at various altitudes, and who hold land personally, the land reforms, repeatedly launched for political purposes with democratic intentions, are a recipe for disaster. Singular is seen as stark poverty, little short of having nothing. A couple have many plots of land, many from her side and many from his side. Hers remain in her name, and his in his, and thus pass to the children. She keeps her name and he keeps his, passing both to the children. In survival terms, these many plots allow for variety in the diet in a good year, and food to eat when there is crop failure at one altitude. The latter is a frequent occurrence. Potatoes, domesticated in the Andes and known in some 10,000 varieties, are regularly cultivated in dozens of varieties by a woman and man together. Some can be freeze-dried, some can withstand frost, and so on. Potatoes there almost always are, from one altitude or another. One man, one house, one plot is not the Andean way.

Sexism, including the naming custom, forms part of a structure within the dominating culture. As part of that structure, many of the imports from Europe have had the effect of reducing women's lives and enlarging men's, even in areas where one might not think to look. These additional imports have the added effect of strengthening the pattern of loss so sharply detailed in the land and name loss, deepening the overall loss of autonomy and even power to fight against each new loss. Some examples might give the flavor of the daily context in which the Jaqi women attempt to maintain or reclaim their status.

According to my texts, the old pattern for music was that the women would sing and men would answer, and that men would play the reeds and women would play the *tinhya*, a small drum. The roles were fully complementary and necessary to each other. European instruments have been assigned entirely to the men, with nothing correspondingly given to the women. Furthermore, on the European model, bands have now been formed that do not require any singing. In many places the ceremonies requiring singing are gradually being lost and/or separated from the men's use of instruments. This means also the loss of the language components of the musical tradition. The modified version, men only or primarily, is what is today marketed as "indigenous" music of the Andes. Thus, music is perceived as belonging only to the men, with women having a small, derivative, occasional part.

There is also the problem of occupation as indicated on identity and voting cards. I remember being quite shocked the first time I saw it. A friend of mine, a farmer, showed me an ID she had been required to get on the coast. It labeled her as "housewife"—a nonexistent role in the Andes. She had been told that was what she was supposed to be! Thus land and agriculture are perceived as belonging only to the men.

One additional anecdote may give the flavor of the problems women face today in "development," based on the behaviors resulting from derivational thinking, in this case through the social sciences as taught from textbooks based on U. S. social science textbooks and European-inspired international notions of development and education.

For Tupe, the government from time to time assigns "developers," depending on the political fashion of the period. Not too long ago a young, idealistic woman sociologist was assigned to help in economic development. She came to Tupe and called a meeting. We all went. The woman sitting next to me fell asleep on my arm—she had already put in a sixteen-hour day by the time the meeting had been called, had walked some ten miles with loads on her back, had irrigated, had herded her cows, sheep and goats, had milked and made cheese, and was tired. The developer came up with a new activity for women—raising rabbits. She talked on and on about how rabbits would be good for the women to raise.

I looked down on the woman leaning against me and wondered when she would have any time. People were courteous and after the meeting I asked some of them what they thought of the idea. Most just laughed, having made no sense of the matter at all. Two young women, active in the municipal organization, talked it over. There was no time to bother with rabbits. No one was ever in the community anyway during the day except the school children, the drunks and the sick. They all agreed that certainly no one had any time for such nonsense. At last one young woman remarked that maybe the men could raise the rabbits, especially the drunks, since they were around the town during the day!

I tried to discuss the matter with the young sociologist, without success. She informed me that in Tupe the men made all the decisions! As far as I could discern, she never once spoke to the women, but confined her conversation to the men that she perceived as being in power. Also, as is common, upon observing women working in the fields, by the application of derivational thinking, she had assumed that such labor was "helping" the men and was in no way essential, that women's time was by definition "vacant." This perception is exacerbated by the translation tradition and the conflicting interpretations of the verb "to help" (*ayudar* in Spanish) and *yanapaña* (Aymara) or *yanhishi* (Jaqaru). The Jaqi verbs are based on the root *yanha*, "companion" (Jaqaru) and do not carry a sense of primary/secondary of hierarchy. The Jaqaru root, furthermore, is verbalized with a suffix meaning "mutually." Thus to say that someone "helps" another, in Jaqaru, means the people work together mutually in companionship. Thus if a woman says she "helps" her husband in the fields it does *not* mean that the work is primarily his, it means the two of them jointly cultivate both her fields and his. That time the developer did not succeed. There are still no rabbits in Tupe.

Stories are numerous, where "development" is fed through the men with no consultation with those who handle the money and with those who would be most affected; see, for example, the work of the Cuzqueña Daisy Irene Núñez del Prado Béjar for examples involving Quechua speakers (1975a; 1975b). In fact, in the Andes, money management is the almost exclusive province of women.

About the same time as the rabbit story, I was called upon to evaluate a similar project for another community. These projects were being pushed as major development from the central Eurocentric government. The whole notion of women having a lot of free time comes, of course, from our western definitions of housework as "not work" and from seeing all other work as done by men, thus obliterating from view the work the women actually do. If women are viewed as derivative of men, a woman and a man working together in the fields is easily and commonly perceived as one man only. This example of derivational thinking involving language and perception is amazing perhaps, when analyzed as I have done here, but is nevertheless common and normal.

CONCLUSION

As the conquerors' languages both reflected and caused the sexism they sought to impose, so also the nonsexist culture of the Jaqi is both reflected in and imposed by the language. Today there is a real possibility that, as a result of past governmental programs and present terrorism, what little has been able to survive these five centuries will be destroyed by violence. The loss of the language may close forever the possibility of thinking and speaking in this one nonsexist way both for the descendants of these self-possessed women and for us.

The differences make a difference. Language patterns that are used on a daily basis give rise to and reinforce different perceptual patterns. I have been the beneficiary of the opportunity to talk with and live with women who have never thought of themselves as derivations of men nor as "belonging to" men, but who have thought of themselves as autonomous productive human beings. In the crush of "world culture" these differences may well be lost. Respect for difference on our part, a profound belief in different and equal, may be the only hope for survival for these differences. As a minimum, we can listen to the voices, few though they be, that are now asking for that respect and for the return of the status held by their foremothers. As part of that ability to listen, we must also understand the blinders our own language places on us. A woman's name is her own; we must not assume we know hers simply because we have met her husband. Her land is her livelihood and her dignity.

NOTES

1. At the time of the conquest, the Andes supported some 20-30 millions in population, without hunger for anyone. Twenty-five years after the conquest, the population was one million and is only now rising again to preconquest numbers, but with extensive hunger and poverty.

2. Methodology is described in the field methods textbook (Hardman & Hamano, 1993).

3. All examples in this paragraph are from the Aymara language.

REFERENCES

Alderete, W. (1992, January/February). The empowerment of Indian women. *Peace and Freedom*, 8-9.

Babb, F. E. (1976). *The development of sexual inequality in Vicos, Peru.* Council on International Studies, Special Study No. 83. Buffalo: State University of New York at Buffalo.

Babb, F. E. (1980). *Women and men in Vicos, Peru: A case of unequal development.* Michigan Occasional Paper No. XI. Ann Arbor: University of Michigan.

Collins, J. (1983). Translation traditions and the organization of productive activity: the case of Aymara affinal kinship terms. In A. W. Miracle (Ed.), *Bilingualism: Social issues and policy implications.* Athens: University of Georgia Press.

Hardman, M. J. (1984, Winter). Gentiles in Jaqi folktales—an example of contact literature. *Anthropological Linguistics, 367-375.*

Hardman, M. J. (1989, Sept/Oct.). White woman's burden. *Free Mind, 32, 5, 2-3.*

Hardman, M. J., & Hamano, S. S. (1993). *Language structure discovery methods: A field manual.* (3rd ed.). Gainesville, FL: Andean Press.

Hardman, M. J. (1993). Gender through the levels. *Women and Language,* forthcoming.

Labov, W. (1966). *The social stratification of English in New York City.* Washington DC: Center for Applied Linguistics.

Miller, G. D. (1977). Tripartism, sexism, and the rise of the feminine gender in Indo-European. *The Florida Journal of Anthropology, 2,* 3-16.

Mita, E. C. de Portugal, J. M., & Montecinos, R. (1992, Fall). Man-woman dualism in the Andean world. *The Newsletter of the Aymara Foundation, Inc. ,* 3-7.

Núñez del Prado Béjar, D. I. (1975a) El rol de la mujer campesina Quechua. *América Indígena, 35,* 2, 391-401.

Núñez del Prado Béjar, D. I. (1975b). El poder de decisión de la mujer Quechua

Andina. *América Indígena, 35,* 3, 623-630.

Rostworowski de Diez Canseco, M. (1983). *Estructuras andinas del poder: Ideología religiosa y política.* Lima: IEP.

Stein, W. W. (unpublished manuscript). Mothers and sons in the Andes: Developmental implications.

15

Language Choice and Use: Influences of Setting and Gender

Kathryn A. Remlinger

Sociolinguistic studies have shown that a connection exists between language use and setting among multilingual speakers (e.g., Hymes, 1968; Labov, 1972; Milroy, 1987). Other research investigating code switching and code mixing has demonstrated how language choice is influenced by the function of the discourse (Lindsay, 1993) and the role relationships—including gender roles—among speakers (Gal, 1984, 1987, 1993; Heller, 1982; Swann, 1988; Valentine, 1985).

Although most sociolinguists exploring the interface of language use and context employ ethnographic methods such as participant observation, few take into account how speakers themselves perceive code switching and mixing. Thus, the implications of speaker perception on language use have not been adequately explored. Furthermore, although many investigations of code switching and mixing have focused on the uses of Indian languages and English (e.g., Singh & Lele, 1990; Vaid, 1980; Valentine, 1985; Verma, 1976), they tend to ignore how language choice is simultaneously influenced by speakers' role relationships, context, function, and topic.

In this essay, I discuss how these dimensions of talk influence language choice and use among female speakers of various Indian languages and American English. This project connects aspects of language, gender, and culture specific to female speakers of American English and five north Indian languages: Bengali, Hindi, Gujarati, Telugu, and Marathi. I address how women from north India see themselves in the United States and Indian societies. Through a combination of qualitative and discourse analyses, I examine how these women see American English and Indian languages affecting their roles in each culture. I am particularly interested in how the women perceive their uses of the languages in relation to each respective culture. Do the women use the variety of languages as participants in both societies? What determines which language they use? Does the use of one language over another reflect intimacy or power within either culture?

Table 15.1
Transcription Key

//	overlap: point at which the first speaker's speech is overlapped by another's, if first speaker continues from overlap point; occurs at a grammatical stopping point in first speaker's speech
[ ]	simultaneous speech: spoken during overlaps
<u>now</u>	underscore indicates stress or emphasis on a word
=	latching speech
( )	inaudible speech, "stage directions," or guess at unclear word
(( ))	non-verbal sounds
?	rising intonation
,	holding intonation
—	interruption, self interruption: interruption if first speaker stops completely or repeats what was being said at the point of interruption, occurs at nongrammatical stopping point in first speaker's speech.
((LF))	laugh

METHODS

The methods I used to gather and interpret the data include a qualitative analysis of observations and interviews of five women, a discourse analysis of a dinner conversation among myself and three women, and a literature review of linguistic and anthropological studies on gender, language, and culture.

Setting is the dominant factor in determining what language participants use (Swann, 1988). Because I wanted not only to learn from the participants about their views of language use, but also to see the language use in action, I observed participants in three settings: domestic, academic, and social (at parties and a bar). In observing the women at home, I noted interactions with children, spouses, and friends.

A second location where I observed the participants is Michigan Technological University's campus: in the Memorial Union Building (MUB), in classes, on the sidewalk, in the library. In these academic settings I have watched how the women interact with each other, with female and male Indian students, with other students, and with their professors. I have carried out these observations as a non-active participant—eating at a nearby table in the union, sitting a few seats away in class, watching interaction among students between classes on the sidewalk, visiting another student in a chemistry lab, pretending to study in the library, and so on.

I have taken the part of participant observer at several parties and in one of the local bars. In these contexts I have been able to interact with the women as well as watch them interact with each other and other students. These settings have enabled me to watch "natural" behavior and listen to "natural" speech in action.

In addition to the above settings, I also observed and informally interviewed three women during a small dinner party. We discussed how the women see their roles in the United States and India, language use, courtship practices in India and the United States, education systems, family structures, and attitudes, values, as well as beliefs on sex, marriage, and courtship held by members of both societies. Although we discussed these same issues when I interviewed the participants, I wanted the women to discuss these topics with each other. I hoped that talking about cultural issues with each other would allow the women more freedom to code switch and/or mix. The discussion also enabled the women to elaborate on ideas that they had discussed during the interviews.

I selected participants for this study based on their diverse backgrounds and roles. Two of the women I observed live with their families in the small university town of Houghton, Michigan. One woman, Pushpa, lives with her husband, who is also from north India, and their two elementary school-aged daughters in an apartment owned by the university. Pushpa takes classes part-time at Michigan Technological University to fulfill teaching certificate requirements. Her first language is Telugu. She is fluent in English and Hindi as well. The second woman I visited, Anaita, lives in a ranch-style house with her husband and their two preschool-aged children. She teaches private Hindi lessons and conducts research on nutrition. Anaita is proficient in English, Hindi, and Marathi, which is her mother tongue. Both Anaita and Pushpa have been in the United States for over seven years. A third woman I observed, Uma, was visiting her fiancé, a graduate student, for several weeks. Uma lives in Bombay and works as an account executive for an import/export company. She speaks Hindi, English, Marathi, and Gujarati, which is her first language.

Of the three other women I interviewed and whom I observed on Michigan Technological University's campus, at parties, and at a local bar, Shanti is a graduate student in chemistry. She has been in the United States for a year. Gita has been in Houghton for eight months. She is an undergraduate student in electrical engineering. Sarada, who has been in Houghton for three years, is a graduate student in business. All but Gita are single, Gita having been married just four days at the time of our dinner. Sarada, Shanti, and Gita are all close friends. Both Sarada and Gita are from the Bombay area and their mother tongue is Marathi. Shanti is from Calcutta. Her mother tongue is Bengali.

Besides having proficiency in these languages, the women are fluent in Hindi and English. In addition, they have studied other languages such as French and Sanskrit in their colleges and high schools. Indian primary education is either taught in English or the local state language; however, it is required by law that Hindi and English be taught in these schools as well. English medium high schools are common, and most universities conduct classes in English. Both Shanti and Sarada attended English medium high schools and colleges. Gita attended an English medium college in Pune, yet her elementary and secondary schools were Marathi medium. Growing up in a multilingual society has enabled these women to be exposed to and to learn a variety of languages.

I conducted two types of interviews. The first set was rather formal in that the tape recorded talk focused on preplanned questions about the women's language use and perceptions of North American and Indian cultures. I held this type of interview separately with Pushpa, Uma, Shanti, Sarada, and Gita. These interviews provided me with cultural, as well as personal information that helped me to develop my analysis of the linguistic data, which I collected during the second type of interview.

I conducted a second type of interview during a dinner at my house with Shanti, Sarada, and Gita. This tape recorded interview was the primary source of my data; I obtained the linguistic data for the study from this interview. Although I had in mind certain questions about language and culture that I worked into the conversation, this interview relied more on "natural" conversation in that talk tended to occur spontaneously. I found the settings and my role as researcher did influence their language use, which I discuss below.

THE STUDY

Coding

I obtained data from the dinner conversation in two ways. First, I noted the content of our talk by keeping a log of the topics we discussed. Second, I analyzed the discourse for the kinds of language used by Gita, Sarada, and Shanti. For example, in coding the transcript of the dinner conversation I noted the use of American and Indian Englishes. I marked the use of American slang, the topic at the time the slang was used, who the speaker was, and for whom the remark was intended. I also coded for instances when I would have expected the women to code-switch yet, they did not. I then analyzed the coded transcripts to determine if patterns existed between the topic, the speaker, and the type of language used.

Results

After transcribing the dinner conversation, I thought at first that I did not have any usable data. I wanted to research code switching, yet at no time did any of the women speak a language other than English, even when I left the room to talk on the phone for about five minutes. Where I expected code switching, all I found was code stasis. Added to this was the fact the women used American English so well that the only indication that they might be from a culture other than that of the United States was the content of their talk. For instance, it is not typical of women raised in the United States to worry about telling their parents that they are dating. Nor would it be typical for them to talk about attending English medium schools. Nevertheless, three patterns developed as I coded the data: the use of American English, the use of Indian English, and code stasis.

In the following excerpt, bold words and phrases mark American English lexicon that Sarada and Shanti use while discussing aspects of Indian university curriculum. For example, where American English uses the word "math" as an abbreviated form of "mathematics," Indian English uses the word "maths." Likewise, the women use American English minimal responses such as "mmhm" and "um." However, what is particularly interesting to me is the women's adept use of colloquial expressions such as the use of "like," "yeah," "you know," "wow," and "stuff." Moreover, Sarada uses the local variant tag question, "eh," at one point in the conversation. Not only do the women use these words, but they use them with a syntax that marks the expressions as being colloquial. For example, the repeated use of "like" as a preposition before a noun, "like chemistry," "like hardware," is a speech pattern typical of young adult Americans. There is no indication in this excerpt that American English is not the speakers' first language. Even the content of the talk could be that of speakers whose first language is American English. (See Table 15.1 for transcription key.)

Shanti:	And all your classes are in your area. // **Like** chemistry I did //, I–I all I studied during the masters was chemistry, nothing else. I had classes in **math** and physics which I had to take, but that was just, I had to **just** pass them, **you know**, chemistry.
Sarada:	**Mmhm**.
Gita:	**Yeah**.
Sarada:	I went to **um** computer engineering college // and all I had to do was **like** hardware, **you know**, applied mechanics, and **stuff** like that. Nothing else. No English, no—no choice basically. When you go to your // first year, this is what you have to take. If you fail it, you'll carry it on to your next // year. // [and you get **like, yeah, yeah**.]

(Later: Sarada is discussing how she has adapted to living in the United States.)

Sarada:	A lot probably has also] to do with our attitude. What I think all of us believe, **you know**, is that **when in Rome, do as the Romans do. You know.** // We have this—this is our chance to be—to do things we can never do at home and see how comfortable we fit into it, **you know**. // That's the way I look at it. I don't know Shanti—if Shanti and myself have [talked about this.]

(Later)

Sarada:	**Wow**, that would be unusual, **eh**?

Another pattern that emerged in my examination of the discourse was the use of Indian English. Although I coded for semantic as well as syntactic examples, the only marker of Indian English was in the word choice, except in the exclusion of articles. However, Sarada only omitted two articles while talking. What's more significant is the vocabulary that she uses. The phrases and words that I have marked below are typical of Indian English. A kind of code mixing takes place as the Indian and American Englishes are woven throughout the conversation. It's also notable that although Sarada has been in the United States longer than either Shanti or Gita, she uses Indian English more frequently. In this part of the conversation, Sarada is talking about how her dad will react when she tells him that she's dating, and that she's dating an American man.

Sarada: If, if it would have been **couple** years ago, like I knew my dad, he wouldn't <u>hear</u> of it. But now considering that I've **stayed away from them couple years**, you know, there's some kind of confidence that builds up, and they say "Ok, she's—she's a ma—she's handling herself alright //. And I have a feeling I'm a lot older, you know, so I don't know. Hm. It's going to be **a study period** for me while I'm here, get to know him again, you know, 'cause I know I have changed and I'm sure he has too, of **the way he looks at me**, you know, he probably **doesn't look at me as** his little girl any more.

(Later, in the same part of the conversation)

Sarada: See, that's what I said. I don't know. It's—I mean—like we use—like now I've been here and I use terms like "going out" and "my boyfriend," and **"my man"** and **"my sweetheart"** so—so easily. It's something I wouldn't <u>dream</u> of doing in a home setting, you know.

A third category that developed in the data was code stasis—times when I would have expected code switching to take place but it did not. I would have expected code switching or code mixing to occur in two cases: (1) when the women discussed aspects or concepts unique to their culture that cannot be talked about in English because no equivalent words exist, and (2) when the women were alone. Below is a segment of a Sarada's talk about how she would explain to her dad that she's dating. Set in bold type are the items representing code stasis.

Sarada: **The hardest part is even saying,** like I was asking Shanti, **even saying something like that,** you know, **'cause you don't say "I'm dating a guy" or "I'm going out with him." All of these terms are** <u>very</u> **American. // So then what do you say? [I like a guy?]**
Shanti: [More like if you'd say, like ( ) this is my boyfriend, you know, that's not done. // I know like uh **we don't say things like that,** and, yeah.]
Sarada: [Yeah, I'm not saying about language Mark, you know. **That's not done.** That is <u>extremely</u> rude.]
Kate: How will you introduce him? // This is my friend?
Sarada: This is my <u>very, very, very, very, very, very good</u> friend, Mark ((LF)). **I don't know** really. It's—I have two big brothers who do most of the talking. See, that's what I said. **I don't know. It's—I mean—like we use—like now I've been here and I use terms like "going out" and "my boyfriend,"**

and **"my man"** and **"my sweetheart"** so-so easily. **It's something I wouldn't <u>dream</u> of doing in a home setting**, you know. // It's—it's not—the only time you introduce a male is either friend or husband, you know ((LF)). There is no in between, I—I don't know. What do you think (to Shanti)? Isn't there? **I mean you don't really say "boyfriend,"** but—

A second point at which I expected code switching to take place was when I left the room to answer the phone. I was gone for about five minutes. Furthermore, the intimate topic of the conversation that took place would also lead me to believe that the women would have switched to Hindi. In the first segment, Gita is talking about how she told her parents about dating Anwar. This is while both she and Anwar were in India. In the second excerpt, Shanti and Gita are discussing their parents' reactions to their dating without intending to marry.

Excerpt One:

Gita:	( ) I told my parents about Anwar, I think, and ((LF)) I just went home and told them. // Yeah. My sister, like she knew, she—before I went—started going around with him. Like, she said, " You know, are you going <u>around</u> with that guy?" I said "No, Na. He's just a friend." ((LF)) //. And then I started going out with him, and then "I think you're going around with him." ((LF)) "I think so too, but <u>now</u>, not before" ((LF))
Sarada:	Uhhuh
Sarada:	((LF))
Sarada:	Wow, that would be unusual, eh? [That would be ( )]
Gita:	[( )] We were just going around and we didn't want to—like—we didn't say like we met today and we're getting married, // anything like that. We were going around. We wanted to see if we, you know, // yeah, so. And for that I had to go out because I stayed school at from seven to five o'clock. And I wasn't a person to sit at home. I would want to see him every day. // We would go out. At seven o'clock we would go out, come back at ten. Obviously my parents weren't in Pune all the time, but ((LF)) they would come, and then they would first call every day at eight o'clock. " ( ) How come you ( ) everyday?" I was like, ah, there's this guy I like, you know. Oh! Dad was like "Really, yah. Well, who is he?" This and that. I said, "I'm not going—I'm not saying I'm marrying him. I'm saying I like him, and we want to go out, but we've not decided. In fact he told me, "Did you promise him anything?" // And I said, "No." He said, "Good. // Just go around, just see if you want to get married to this person."
Sarada:	Yeah.
Sarada:	Yeah. Wow.
Sarada:	Hmm.
Sarada:	((LF))
Sarada:	((LF))
Sarada:	That is very unusual . . .

Excerpt Two:

Sarda: [( )] I'm trying to tell my dad that "Hi. This is my very good friend, Mark.
             I'm interested in him, but I don't think I am going to marry him."
Shanti: "Fuck. You're going out with him and you don't know if you're going to
             marry him?" ((LF))
Gita and Sarada: ((LF))
Sarada: You know?! It's like that would be absolutely—I think he would take it
             better if I said, you know, "This is it. I'm going to marry him." [You
             know, ( )]
Gita: [( )] don't decide before you know if you're going to like him you know
             ((LF)), for the rest of your life.
Sarada: Yeah.

In addition to these three categories, the data also revealed information on the interplay of language and culture that I have triangulated with data from my observations and the interviews in the analysis section of this paper. Three main aspects of language and culture emerged: (1) how the women use language and how they see language affecting their roles in each culture, (2) how culture is maintained through language and language through culture, and (3) what language use reflects about the relationship between gender roles and culture.

ANALYSIS

The context of a speech event tends to be the determining factor in language choice and use. This proved to be true in my study where the context of the speech event, the dinner at my house, seemed to affect the language use and choice of the three women. The setting was such a strong influence that even when the topic may have called for code switching or mixing, in addition to when I was not present to participate in the conversation, the women, who normally would speak Hindi with each other, unfailingly used English.

The most significant aspect of their language use is their adept use of American English. Outside of the content of the conversation, there is little indication that American English is not the first language of these women. Their ability is so good that when the situation enabled them to code switch, they did not. In fact, one of the speakers, Shanti, switches to a different American English register. She uses the exclamatory "fuck!"

From the data it appears that the overriding factor in determining language choice is the setting. I had heard these women speak Hindi when I was present, yet these instances were in more "neutral" settings—the MUB, parties, the bar, on the campus sidewalk. When I asked Gita a few days after our dinner why they didn't code-switch during the dinner, she explained that, even though I was out of the room a few times, it would have been rude for them to speak in anything except English, because they were at my house. She added that, had the dinner been held at any of their own homes, they would have felt more comfortable speaking Hindi.

Analysis of the data reveals that the speakers are well aware of how they use each language and for what purposes: whether to show respect to parents or teachers, to show intimacy with friends, to maintain power in an argument. The interesting aspect of their language use is that different languages are used for the same purposes. For example, both Uma and Shanti told me that using English with their mothers, unless discussing some technical aspect of their fields, would be disrespectful. Speaking English would alienate their mothers in that their knowledge of English is limited yet proficient enough to understand and carry on a conversation. Not speaking their first language with their mothers would signal a strain in their usually close relationship. However, both women said that they tend to speak their first languages as well as English with their fathers. Both of their fathers conduct business in English, so they are comfortable using it. But more important, the women have a less intimate relationship with their fathers than they do with their mothers, so speaking English with them would not endanger their relationship. Similarly, using Hindi or another Indian language with Indian professors on campus would be disrespectful in that it would connote a level of unacceptable intimacy. In order to maintain aspects of these relationships, the women control the codes according to norms of respect and intimacy. Their role relationships, topic, and situation coordinate to determine code use.

Related to intimacy and status is group solidarity and individual identity. Through assertion of identity, the women help to build and maintain their status with language use. For example, Uma told me that when she argues she prefers to use English. Not only does this reflect her education background and social status (typically only upper-class families are able to send their children to English medium school), but using English in a confrontation gives her an edge over the other person, who most likely would not know English as well as she does. Uma is aware of the cultural value of English and how her use of it enables her to reveal her status, which may also be a way of intimidating the addressee.

The women also use language to maintain group solidarity. All of the participants told me that they use Hindi with other Indian friends, yet use English or English/Hindi mix with acquaintances. For example, Shanti shares an office with another Indian graduate student. Although they both know Hindi, they use English to talk with each other, even when they are discussing Hindi films or music, Indian politics, or current events. Shanti indicated that because she and her officemate are not close friends, they will use English with each other. In contrast, if one of Shanti's close friends were to greet her in English and maintain the conversation in English, she would be hurt. The language choice would signal a rift in their relationship.

In addition to signaling role relationships, language use and choice reveals how women from one culture adapt to living in another without assimilating completely. This is revealed in part through the content of the dinner conversation. Although the women appear to be "Westernized" through their dress, mannerisms, speech, behaviors, interaction with aspects of North American culture, they maintain strong ties with their respective Indian cultures. As Sarada said when I asked how she saw herself in Houghton, she said that she seems to "do as the Romans do." However, these women accommodate the culture without assimilating. For example, each of the women has a shrine in her home where she practices *puja*, honoring personal and family dieties. They cook traditional Indian foods. They listen to Hindi music and watch videos of Hindi films and taped Indian television programs.

Just as language use and choice is influenced by context, so are cultural behaviors. Although their public lives bring them into an English speaking culture, aspects of the private lives of the participants are similar to those that they would traditionally lead in India. At home the women tend to speak their mother tongues or Hindi, eat foods native to their respective regions, practice the religion of their families. However, this private life exists for them because as women they are expected to maintain traditional aspects of their culture. The women are responsible for maintaining the shrines, cooking the foods, teaching the children the "mother tongue," whereas the men are responsible for the public sphere. The sons, brothers, fathers are expected to know and use English. The daughters, sisters, mothers are expected to know and use the mother tongue with each other. Language use is influential in reinforcing cultural values, attitudes, and beliefs. The data from the observation interviews show that these attitudes, values, and beliefs are divided along gender lines.

Just as language helps to maintain relationships of power and solidarity, it is a force in maintaining the culture. The mother's role as keeper of culture is evident in that the children speak their mother's first language, the mother tongue. The participants repeatedly corrected me when I referred to their mother tongue as their first language. They perceive English as their first language; it is what they first learned to read and write. Shanti, Sarada, Gita, and Uma all told me that their children's mother tongue will be that of their own: Bengali, Marathi, and Gujarati respectively. Even if the children are raised in the United States, they will first speak the language of their mothers. Both Anaita's and Pushpa's children speak Marathi and Telugu in addition to English. The women have told me that if their children are not able to speak their mother tongues, then they will lose insight into their Indian heritage. The children will not be able to speak with the required respect to their grandparents.

The link to heritage through language is broken more readily with boys than girls. For example, Shanti's brother reads and writes English better than their mother tongue, Bengali. Their parents haven't insisted that he learn to read and write Bengali as they did with Shanti. Perhaps this is because as a female Shanti will be responsible for passing on the language to her children. Likewise, Anaita tends to speak English more often with her son than she does her daughter.

This code switching has implications for status and intimacy that is determined through particular role relationships. Could it be that the mothers are establishing these relationships with their children? It seems that they are, and in doing so they are also establishing role relationships between the genders. The language choice indicates the maintenance of gender roles according to private and public social spheres as well as to levels of status and intimacy. It follows then that language does play a part in shaping cultural ideology.

CONCLUSION

The situation of contemporary Indian culture is such that members must not only know multiple languages, they must also know when and how to use them. Interaction in the public sphere requires women and men to know English as well as Hindi, whereas interaction in the private domain demands that speakers use the language spoken by their mothers. Evidence of language use and role relationships shows that the public belongs to the males; the private traditionally is the females' domain. The reciprocal nature of language and culture is revealed in part through language choice and use, which are influenced by the cultural aspects of context and gender.

ACKNOWLEDGMENT

I owe many thanks not only to the women who let me into a part of their lives so that I could conduct this study, but also to Prashanth Narasimha for his patient listening to hours of taped conversation. Without his ears I would not have heard what was actually said during parts of the dinner conversation. Thanks also to Vicky Bergvall for helping me hear what the data were saying.

REFERENCES

Gal, S. (1984). Peasant men can't get wives: Language change and sex roles in a bilingual community. In J. Baugh & J. Sherzer (Eds.), *Language in use: Readings in sociolinguistics* (pp. 292-304). Englewood Cliffs, NJ: Prentice-Hall.

Gal, S. (1987). Code switching and consciousness in the European periphery. *American Ethnologist, 14* (4): 637-653.

Gal, S. (1993). Diversity and contestation in linguistic ideologies: German speakers in Hungary. *Language in Society, 22* (4): 337-359.

Heller, M. (1982). Negotiations of language choice in Montreal. In J. J. Gumperz (Ed.), *Language and social identity* (pp. 108-118). Cambridge: Cambridge University Press.

Hymes, D. (1968). The ethnography of speaking. In J. Fishman (Ed.), *Readings in the sociology of language* (pp. 99-138). The Hague: Mouton.

Labov, W. (1972). *Sociolinguistic patterns.* Philadelphia: University of Pennsylvania Press.

Lindsay, C. (1993). Welsh and English in the city of Bangor: A study of functional differentiation. *Language in Society, 22*(1): 1-17.

Milroy, L. (1987). *Language and social networks.* Oxford: Basil Blackwell.

Singh, R., & Lele, J. K. (1990). Language, power, and cross-sex communication strategies in Hindi and English revisited. *Language in Society, 19* (4): 541-546.

Swann, J. (1988). Talk control: An illustration from the classroom of problems in analyzing male dominance of conversation. In D. Coates & D. Cameron (Eds.), *Women in their speech communities* (pp.122-140). London: Longman.

Vaid, J. (1980). The form and function of code-mixing in Indian films: The case of Hindi and English. *Indian Linguistics, 41* (1): 37-44.

Valentine, T. (1985). Sex, power, and linguistic strategies in the Hindi language. *Studies in the Linguistic Sciences, 15* (1): 195-211.

Verma, S. K. (1976). Code-switching: Hindi-English. *Lingua*, *38* (2): 153-165.

Part III

EXPANDING GENDER RELATIONS

The final section of this book is concerned with the future of gender relations. In it, authors argue that an exclusive focus on gender differences is limited. These essays suggest new paradigms and frameworks for examining the intersections of communication, language, and gender. Moving beyond analyzing and critiquing what *is* the case, each presents possibilities for thinking about (and bringing about) what *should be* the case.

Lisa Merrill and Denise Quirk, in "Gender, Media, and Militarism," highlight the masculine nature of the metaphors used to undergird U. S. involvement in the Persian Gulf War. After explaining how men who opposed the war were called "faggots" and women who resisted were labelled "dykes," Merrill and Quirk forcefully urges women and men to resist patriarchal cultural impulses, especially when they are life-negating.

Tracing the history of frameworks that position women and men as opponents, Linda Perry calls for women and men to seek out and to mine the resources of their common humanity. As long as masculine perspectives hold privilege in Western culture, achieving commonality will be difficult.

The next two chapters show how women who hold political power are changing the symbolic climate--in Ireland and in the United States--finding ways to accommodate *both* female and male points of vision. Kathleen Watters explains how Mary Robinson, president of Ireland, influenced voters with her integrated vision of motherhood, personhood, and nationhood. Robinson praises women voters who "instead of rocking the cradle, rocked the system" (p. 199) and male voters who were able to expand their understanding of "woman" to include "president." In a similar vein, Sullivan and Goldzwig argue that female politicians in the United States are affecting public discourse and decision making through convincing the American public that the big issues are those that touch human beings directly. Sullivan and Goldzwig develop a "postmodern ethic" that assumes the feminist ideal of "decision making grounded in personal experience, context, and maintenance of relationships" (p. 209)

In the final chapter, Lynn Turner and Helen Sterk return to issues raised in the Introduction. These are issues of profound change in the ways in which communication, language, and gender scholarship must attend to the human community, composed as it is of women and men who have become more polarized, more estranged from one another instead of more united, to face the challenges of a future technology that enables us to isolate ourselves in our rooms, meeting over modems instead of over lunch; intense nationalistic loyalties, blinding us to our common destiny; reproductive choices, which can allow us to choose whether to conceive or to bear children, as well as to extend our reproductive life well past menopause; and a tense climate of cultural diversity, in which some forms of difference are tolerated, but not others.

Differences That Make a Difference ends with a vision of reconciliation based on the recognition that no matter how many differences seem to intervene between women and men, our common humanity unites us.

16

Gender, Media, and Militarism

Lisa Merrill and Denise Quirk

Individuals are led to affiliate with or oppose political actions largely on the basis of how those actions are (re)presented. In a publisher's note to Pam McAllister's *You Can't Kill the Spirit*, an anthology of stories of women and nonviolent action, David H. Albert (1988) of New Society Publishers notes:

> We know of course that events can be retold in a host of different ways and from a myriad of perspectives. But there is something suspect, even sinister, when the events to be retold, despite the differences in the perspectives of the historians, seem to have so many common elements: the major actors are all (or virtually all) male, their actions almost always result in the death of others—often in large numbers—and the results are measured in their short- or long-term effects upon a dominant church, state or class or in the way goods and services are exchanged. (p. x)

In the essay that follows, we explore some of the ways the mediated coverage and analysis of the Persian Gulf War drew upon gender-stereotyped dichotomies that equate militarism and Western technology with masculinity; negotiation, nonviolent resistance, and protest with passivity and femininity; and assumed a hegemonic political worldview that cast the former constellation of values within "the national interest" and characterized the latter as a threat to "national security" or "our [sic] way of life."

As Mary Ellen Brown (1989) explains, "The concept of hegemony, developed by Gramsci (1971), refers to the exercise of social and cultural leadership by the dominant classes. Dominant classes win support for their ideological positions through cultural and social influences rather than through coercion, and in this way exercise their political and cultural leadership" (pp. 161-162). Although clearly the unprecedented press restrictions imposed by the United States Department of Defense during the Gulf War were coercive, for the majority of American viewers and readers the information provided by journalists and the absence of critical discourse on American foreign policy served the hegemonic process.

What were the words and images that encouraged support for and complicity with President Bush's decision to go to war, and how do these symbols relate to American gender stereotypes?

USING MASCULINITY AND
METAPHOR TO SERVE THE WAR EFFORT

Let us start by briefly noting earlier political rhetoric in contrast with the arguments offered to support war in the Persian Gulf. At the July 1984 Democratic National Convention, Governor Mario Cuomo of New York claimed that his party spoke for "reasonable people who are fighting to preserve our very existence from a macho intransigence" (p. A16) on the part of politicians who refuse to discuss responsibly the possibilities and dangers of nuclear war. In ascribing the threat of nuclear holocaust to a "macho intransigence," Cuomo was equating global militarism with a specifically male model of aggression: to be intransigent is to be unwilling or unable to compromise, to reconcile, or to come to an agreement (Borisoff & Merrill, 1992, p. 94). Yet seven years later, this very behavior was exemplified by George Bush's decision to "draw a line in the sand" and refuse any overtures at negotiation, a decision lauded by much of the American public.

How does one account for the press reportage of and public response to such overt macho posturing as evidenced in Bush's exhorting his political adversaries to "read my lips" or "make my day?" Perhaps the answer lies as much in the intended association with the popular-culture depiction of Clint Eastwood's Dirty Harry's metaphorical stance as in the swagger and language of the "tough guy" who takes pleasure in destroying the "crook." In fact, the headline under a stern picture of Bush in the Sunday *Times* [London] was "Make my day." Under this ran the subheading, "Tough guy Bush challenges Saddam to duel in the desert." Another photograph of Bush was printed with the caption "From wimp to warrior, George Bush's decisive handling of the Gulf crisis has won him the admiration of Pentagon chiefs" (cited in Beneke, 1990, p. 5).

As with the mythos embodied in the traditional American Western, the Dirty Harry persona offers spectators the opportunity to identify with a lone male hero who embodies the common man. This "common man" or working-class hero has become a popular-culture icon for much of the disenfranchised, anti-intellectual American populace. We contend that one of the many metaphors present in the press coverage of the Gulf War was one that linked George Bush or "Stormin' Norman" Schwartzkoff with the same macho ideals noted above and then equated that notion of masculinity with U.S. and Allied military "success" in the Persian Gulf.

Media images equated military success and sexual conquest, assuming a universal identification with a specifically male sexual response. Just as conquest is associated with masculinity, failure at conquest—being conquered—is equated with being emasculated. This parallel between male sexuality and militarism was made repeatedly by broadcast journalists covering the war. John Gottlieb (1991), for example, noted in his article "The Sexual Connection," that reporters and military officers described a U.S. attack on Iraqi tanks as a "hard" kill. The Iraqis "penetrated Saudi Arabia"—their first "thrust" into that country. Bush constantly referred to the "rape of Kuwait." Gottlieb also noted the sexual quality in the visual broadcast images of American military action. In the Pentagon's "bomb's-eye-view videotapes . . . a long, flying projectile climactically made contact with its target . . . and exploded. Even those of us who were against the war felt a tinge of exhilaration and release" (p. 39). In fact, the military's encouragement of the association of male sexual build-up and release with the use of weaponry can be seen in the fact that navy pilots on the *U.S.S. Kennedy* in the Persian Gulf told an Associated Press reporter they had been watching pornographic movies before flying bombing runs (Gottlieb, 1991).

Why would this specifically macho, psychosexual posturing be embraced almost uncritically by the mainstream media and so many sectors of the American public? Linguist George Lakoff (1990) attributed this complicity to "the fairy tale of the just war."[1] According to Lakoff, "The most common discourse formation in the West where there is combat to settle moral accounts is the classic fairy tale." In fairy tales, a villain commits a crime against an innocent victim. The hero, either alone or with helpers, journeys to battle the villain and rescue the victim. The hero is rational, but the villain is unreasonable and must be defeated. Lakoff claims that "the enemy-as-demon metaphor arises as a consequence of the fact that we understand what a just war is in terms of this fairy tale" (p. 5). Lakoff's metaphoric construction personifies each of the nation-states whose interests were threatened in the gulf crisis. While Lakoff does not explore the gender implications in these personifications, the hero in the classic fairy tale is male, and the victim is an unprotected female.

As the gulf crisis developed, the Bush administration tried to justify going to war through the use of two separate metaphoric scenarios. In the "rescue scenario," Iraq is the villain; the United States is the hero; Kuwait is the victim; and the crimes are kidnapping and rape. In his speech to the American public announcing the war with Iraq, President Bush (1991) said, "While the world waited, Saddam Hussein systematically raped, pillaged and plundered a tiny nation no threat to his own" (p. 226). By presenting Kuwait as a helpless female victim, Bush equated the American military with chivalrous male protectors of womanhood.

Lakoff describes the second fairy-tale scenario as the "self-defense" scenario. In this metaphor, Iraq is the villain, the United States is the hero, the United States and other industrialized nations are the potential victims, and the crime is a death threat based on possible Iraqi control of oil or development of nuclear weapons. In the same speech cited above, Bush asserted: "While the world waited, while Saddam stalled, more damage was being done to the fragile economies of the Third World, the emerging democracies of Eastern Europe, to the entire world, including to our own economy" (p. 226). Repeatedly, during the months building up to the war, Bush warned that U.S. "vital national interests" and maintenance of "our way of life" were dependent upon a military victory in the Persian Gulf.

This strategy was effective in soliciting support for U.S. intervention in part because of the media's harkening back to Vietnam as, according to Lynda H. Boose (1993), "a war that had emasculated a generation of American men by stigmatizing them as losers" (p. 80). Since the potential victim—or loser—is depicted as emasculated, the posture of the U.S. military within this framework was to protect one's (male) self from becoming or being seen as feminized. In calling upon images of Vietnam, the media helped garner public support for a possible victory in the gulf as an opportunity for the United States to regain its status of male hero. The classic male hero is characterized as having a moral and intellectual superiority over the villain; in late twentieth-century militarism, this superiority is linked with the technological advances ascribed to Western nations.

Lakoff notes that when a nation is conceptualized as a person, maturity for the state is frequently equated with industrialization; unindustrialized nations are considered "underdeveloped" (p. 4). Industrialized nations frequently are assumed to be more highly developed morally as well as technologically. For example, conservative columnist and commentator George Will expressed the hope that the war in the Persian Gulf would "pry parts of Arabia into participation in the modernity that is capable of such *technological prowess* and moral purpose" [emphasis ours] (cited in Cockburn, 1991, p. 14). To refer to technological advances as "prowess" is to imbue the process of industrialization with a sexual character and then attach to that characterization a moral purpose. Hence, the media, taking their cue from the Pentagon, repeatedly adopted the jargon that cast Western weapons of mass destruction as "smart weapons" capable of executing a "surgical strike," while referring to Iraqi weapons (originally produced by many of the same Western nations) as the more guttural sounding "Scud missiles." For example, in the first days of the war, NBC newscaster Arthur Kent (1991) said of the Scud missile, "It's an evil weapon, but not an accurate weapon." Thus, the United States, and by extension its weaponry, was presented as rational, accurate, civilized, and "smart," while the Arabs were presented as emotional, irrational, and underdeveloped. This dichotomy echoes stereotypical gender differences.

ENLISTING IMAGES OF
WOMEN TO SERVE THE WAR EFFORT

Images of American women in the military during the Persian Gulf War were presented as "evidence" of Western progress and moral superiority by implying that the more industrialized, masculinist nations allow more freedom for women. As Cynthia Enloe (1990) noted:

> American coverage of the gulf crisis has been framed by a contrast between the liberated American woman soldier and the veiled Arab woman . . . . By contrasting the allegedly liberated American woman tank mechanic with the Saudi woman deprived of a driver's license, American reporters are implying that the United States is the advanced civilized country whose duty it is to take the lead in resolving the Persian Gulf crisis. Women of both countries are being turned into currency with which men attempt to maintain the unequal relations between their societies (p. 32).

Thus, the actual or imagined experience of women was reduced to a symbol that was appropriated in the service of an ideology or military ethos. The ideology that depicts "our" women as more developed (or more civilized) than "their" women exploits women as symbol—as currency—as property (of an implicitly male nation) to be protected. These media images that present women as symbols or trophies assume the spectator's universal identification with a specifically male experience of ownership.

How did the media lead women to affiliate with this assumed male ethos? The collective psyche of a nation is to some extent constructed by the "threat" of war; when faced with such a threat, the patriarchal structure is reified by what Sara Ruddick (1993) calls the "myth of manly protection," a myth that is "sustained by androphilia." She claims that the "loyal military female . . . is androphiliac. In the midst of battle excitement, she eroticizes 'our' heroes, memorializes 'our' just warriors, and matronizingly cheers 'our' boyish adventurers" (p. 113).

Women are traditionally defined by and through their relationship to men, a relationship that in a patriarchal culture is inherently dependent. Because both the feminine and victim positions necessitate a protector or hero, masculinist culture requires this dependency. Just as the fairy-tale hero (whether in Lakoff's work or as a cultural icon) is implicitly male, so too is the "patriot." Patriotism is a gendered concept that assumes a universal identification with values that are implicitly "masculine." This construction affords women only a supportive role—as adjunct rather than actor; women's actions that serve a political ideology can be marked with adjectives such as "patriotic" or "heroic," but the actor/noun (as subject), or "patriot," is assumed to be male. Yet, the patriot's action is co-constructed by an audience whose encouragement contributes to the definition of the act as worthy or valuable. As Boose (1993) points out, "Heroism must be conferred by a woman—without whose cheers it cannot be constituted . . . " (p. 86). Women's participation is enlisted, according to Lesley Merryfinch (1981), by convincing the public that "their interests are identical with those of the military. Good citizens are supposed to be proud and not unduly critical of their country" (p. 10).

Throughout history, androphiliac images of gender-appropriate behavior and occupations have varied with the efficacy of a given notion for the dominant interests in the society at the time. Thus, during World War II, women were encouraged to leave the home for work in factories, taking jobs that previously (and subsequently) were considered only appropriate for men. Rather than liberating women from sex role–stereotyped conventions, however, women's nontraditional work was depicted in conservative terms as "supporting the war effort." Once the war ended, Rosie the Riveter was replaced by Donna Reed, and women were encouraged to leave the workforce to the returning male breadwinners. However disparate each of these options for women appear, both served hegemonic values and were justified by love for "our boys overseas."

By the time of the gulf crisis, the hegemonic interests were served by women actually enlisting in the military. More than 32,000 women (Miller, 1991) were in the U.S. armed forces at this time, largely because of the military's aggressive recruitment policies following the end of the draft in the 1970s. The images from the front lines in the Persian Gulf War were tailored to allow for the inclusion of servicewomen in the region. One of the reasons for the Department of Defense's restrictions on the press, as Walter Goodman noted in early January 1991, was that "the prospect that even one or two of the many women (some of them mothers!) now in uniform [would] be killed [sent] shudders through the Pentagon" (p. D8). Consequently, viewers and readers of the U.S. press did not witness or read very much about American servicewomen (or men) killing or being killed. Instead of a report of the Iraqi deaths, the American and British public heard of "minimized collateral damage." Deaths and injuries of American women and men were also virtually unmentioned by the American media. The effect of such manipulated and sanitized press coverage served the "war effort" by rendering these images palatable to a patriarchal civilian constituency.

Largely absent from any lengthy discussion in the U.S. press were the implications for families of American servicewomen called to active duty in the Persian Gulf, such as presentations that might cast in oppositional terms women's traditional roles as wives or mothers and their being called away to military service. These images would have been impossible to exploit for the military's rhetorical purposes had readers and viewers been presented with the actual purposes served by women and men in militaries, to kill or be killed. Any other images—for example, of women actually serving in field positions—would have refuted the traditional notion of womanhood.

In the military, despite the liberated opportunity depicted in the media, the reality of women's experience is that they are largely limited to traditionally subordinate positions. The sexual division of labor within the military echoes the sexual division of labor within the larger society: women are most likely to serve in clerical, administrative, nursing, and communications roles in an even more rigid sex-role division than in civilian life and without civilian women's rights. By joining the military and/or identifying with an aggressor through the adoption of military uniforms, symbols, and rituals, women initially may feel more powerful; as though in this one endeavor they can "be all that they can be." As Astrid Albrecht-Heide (1981) notes: "'Identification with the aggressor' is not only found among those women who themselves become soldiers, but also among military wives and even women completely outside the military who applaud military violence by admiring uniforms, military parades, and so forth" (p. 85).

CHALLENGING THE STEREOTYPES

Just as the images of women in the military offer some women a superficial relationship to power by virtue of the association between the military and "maleness," so men who refuse to participate in militaries (or indeed, in any acts demeaning and dehumanizing women) are frequently regarded as "emasculated" or homosexual by a culture that equates masculinity and violence. As Carol Cohn (1993) notes:

'Fag' imagery . . . also appears in popular 'political' discourse. The Gulf War was replete with examples. American derision of Saddam Hussein included bumper stickers that read 'Saddam, Bend Over.' American soldiers reported that the 'U.S.A.' stenciled on their uniforms stood for 'Up Saddam's Ass' . . . . Over and over, defeat for the Iraqis was portrayed as humiliating anal penetration by the more powerful and manly United States. (p. 236)

From the war buildup through the welcome home parades, male peace activists, resistors, protestors, and conscientious objectors were frequently verbally attacked and referred to as "faggots" by those enraged at their refusal of this bastion of male power (Vic Scutari, "Americans Removing Injustice, Suppression, and Exploitation," personal communication, March 12, 1991). Similarly, women who refuse to acquiesce to males in the family, the workplace, or the military are often labeled "dykes" and subject to homophobic witch-hunts. Thus, the relationship between gender-specific behavior and militarism is reinforced by the homophobia to which violators of the established norms are subjected.

By refusing to acquiesce to male authority and reify masculinity through androphilia, women threaten to unmask the masculinist interests embedded in both the social construction of patriotism and the myth of manly protection. The construction of the gendered, heterosexist state depends on women's participation—or identification with—the whole ethos that equates militarism with masculinity. Yet, ultimately, identifying with one who has power over one never results in true empowerment. Rather, as Carolyn Heilbrun (1987) notes, "Power is the ability to take one's place in whatever discourse is essential to action, and the right to have one's part matter" (p. 18).

NOTE

1. Lakoff felt such urgency to present his study of the metaphors he saw being used to justify U.S. and Allied intervention in the gulf that he elected to employ international computer networks that afford instantaneous and interactive communication, rather than traditional one-directional publishing venues. On December 31, 1990, just two weeks before the January 15 deadline, Lakoff transmitted his study to colleagues and interested parties via BITNET.

REFERENCES

Albert, D. H. (1988). Publisher's note. In P. McAllister, *You can't kill the spirit* (pp. x-xi). Philadelphia: New Society.

Albrecht-Heide, A. (1981). The peaceful sex. In W. Chapkis (Ed.), *Loaded questions: Women in the military* (pp. 83-87). Amsterdam: Transnational Institute.

Beneke, T. (1990). An interview with Daniel Ellsberg about the Middle East crisis. *Thinkpeace, 6*, (3), 1-6.

Boose, Lynda H. (1993). Techno-muscularity and the "boy eternal": From the quagmire to the gulf. In M. Cooke & A. Woolacott (Eds.), *Gendering war talk* (pp. 67-106). Princeton: Princeton University Press.

Borisoff, D., & Merrill, L. (1992). *The power to communicate* (2nd ed.). Prospect Heights, IL: Waveland.

Brown, M. E. (1989). Soap opera and women's culture: Politics and the popular. In K. Carter & C. Spitzack (Eds.), *Doing research on women's communication: Perspectives on theory and method* (pp. 161-190). Norwood, NJ: Ablex Publishing.

Bush, G. (1991, February 2). War with Iraq: Enforcing the U.N. resolutions [Transcript of January 16, 1991, speech]. *Vital Speeches of the Day, 57* (8), 226-227.

Cockburn, A. (1991). Moral bluster. *New Statesman & Society, 4* (137), 14-15.

Cohn, C. (1993). Wars, wimps, and women: Talking gender and thinking war. In M. Cooke & A. Woolacott (Eds.), *Gendering war talk* (pp. 227-246). Princeton: Princeton University Press.

Cuomo, M. (1984, July 17). Transcript of keynote address by Cuomo to the convention. *The New York Times*, p. A16.

Enloe, C. (1990, September 25). Womenandchildren: Making feminist sense of the Persian Gulf crisis. *The Village Voice*, pp. 29-30, 32.

Goodman, W. (1991, January 10). Gulf tensions: TV's cause and effect. *The New York Times*, p. D8.

Gottlieb, J. (1991, April). The sexual connection. *The Progressive*, p. 39.

Heilbrun, C. (1987). *Writing a woman's life.* New York: Norton.

Kent, A. (1991, January 17). NBC nightly news [Television newscast]. WNBC, New York.

Lakoff, G. (1990). *Metaphor and war: The metaphor system used to justify war in the gulf.* Distributed by author via BITNET [lakoff@cogsci.berkeley.edu].

Merryfinch, L. (1981). Militarization/civilianization. In W. Chapkis (Ed.), *Loaded questions: Women in the military* (pp. 9-13). Amsterdam: Transnational Institute.

Miller, M. (1991, April/May). AAUW members in the gulf war. *American Association of University Women Outlook*, p. 5.

Ruddick, S. (1993). Notes toward a feminist peace politics. In M. Cooke & A. Woolacott (Eds.), *Gendering war talk* (pp. 109-127). Princeton: Princeton University Press.

17

Difference, Dominance, and Dialectics: A Call for Change

Linda A. M. Perry

Researchers of female and/or male experience are also participants as male or female communicators. Thus, while we as researchers may believe our stance should be objective, it always is subjective. Our life experiences shape our beliefs, and our beliefs shape our research interests, methods, and perspectives. As such, there is a reflexive process between experience and theorizing about experience. Researchers have studied female and male relationships through two primary theoretical perspectives which undoubtedly reflect their own experiences: the difference (or cultural) perspective and the dominance (or power) perspective.[1] The difference perspective claims that male and female experiences are derived from separate cultures and/or from the genetic makeup of females and males. The dominance perspective claims that these differences between males and females are artificial and create power distinctions such that males are in more dominant positions and females in more subservient positions.

As a child and young adult, my orientation was one of difference—I learned to act within the constraints of being female because I believed the distinctions between male and female actions were biologically mandated. As I matured, my life experiences provided revelations that caused me to hold a dominance orientation. I recognized that what had been sold as a product of nature was more the result of being socialized into a male-dominated society. As I gained self-direction, I came to recognize that sex stereotypes and the resultant behavioral expectations are socially bound and mutable.

Being true to my own life experiences in this essay, I address the problems inherent in these two perspectives and suggest a third, the dialectic perspective. First, the difference perspective is explored briefly by filtering it through the "acid test" of my reality. Next, the dominance perspective is similarly addressed. I do not cover all aspects of these perspectives but instead focus on some of the issues that arise when we locate ourselves as proponents of either orientation. Finally, I advance the dialectic perspective on male/female experience. After years as a feminist and an advocate for change, I have embraced this new perspective, which echoes the difference and dominance perspectives while moving into a more holistic orientation toward studying female and/or male behavior.

THE DIFFERENCE PERSPECTIVE

Most researchers would agree that isolating differences between the sexes is both interesting and important. We can readily identify with differences because we live them. For example, whether by nature or nurture, many males seem to have great fondness for hanging out in packs and many females seem to enjoy sharing their intimate thoughts and aspirations with each other. Carol Gilligan (1982) and Deborah Tannen (1990) both espouse a difference perspective. Gilligan looks at rights versus responsibility: men operate from an orientation based on rules, rights, and hierarchies; women operate from a perspective based on care, responsibility, and web-like connections between people and among events. Tannen looks at symmetry and asymmetry: women are concerned with intimacy so symmetry is their style; men are concerned with status so asymmetry is their style.

Gilligan argues that the differences between male and female ways of being are problematic because our culture has designated the male model of behavior as the norm and female as abnormal. She further argues that female behavior is based on an ethic of care which cannot be fairly judged against the male ethic of justice. She claims because men and women are different, researchers should use alternative methods for exploring their experiences. While this strategy helps researchers to better define female and male behavior, including differences in their moral development, it does little to address the day-to-day problems resulting from the power imbalance between males and females.

Tannen argues that females and males have different ways of being because they grow up in different "cultures." She notes that males grow up in a culture concerned with competition and learn to separate themselves from others while females grow up in a culture concerned with connectedness and learn to bring themselves closer to others. These differences between female and male ways of being create opposing ways of communicating which, in turn, exacerbates problems between males and females. Tannen says these differences are problematic, but they can be overcome through simple negotiation of communication styles. Males can learn to use more intimate talk and women can learn to accept men's distancing behaviors as stylistic and not necessarily reflective of their level of care. This suggestion oversimplifies the problem because it ignores the fact that men, who are in the more advantageous position, have little motivation to change.

As a young child, I recognized the differences between being a girl and being a boy. I believed being a boy was more fun because boys could play softball and basketball, stay out later, go further away from home after school and so forth. I believed being a girl was not much fun because girls engaged in passive play, such as playing with dolls and playing house. I believed I would rather be male. Males had more freedom; they had more independence; they seemed to be more respected; in sum, they had more power. Looking back on it, I realize I did not have penis-envy, I had power-envy. I never questioned that power differentiation, however. I was accepted as "one of the guys" as a young child. But, as I grew older, my male peers gained more freedom and I "became" a girl. And, I did not put up a fight. When one is raised to believe that male privilege is based on genetic propensities, one comes to accept the consequences with minimum resistance. After all, most children want to fit in with the group. Therefore, girls experience strong motivations to adopt feminine behaviors and most boys to adopt masculine behaviors. And, although one might have moments of resistance, the cultural rules and meta-rules will more than likely quiet that discontent. The outcome is enculturated denial of the power males have over females by masking it as biologically mandated.

Laing (1972) says that we obey social rules by adopting social roles even when the rules and roles may limit or damage our self-direction. When a female disobeys the social rule to be feminine by behaving too powerfully or dominantly, she is labeled a "tomboy," a deviant role. When a male disobeys the social rule to be masculine by behaving too subservient or nurturing, he is labelled a "sissy," also a deviant role. Deviant males and females experience alienation through deterrents and punishments and come to believe they must be either bad or mad for behaving differently than the gender role they have been assigned. To remove themselves from the resultant cognitive dissonance (wanting to fit in the group but behaving in deviant ways that alienate them from the group), they must deny who they are. Denial involves obeying rules, meta-rules and meta-meta rules. The adoption of sex-stereotyped behaviors through denial progresses as follows:

1. Rule: Behave according to sex role expectations.

2. Meta-rule: Act as though you are behaving according to sex role expectations because they are based on nature and not on social rules.

3. Meta-meta-rule: Forget that the rule and meta-rule exist (denial). To question these is to return to a deviant, alienated position.

Because generations of people have lived their lives in denial, those who become conscious are often met with suspicion and isolation. For example, I attended a presentation by Anne Wilson Schaef who wrote *Meditations for Women Who Do Too Much* (1990) and other feminist works. As Dr. Schaef outlined the ways in which women are objectified, ignored, and abused worldwide, many women and men walked out on her presentation. Feminists who speak out are labelled as maladjusted men haters because they do not obey the rules and meta-rules, so are subjected to deterrents and punishments. It is highly possible (or probable) that those who left Dr. Schaef's presentation were so entrenched in denial that they discounted her and her words and left in disgust. By walking out during her presentation, they were punishing Dr. Schaef for not following social rules for the female sex stereotype. These were the people who most likely needed to hear her message more than those who stayed. As argued above, we come to obey the rules and meta-rules to avoid cognitive dissonance and alienation. Certainly, it was much more comfortable for those people entrenched in denial to leave Schaef's presentation early than to try to fit what she had to say into their cognitive set.

Overcoming adherence to long-forgotten rules and being able to withstand the alienation that comes with consciousness takes a cataclysmic event—something has to happen that jars one into another reality. To move from accepting a difference perspective to one of dominance often takes just that, a revelation that changes the way one sees the world.

REVELATION: FROM DIFFERENCE TO DOMINANCE

Laing (1972) says that "unless we can 'see through' the rules, we can only see through them" (p. 105). Unless we can see that the differences between men and women give males abusive power, we act as though these differences are benign, as just the way nature intended life to be. The only way to "see through the rules" is through revelations that expose the real dangers of the difference perspective—dangers for both people of the street and researchers of human interaction. These revelations take many forms.[2] Maybe you see your lover with someone else, or maybe you or a loved one is beaten badly enough to be taken to the hospital. Perhaps you see a movie and identify with the obedient and misused woman. Or, perhaps you read a book with whose characters you closely, and uncomfortably identify.

For me, that revelation came from reading *The Women's Room* (French, 1977) one year after my first husband and I divorced. Through identification with the lead characters in French's novel, I became more and more angry as I awoke from the dream of denial. I thought I had been angry a lot in my life, but I didn't know what anger was. Being angry is not simply acting out by shouting or pouting, it is an internal emotional/physical response that occurs when you realize that while you were following the rules (rules of which you may not have been aware), you were being lied to, mistreated, and made to feel guilty and confused. When women are not allowed to express their legitimate anger, they hide behind facades. When these facades crack, women feel guilty because they have broken the rule that says women may not express anger. When revelations occur that force women to internalize their anger, women (such as me) come to understand they have been following deeply embedded, long-forgotten rules and meta-rules—rules they had no part in creating, and which should now be broken.

Once a woman has experienced this kind of revelation, she no longer can accept as given the stereotypical behavioral differences between women and men. She comes to recognize that this is a difference that makes a difference. She also comes to know that the outcome of adhering to a belief in the difference perspective without recognizing its possible outcomes can be disastrous. These rule-based differences affect every aspect of life from equal opportunity, to personal decision making, to rights to walk alone in the evening, to child-support legislation, to simple respect.

Once women wake up from the denial dream, the dream turns into a nightmare. In response to my own personal revelation, I moved from a difference perspective to a dominance perspective on female and male experience. Through revelations about the outcomes of the difference perspective, I, and most likely women like me, learned not to trust the system, not to trust my own perceptions, and certainly not to trust men. By going through revelations, one quite possibly becomes more aware, more angry, and more secure. As such, these revelations and the resultant anger have been the stepping off point for me and many women to become feminists. It is, however, harmful to women and to the world itself if legitimate feminist anger cannot be transformed from its anti-male position. To better understand that transition, let us look at the differences between males and females through the dominance perspective.

THE DOMINANCE PERSPECTIVE

At a minimum, the dominance perspective argues that many of the perceived differences between men and women are based on inequitable power distribution between the sexes (Spender, 1984). Additionally, those power inequities create a system in which women become "invisible" and "mute" (Kramarae, 1981). Most people do not want to be dominated and most domineering people do not claim the title overtly. Because dominance often is disguised as difference, one must transcend the "safety" of denial and recognize that believing in sex-role distinctions allows sex-based dominance. And, where the difference perspective relies on social rules and roles for existence and maintenance, the dominance perspective is played out through attributions and injunctions.

It is easy to create and/or maintain inadvertently the very actions we wish to extinguish. Laing (1971) explains that attributions based on female and male sex stereotypes actually may perpetuate them. For example, if a little girl is attributed (labelled) to be a " sweet little lady," she also receives the injunction (command), "be a sweet little lady." The little girl learns the action expectation for females through the attributions she receives. Little boys also receive attributions and injunctions that create and sustain masculine actions of dominance and powerfulness. Thus, both males and females are caught in double binds. If males enact feminine behaviors (nurturance and dependent) they are not "real men." If males enact masculine behaviors (aggression and dominance), they are bad people. If females enact masculine behaviors, they are seen as unattractive. If females enact feminine behaviors, they lose control over their destinies. The outcome of females learning to be feminine and males learning to be masculine has ramifications for both males and females. Part of the evolution in feminist thought is to recognize that society in general, and not men or women specifically, maintains power distinctions between males and females.

Living our lives according to either the difference or the dominance perspectives on female/male relationships presents significant limitations and drawbacks. The difference perspective is limited by its reliance on sex stereotypes, as is the dominance perspective. And, while both perspectives support differing levels of change, they are both tied to a polarizing dichotomy between men and women. That is, they are based on a traditional heterosexual model in which women and men are at opposite ends of a sex-biased and power-based dichotomy. Thus, researchers who focus on either of these orientations limit what they find. A third perspective that removes emphasis on sex stereotypes and advocates a more encompassing and holistic view of women and men is needed. I believe a dialectic perspective fills just such a need.

THE DIALECTIC PERSPECTIVE[3]

Reading the works of Virginia Woolf, Mary Wollstonecraft, Betty Friedan, Gloria Steinem, and so forth allows recognition that the difference and dominance perspectives, in one form or another, span history. It is time to bring women and men into a common group, the human race, to begin to focus on ways to heal the wounds created by severing our experiences into divergent and competing ways of being. Because of heterosexual stereotypes, "masculinity" is most often exclusively mapped on males and "femininity" is most often exclusively mapped on females. This does a disservice to humans because femininity and masculinity are not the province of one sex or the other but of both sexes in varying degrees. When researchers discuss male rather than masculine behaviors, female rather than feminine behaviors, they add to the alienation between women and men. Discussing femininity and masculinity as human attributes can help researchers to begin to close the gap between men and women. So doing represents the third perspective on human gendered experience—dialectic. In the context of this perspective, men are the dialectic necessity of women; women, the dialectic necessity of men. That is, women and men need each other to balance the human system. Also from this perspective, femininity is the dialectic necessity of masculinity; masculinity, the dialectic necessity of femininity. That is, masculinity and femininity need to be embraced both within and between females and males. As such, a dialectic perspective suggests (at a minimum) the following three tenets:

(1) There are both women and men in our culture. To overvalue one is to undervalue the other. Sometimes, in our determination to research female and/or male experience and/or interaction, we come to value one sex over the other. As Ellen Dubois argues when addressing problems with research that focuses solely on women's experience, "Single-minded focus on women's own culture brings with it the risk of ignoring the larger social and historical developments of which it is a part and does not address the limitations of the values of women's culture" (cited in Kerber, Greeno, Maccoby, Luria, Stack, & Gilligan, 1986, p. 308). It is important to remember that while women and men share attributes as parts of the superordinate system, they each have their own biologically induced attributes. To resolve the problems inherent in researching gendered experiences, we must recognize human gender differences as valid without also embracing blind obedience to the old sex-role stereotypes. The dialectic perspective allows males and females to become the true complements of each other (yin/yang) in a holistic setting in which equal opportunity becomes a given.

(2) While human experiences of gender may differ, they can be linked through the adoption of masculine and feminine orientations by both and either sex. Masculinity is enacted by both males and females. Extreme masculinity results in dominant, violent, and dangerous behavior. A social system that supports masculinity out of balance with femininity—one that condones it and espouses it through domestic violence, political stances, and mass media representations—is systematically problematic. We need to explore new labels for masculine actions so that males *and*

females have socially acceptable access to them when situations demand it.

Femininity is enacted by both females and males. Extreme femininity results in subservient, passive, and powerless behavior. A social system that supports femininity out of balance with masculinity—one that makes it less admirable than dominance and compounds the problem by mapping it almost exclusively on females—is systematically problematic. We need to explore new labels for feminine actions so that females *and* males have socially acceptable access to them when situations demand it. In sum, cultural interactions should be able to evolve in which both sexes can choose masculine and/or feminine behaviors without being forced to choose one over the other.

(3) To accept a dialectic perspective means also to explore and espouse issues of trust and risk-taking in relation to gender issues. In the past, trust has been a double-edged sword for women and men. Society has always trusted men to adhere to their assigned masculine roles and women to adhere to their assigned feminine roles, even when doing so was detrimental to themselves, each other and society at large. A new form of trust is greatly needed between males and females to help us move beyond sex-stereotype mandates to make possible a true cultural paradigm shift into equality. This shift would free females and males from blindly adhering to the difference perspective that relies on accepting socially mandated rules and roles for each sex. This shift would also free males and females from adhering to a dominance perspective that maintains power distinctions between males and females through attributions and injunctions. It is time for females and males to risk deterrents and punishments and move into a holistic manifestation of masculine and feminine behaviors. It is also time for researchers to lay down their shields of difference and dominance and refocus on a dialectic perspective on human interaction.

CONCLUSION

The difference perspective on male/female behavior is the result of blind obedience and denial. Through revelations about the harm in adhering to the difference perspective, the dominance perspective emerges. A dialectic perspective defines women and men as interlocking subsystems within the superordinate group called humanity. This perspective requires acknowledgement of both the values and problems inherent in the present sex-role stereotypes and the perspectives from which they are studied.

In order to espouse a dialectic perspective, societal understanding of the gender system must change. To move human experience and the study of it forward, it is time to focus on both common and distinctive experiences of females and males and to address masculine and feminine behaviors in the context of varying sexual orientations (females and males with a feminine perspective, males and females with a masculine perspective), rather than according to a woman/man dichotomy. Blind acceptance of roles socially mandated through rules and meta-rules for male and female behavior disguised as biologically bound behaviors minimizes cultural and personal responsibility to change the system and the resultant stereotypes. In sum, the dialectic perspective on female and/or male experience is both grounded in and transcendent of the interplay between the difference and dominance perspectives.

NOTES

1. The difference and dominance perspectives as described herein are defined narrowly for the sake of argument. Thus, the works of Gilligan, Tannen, Spender, and Kramarae are referenced without full representation.

2. The following examples are based on female experiences, because those are the dilemmas I know best.

3. Some may argue that ecofeminism already encompasses attributes of the dialectic perspective. While in many ways that is true, connecting a holistic model to a female-centered (feminist) orientation still maintains divisions between women and men.

REFERENCES

French, M. (1977). *The women's room.* New York: Summit Books.

Gilligan, C. (1982). *In a different voice.* Cambridge, MA: Harvard University Press.

Kaplan, A. (1964). *The conduct of inquiry.* New York: Harper & Row.

Kerber, L. K., Greeno, C. G., Maccoby, E. E., Luria, Z., Stack, C. B., & Gilligan, C. (1986). On in a different voice: An interdisciplinary forum. *Signs: Journal of Women in Culture and Society, 11* (21), 304-333.

Kramarae, C. (1981). *Women and men speaking: Framework for analysis.* Rowley, MA: Newbury House.

Laing, R. D. (1971). *Self and others.* Middlesex: Penguin.

Laing, R. D. (1972). *The politics of the family.* New York: Vintage Books.

Schaef, A. W. (1990). *Meditations for women who do too much.* New York: Harper & Row.

Spender, D. (1984). Defining reality: A powerful tool. In C. Kramarae, M. Schultz, & W. M. O'Barr (Eds.), *Language and power* (pp. 194-205). Beverly Hills, CA: Sage Publications.

Tannen, D. (1990). *You just don't understand: Women and men in conversation.* New York: William Morrow.

18

Visionary Language: The Voice of Mary Robinson

Kathleen B. Watters

On November 8, 1990, Mary Robinson, an independent candidate, was elected Ireland's first woman president. Robinson's emergence as a viable national candidate and her surprising victory over nominees of the entrenched political parties would, perhaps, be remarkable in a majority of the world's democratic nations. But in Ireland, a country often characterized as a nation dominated by a conservative, parochial social and political life, Robinson's achievement has been regarded as no less than stunning. Two days *before* the election the *Irish Times* said of Robinson, "She has possibly done more, with words alone, to induce change in Ireland than any other politician" (McKittrick, 1990, p. 19). Robinson's rhetoric made a difference both during the campaign and as she assumed the office of president of Ireland.

Placing Robinson's candidacy in its cultural and political context, she would surely be an improbable choice, and perhaps, even a preposterous one. From the start of her campaign, she was regarded as an unlikely candidate, much less a future head of state. Irish bookmakers, quoted with far greater frequency in the national press than public opinion polls, placed her at 100 to 1 odds in handicapping the election ("Irish bookies," 1990, p. 14).

While Robinson's candidacy was exceptional on the basis of gender alone, its distinction was heightened by her public identity as a champion for women's rights, divorce and family law reform, and accessible contraception and abortion information. In Ireland, these issues are not only socially taboo but the subject of puritanical laws promulgated by both the State and the Catholic Church. An Irish journalist summarized the inconsistencies between candidate and culture this way: "She is a woman in a country whose politics are dominated by men; she is a feminist in a land where such activities are often scorned; she is a radical in a conservative society; she is an outsider in activities characterized by cronyism; and she is sympathetic to the Protestants of Northern Ireland, who are often detested in the Irish Republic" (Tuohy, 1990, p. 16).

The candidates and messages of many national political campaigns attempt to go beyond slogans and sound-bites to construct and communicate an encompassing vision for the nation and its citizens. For some candidates the messages can be contradictory as they confront a pluralistic society of competing constituencies and, as a result, the vision becomes lost or obscured. Robinson's campaign discourse is a striking illustration of consistency and evolution in the political arena. During the campaign and in her Inaugural Address, Robinson's messages represented the fusion of "womanhood," "personhood," and nationhood. The concepts of "womanhood" and "personhood" have been viewed as opposing and distinct ideological frames *within* feminist movements (Campbell, 1983; Wood, 1994). However, Robinson's rhetoric reveals a synthesis and extension of these concepts in the broader context of a national political life. This synthesis, and its extension to nationhood, constitutes Robinson's distinctive vision.

Robinson describes her vision as a means to empowerment for women in Ireland and for others who are disenfranchised or exiled from full participation or membership in national life as citizens. The vision espouses the values, beliefs, and goals of citizenship and participation. The following discussion offers a rhetorical explanation for Robinson's influence and electoral victory. First, it examines Irish political culture and Robinson's role in the 1990 Irish presidential campaign; and second, it presents an analysis of her fusion of womanhood, personhood, and nationhood into a distinctive vision for a "new" Ireland.

IRISH POLITICAL CULTURE
AND ROBINSON'S CAMPAIGN

Robinson's campaign rhetoric challenged the traditional political parties in Ireland. Her vision challenged the nation's dominant political culture founded in the historical and victorious struggle for independence, the almost mythical ties of two major political parties to the Civil War, and the unique presence and influence of the Catholic Church as a cultural institution. Unlike the vast majority of Western democracies, Ireland is an old country and a young nation. When Robinson assumed office in 1990, the Irish Constitution had been in place only 54 years. It is within this political and cultural context that Robinson enacted and spoke to the "womanhood" idealogy and unified it with personhood and nationhood.

Robinson was a former member of the Irish Senate and—by self-description and reputation—a feminist. In 1990, a cry for a reinvigorated presidency by minor political parties and a timely political scandal (labelled "Dublingate," involving the leading presidential candidate) presented an unusual opportunity for Robinson, who had forsaken a party label to mobilize support as an independent candidate (rare in Ireland's electoral practices).

Since 1922, the practice and philosophy of Irish politics have been defined by two centralist parties: the dominant Fianna Fail (Soldiers of Destiny) and the principal minority party Fine Gael (Family of the Irish). One commentator compares the Irish political parties to their American counterparts in this way: "Think of Fianna Fail as conservative, populist Democrats and Fine Gael as moderate, progressive Republicans, and you'll have workable analogy" (Walker, 1990, p. 11).

Robinson's election would mark not only the first woman president, but the first president elected from outside the Fianna Fail. Running as an independent, she enjoyed the backing of two "liberal/leftist" minority parties, the Labour Party and Workers Party, who enjoy limited public support and have small representations in the Irish Parliament. A Fianna Fail party official and member of Parliament later remarked, "It's a culture shock to have someone . . . beat the two major parties. It's never happened. It's significant and forces everyone to take a look at themselves" (Rule, 1990, p. 4).

Both in style and content, Robinson's campaign was as unconventional as her candidacy. Despite "American-style" campaign strategies and the aggressive marketing of candidates now firmly established in Irish political contests, Robinson's campaign was the antithesis of modern image politics. Lacking funds and outspent by her principal rival at a ratio of almost 10 to 1, and with little access to the paid media advertising thought essential to a candidate's success, Robinson's campaign relied on a grass-roots strategy mobilized by a relatively small campaign staff and dependent on a national network of volunteers, activists, and friends (Cooke, 1990, p. 18). Her campaign was also the antithesis of the "stroke" politics of Ireland, the ingredients of stroke politics being "blarney and booze, cracker-barrel jokes, and also the odd spot of character assassination, petty patronage, and Clan loyalties. And the binding glue of all of this, fierce male kinship" (Gwyn, 1990, p. H1).

Robinson's "walkabouts" became the candidate's distinctive vehicle, traveling by bus with loudspeaker and banners across the country. By some accounts she visited every city, town and village of any significance as many as three times. One reporter traveling with the candidate in the final days of the campaign described the scene:

Here's to you, Mrs. Robinson, the Simon and Garfunkel tune wafts from the loudspeaker of her campaign bus without the words. [The lyrics] would be awkward for this Mrs. R, who though still a Catholic, introduced her Family Planning Bill in 1970. It did not prosper, but she made herself notorious overnight . . . . Her campaign bus rolled into another little grey town, Gorey, and stopped outside Byrne's funeral parlour, which offered a bike for sale. On a cold November day there were many hands to shake, apart from a young fishwife at a stall whose hand was too fishy, garrulous women shoppers who declared that it was time a woman got in, though they never voted Labour before. (Grove, 1990, p. 1 Features)

"The faded flags of the civil war" was Robinson's shibboleth, first, to identify the traditional parties and their candidates and, second, to depict the Ireland of men and guns.[1] Throughout the campaign, Robinson urged voters to "step out from the faded flags of the civil war and vote for a new Ireland." Following her election, Robinson praised "the moral courage" of citizens who voted for a "new Ireland."

WOMANHOOD, PERSONHOOD, AND NATIONHOOD

Robinson's rhetorical fusion attempted to resolve the conflict between womanhood and personhood suggested by scholars (Campbell, 1983, 1989; Wood, 1994). Womanhood ideology honors femininity, the "cult of domesticity" and argues the moral superiority of women (Wood, 1994, p. 95). Personhood rejects womanhood and femininity beliefs as oppressive and a denial of participation, membership and, in effect, citizenship in society. Personhood ideology or "liberal" feminism asserts that women and men are entitled to the same rights and opportunities in all spheres of society (Wood, 1994). Liberal feminism seeks to "free women from oppressive gender roles—that is, from those roles that have been used as excuses or justification for giving women a lesser place, or no place at all, in the academy, the forum, and the marketplace" (Tong, 1989, p. 28).

Robinson's rhetorical synthesis begins with herself as a candidate for president of Ireland. During her seven-month campaign for the presidency (the longest in Irish presidential history), Robinson embodied and enacted the role she advocated for women as citizens: "All of us need to embrace the idea that mothers can be Taoiseach (prime minister) or, yes, even President. We must abandon now the outmoded traditions that still dictate that it is somehow inappropriate that a mother should seek paid employment, that there are jobs and roles that women must be excluded from."

Robinson speaks of women as mothers. She selects the most revered gender role of women and argues not that women enjoy citizen membership and participation as a measure of their equality with men, but that mothers have the opportunity and right to seek additional roles as full citizens. By arguing that "mothers" could be prime minister, president, and "seek paid employment," Robinson attempted to make her own candidacy and her message more tolerable to the Irish electorate. In a country where 96% of the population is of the Catholic faith and the relationship between church and state is entwined, the image of women as mothers is not only more acceptable to voters—it also extols the essence of womanhood ideology. Using womanhood as the starting point and merging it with personhood and, ultimately, nationhood allowed Robinson to launch her candidacy, to be heard, and to advocate change within the context of a Catholic country.

Robinson's use of womanhood values, as enactment and inception for her vision, is also significant in a nation where a woman's role in the home is affirmed in the 1937 Irish Constitution. Article 41 of the Constitution declares, "The state recognizes that by her life within the home, woman gives to the state a support without which the common good cannot be achieved. The state shall therefore, endeavour to ensure that mothers shall not be obliged by economic necessity to engage in labour to the neglect of their duties in the home." Recognizing the role of women prescribed in the Constitution, Robinson argued that the nation is a home for its citizens and mothers should be part of the political life of the nation.

Integral to Robinson's rhetorical fusion and vision is a definition of nationhood derived from an active recognition and respect by the State and its policies for citizens. In Robinson's interpretation, pluralism became the counterpart of nationhood, and inclusion, equality, tolerance, and opportunity the precepts for the State and its citizens. Thus, Robinson grounds nationhood in "personhood," the recognized rightful and active participation of an individual in social, political, and economic life. But Robinson goes beyond this relationship to articulate a vision of nationhood and personhood that encompasses the values of "womanhood," a feminist profile of national purpose. In this fusion lies a redefinition of a government's responsibility toward its people and a more inclusive political system.

In constructing the rhetorical fusion, Robinson also attempted to transform citizen perceptions by offering contrasting portrayals of Ireland as part of the community of nations. She described her candidacy as a choice "between old strokes and new moves . . . between Ireland as an old, backwater republic of nudge and wink or Ireland as a young, shining state of the new Europe" (Eichel, 1990, p. A3). One observer commented that she effectively cast the presidential election as a choice "between two diametrically-opposed symbolic images of Ireland: The old and the new, the conservative and the progressive, the inward-turned traditional and the outward-looking modern" (Gwyn, 1990, p. H1).

A journalist, Mary Holland, wrote about Robinson's campaign messages as a choice between an "ascribing society" and an "achieving society." In Holland's words, an "ascribing society is one in which people judge themselves and one another by old traditions and connections . . . [A]n achieving society is one in which people value one another by personal accomplishment or self-realisation" (Holland, 1990, p. 21). Throughout the campaign, Robinson spoke of her "commitment to pluralism," and the value of tolerance. She used this call to argue that traditional politics and the Catholic Church are exclusionary, intolerant and unjust. As counterpoint to this characterization, Robinson spoke repeatedly of "equality and excellence" having a "home" in society and in her presidency. She declared that the women of Ireland were, in fact, "exiles at home," and promised them, "You have a voice. I will make it heard." Robinson also assailed the Catholic Church's role and influence in the major political parties, charging that the "patriarchal, male-dominated presence of the Catholic Church subjugates women in Ireland" (Frankel, 1990, p. A20). In Robinson's view, an "achieving society" would embrace and respect all citizens, and extend justice and opportunity to all.

Robinson regarded her victory as a major advancement toward an achieving society; "My election was on the exact first anniversary of the fall of the Berlin Wall. Something has crumbled away in Ireland too" (Cooke, 1990, November 10, p. 2). What "crumbled away" was the "outmoded traditions" that excluded women from public life, the political culture of the Civil War, and the intolerance of the Catholic Church. In her victory speech Robinson stated:

> I was elected by women and men of all parties and none, by many with great moral courage who stepped out from the faded flags of the civil war and voted for a new Ireland, and above all by the women of Ireland, *mna na h-Eireann*, who instead of rocking the cradle rocked the system, and who came out massively to make their mark on the ballot paper and on a new Ireland.

Within a few weeks of her victory at the polls, Robinson delivered her Inaugural Address. It represents the culmination of the rhetorical fusion and suggests how, as president, she will advance her vision of a new Ireland.

PRESIDENT ROBINSON'S VISION

The president in Ireland is considered the "First Citizen." The office is defined around this notion rather than one of executive powers. Consistent with the office she sought, Robinson's vision interpreted nationhood by unifying the ideological friction between womanhood and personhood. In this fusion women (and others who Robinson argued are exiled and disenfranchised) become full citizens and are accorded participation and rights in social, political, and economic life. In her inaugural address, Robinson described the vision as "the quest for equality and excellence," and advanced her union of womanhood, personhood, and nationhood:

> What I promised as candidate I mean to deliver as President. Aras an Uachtaran will, to the best of my ability become a home as well as a house; a home for all those aspirations of equality and excellence. The Ireland I will be representing is a new Ireland, open, tolerant, inclusive. Many of you who voted for me did so without sharing all of my views. This, I believe, is a significant signal of change, a sign, however modest, that we have already passed the threshold to a new pluralist Ireland.

Robinson spoke of the "new" Ireland as inclusive and tolerant—a nation striving for equality and compassion. The unstated contrast was the "old" Ireland of injustice, mediocrity, exclusion, and intolerance represented by the Catholic Church and the traditional political culture. Robinson described the "face of modern Ireland" that she will represent:

> In my travels throughout Ireland I have found local community groups thriving on a new sense of self-confidence and self-empowerment. Whether it was groups concerned with women's support, employment initiative, adult education or environmental concern, one of the most enriching discoveries was to witness the extent of this local empowerment at work.

Recognizing the president's role as "First Citizen," Robinson speaks of herself and her presidency as a symbol within the context of the vision:

> We have exiles at home; all those who are at home but homeless; the poor, the sick, the old, the unemployed, and above all the women of Ireland who are still struggling on the long march to equality and equity. To all those who have no voice or whose voice is weak I say: take heart. There is hope. The old Irish term for Province is *coicead*, meaning "fifth"; and yet, as everyone knows, there are only four geographical provinces on this island. So where is the Fifth? The Fifth Province is not anywhere here or there, north or south, east or west. It is a place within each one of us - that place that is open to the other, that swinging door which allows us to venture out and others to venture in. If I am a symbol of anything I would like to be a symbol of this reconciling and healing Fifth Province.

In the conclusion to her inaugural address, Robinson spoke of how she will champion the "new" Ireland:

I will rely to a large extent on symbols. But symbols are what unite and divide people. Symbols give us our identity, our self image, our way of explaining ourselves to ourselves and to others. Symbols in turn determine the kinds of stories we tell; and the stories we tell determine the kind of history we make and remake . . . . I want this Presidency to promote the telling of stories—I want women who have felt themselves outside history to be written back into history, in the words of Eavan Boland, finding a voice where they found a vision. May God direct me so that my Presidency is one of justice, peace and love.

Robinson's campaign rhetoric represented the development of a rhetorical synthesis. Her Inaugural Address embodied the culmination of that fusion into a vision of inclusion, equality, tolerance, and opportunity for Ireland and its citizens. The vision represents an effective illustration of how womanhood and personhood were reconciled and cast in terms of nationhood. In Robinson's vision womanhood, personhood, and nationhood become the force for redefinition and revision of society. Robinson spoke of her candidacy as an enactment of a vision; she spoke of her election as an endorsement of a vision; and as president, she speaks of herself as the voice for a vision. Her success at the polls and her acclaim in office suggest that her vision has captured the reality and aspirations of the Irish people.

NOTE

1. Unless otherwise referenced, all quotations attributed to Mary Robinson are taken from the written texts of speeches she made during October and November of 1990. Texts of Robinson's victory speech and her inaurgural address (delivered December 3, 1990) were provided by the Irish Embassy in Washington, D. C. Texts of campaign speeches were provided by Robinson's campaign organization.

REFERENCES

Campbell, K. K. (1983). Femininity and feminism: To be or not to be a woman. *Communication Quarterly, 31*(2), 101-108.

Campbell, K. K. (1989). *Man cannot speak for her: A critical study of early feminist rhetoric.* New York: Greenwood Press.

Cooke, K. (1990, November 10). Robinson to be Ireland's first woman president. *Financial Times,* p. 22.

Cooke, K. (1990, December 6). And here's to you—Irish presidential election. *Financial Times,* p. 18.

Eichel, L. (1990, November 10). Ireland election. *Toronto Star,* p. 3A.

Frankel, G. (1990, November 10). Socialist feminist wins Irish presidency. *Washington Post,* p. A20.

Grove, V. (1990, November 4). Contrary Mary could break the Irish mould. *Irish Times,* section: Features.

Gwyn, R. (1990, November 11). Irish voters look forward, reject blarney. *Toronto Star,* p. H1.

Holland, M. (1990, November 7). *Irish Times,* p. 15.

Irish bookies. (1990, November 12). *Financial Times,* p. 14.

McKitrick, D. (1990, November 6). Editorial page. *Irish Times,* p. 19.

Rule, S. (1990, December 27). New president sees a "new Ireland": could she be a startling beginning? *The New York Times,* p. 4

Tong, R. (1989). *Feminist thought.* Boulder, CO: Westview Press.

Tuohy, W. (1990, November 11). Robinson is feminist and political outsider: Voters chose her anyway. *Los Angeles Times,* p. 16.

Walker, R. (1990, December 12). An island off the coast of an island. *Christian Science Monitor,* p. 11.

Wood, J. T. (1994). *Gendered lives: Communication, gender and culture.* Belmont, CA: Wadsworth.

19

Constructing a Postmodernist Ethic: The Feminist Quest for a New Politics

Patricia A. Sullivan and
Steven R. Goldzwig

I could not bear to turn every human contact into a photo opportunity. Nor could I bear to be separated by people who were well-meaning but trying to protect me. I would shrivel. I learned a lot about Pat Schroeder, and that's why I'm not a candidate for President.
— U.S. REPRESENTATIVE PATRICIA SCHROEDER (Quoted in Weaver, 1987, p. 1A)

An uneasy relationship exists between feminism and postmodernism. Anne Balsamo (1987) acknowledges tensions, but stresses in her essay, "Un-Wrapping the Postmodern: A Feminist Glance," that obvious connections exist between the concerns of feminist theorists and postmodernist theorists. When she examines points identified by Jean-Francois Lyotard, for example, she senses "a nagging familiarity" (p. 65). She feels that feminists should embrace postmodernism's concerns with "the loss of credibility of the master narrative of modernism, and more broadly, the question of the legitimation of knowledge," as well as challenges to "the universality of grand theory" (p. 65).

However, although the concerns of postmodern theorists and feminist theorists seem to dovetail, Balsamo says she hesitates to draw parallels between their research. She claims: "The postmodernists fail to engage feminism directly. It is not, for example, that the voluminous feminist work which identifies the gender politics inherent in the legitimation of knowledge is recast as evidence of the incredulity toward meta-narratives; the work is ignored" (p. 65). With Lana Rakow (1985), Balsamo addresses the possibility that poststmodernist theory may be "another masculine invention engineered to exclude women" (p. 64).

Balsamo closes her essay by asking whether a space exists for feminism in postmodernism. She also suggests that feminists cannot wait to be invited to "comment on the cultural phenomena of our 'age'" (p. 69). Feminist theorists must cast aside suspicions and fill in what appear to be obvious gaps in postmodernist theorizing. She proposes that feminists must test and—if necessary—expand postmodernist critical boundaries. If "the postmodernist project [is defined as]—the search for the partial, the other, the silenced," (p. 70) then feminist theorists must join this project.

In a more recent essay, Cathy Schwichtenberg (1992) agrees with Balsamo's contentions and suggests that although Jean Baudrillard's (1983a, 1983b) postmodernist theory might "seem to have nothing in it for women, looks are deceiving" (p. 123). She argues that his "concept of simulation" is useful for feminist theorists.

> Simulation begins with the liquidation of all referentials, and a new culture of surface emerges out of the rubble. This new postmodern culture lacks all references to a fixed and stable reality. When played out in a postmodern feminist key, this bi-polar collapse into fabrication poses a challenge to the male/female polarities of sexual difference, which have by now proved to be an impasse for feminist theory. (p. 123)

In this essay, we attempt to create a space in postmodernism for feminist theorizing concerning political communication. With Balsamo, we search for "the partial, the other, the silenced," and with Schwichtenberg we seek new reference points which we will apply to political communication. First, we discuss conceptual links between postmodernist theorizing and feminist theorizing that illuminate our approach to political communication. Second, we outline cultural feminist responses to Enlightenment philosophies that inform the postmodernist political ethic we are forging. Third, we map a postmodernist feminist ethic based on a female-identified value system as defined by cultural feminists.[1] Finally, we explore possibilities for actualizing a postmodernist feminist ethic in U. S. political discourse.

POSTMODERNIST THEORIES
AND FEMINIST THEORIES

For the purposes of this essay, we address the intersections of feminist and postmodernist thinking in responding to the formation of new shapes of political life. Jane Flax (1990) defines the postmodern period in Western culture as marked by a recognition that "a 'shape of life' is growing old" (p. 39). Because feminist theorists also respond to "a 'shape of life' [that] is growing old," Flax envisions philosophical links between feminist theorists and postmodern theorists. With Flax, we recognize that "feminist theory is not a unified or homogeneous discourse" (p. 40); however, we also agree that—regardless of ideological bent—feminist theory has as its goal "to analyze gender relations" (p. 40). Postmodernist principles may assist the feminist critic in "reevaluating and altering our existing gender arrangements" (Flax, p. 40). Flax refers to feminist theory "as a type of postmodern philosophy," because it "reveals and contributes to the growing uncertainty within Western intellectual circles about the appropriate grounding and methods for explaining and interpreting human experience" (p. 41). Feminists join postmodernists in questioning "beliefs concerning truth, knowledge, power, the self, and language that are often taken for granted within and serve as legitimation for contemporary Western culture" (Flax, p. 41).

Postmodernist thinkers foreground and question a number of Enlightenment beliefs that pervade Western (particularly U. S.) culture. These beliefs provide the backdrop for our discussion of political communication from a feminist standpoint. Postmodernist thinkers call into question the privileging of reason in moral decision making; they question the assumption that reason "can provide an objective, reliable, and universal foundation for knowledge" (Flax, p. 41). A corollary of this assumption is that "the right use of reason will be 'true'—for example, such knowledge will represent something real and unchanging (universal) about our minds and the structure of the natural world" (Flax, p. 41). From this Enlightenment perspective (best represented by the Kantian categorical imperative), the force of law is "transhistorical" (Flax, p. 41). Human beings act morally when they adhere to laws or abstractions that transcend their own experiences. Society benefits when knowledge or truth is "grounded in universal reason, not particular interests" (Flax, p. 42). From this perspective, the world of public, disinterested, "rational" discourse is clearly distinguished from the world of personal, emotionally engaged, "irrational" discourse.

Although many feminist thinkers hesitate to align themselves with postmodernist thought, believing it to be "another masculine invention engineered to exclude women," we shall demonstrate the correlation between the two enterprises in the next section of this essay. Feminist theorists who contrast male-identified Enlightenment approaches to moral reasoning with female-identified "irrational" approaches to moral reasoning are traveling the same theoretical path as postmodernist theorists. The next section of this essay provides a context for understanding the link between postmodernist and cultural feminist thought.

CULTURAL FEMINIST RESPONSES
TO ENLIGHTENMENT THOUGHT

Cultural feminists challenge Western Enlightenment dualities that have privileged the mind over the physical body. While the mind was seen as what set humans apart from animals, as essentially "human," the body was viewed as

> a connection to the animal and natural world and as a hindrance to free thought. Conceived in this way, the mind enabled humans to conquer and overcome physical limitations of environmental and physical barriers to human progress and cognitive development. The physical body thus received relatively little philosophical attention. (Cirksena & Cuklanz, 1992, p. 33)

These dualities marginalized women in a number of ways. Because of their role in childbirth, women were associated with the natural world as opposed to the world of reason. Therefore, women were perceived as unsuited to intellectual work. Women's roles were circumscribed in accordance with their role in childbearing: "the important attributes of women were thought to be physical rather than mental" (p. 33). Because women were not seen as part of the "disinterested" and abstract world of reason, "they were devalued as less human than men" (p. 33).

Thus, women and their natural pursuits were relegated to the private world, the world of the home, while men and their intellectual pursuits were assigned to the public realm. The Enlightenment legacy, in the form of dualities, was used to justify the exclusion of women from important intellectual work, including politics (Cirksena & Cuklanz, 1992, pp. 33-34). A number of feminist cultural theorists argue that, because women were socialized to perform particular caring tasks in the home or workplace, they developed a different value system from that of men. Furthermore, they suggest that the public sphere, including the world of politics, would be transformed if values associated with women informed communication and moral decision making.

FEMINIST CULTURAL THEORISTS
AND THE TRANSFORMATION OF POLITICS

Feminist cultural theorists, including Gilligan (1982); Belenky, Clinchy, Goldberger, & Tarule (1986); Noddings (1984, 1989); and Ruddick (1989), argue that, in Gilligan's terms, "male and female voices typically speak of the importance of different truths" (p. 156). Gilligan, as the earliest articulator of female-identified and male-identified value systems, established definitions that have been embraced by other feminist cultural theorists. Although Gilligan is a prolific writer, the controversy surrounding her work centers on *In a Different Voice: Psychological Theory and Women's Development* (1982). *In a Different Voice* and Gilligan's subsequent works argue that women and men orient themselves to the world differently, and that this difference is reflected in their approaches to moral decision making. Women "define their identity through relationships of intimacy and care" (1982, p. 164).[2]

Belenky et al. (1986) extend Gilligan's work to identify approaches to moral decision making that blend concerns for "care" and "rights." A separate epistemological approach to moral decision making that is more frequently but not exclusively identified with men corresponds with Gilligan's "rights" ethic and embodies classic Enlightenment values. People operating out of a separate epistemology rely on abstract standards in making decisions. A connected epistemological approach to moral decision making, on the other hand, corresponds with Gilligan's "care" ethic and represents an approach unrecognized by Enlightenment thinkers. For "connected knowers," "truth emerges through care" (p. 102) and attention to the "relationships between knowers and the objects (or subjects) of knowing (which may or may not be persons)" (p. 102). Connected knowing "is just as *procedural* as separate knowing, although its procedures have not yet been as elaborately codified" (p. 121). The "constructed knower" is a "passionate knower" who blends the two epistemological approaches and recognizes "that answers to all questions vary depending on the context in which they are asked and on the frame of reference of the person doing the asking" (p. 138).

Nel Noddings (1989) and Sara Ruddick (1989) embrace the findings of Gilligan and Belenky et al. (1986), but make more direct remarks concerning the necessity to transform political decision-making processes in accordance with female-identified value systems. In *Women and Evil*, Noddings challenges Western philosophical ideals, as these are embodied in Greek and Enlightenment thought, that frame approaches to moral reasoning in U. S. culture and "ignore many of the questions so important to women" (p. 187). She distinguishes an "ethic of principles" from an "ethic of relations" (see especially pp. 180-206). An "ethic of principles" is grounded in patriarchal principles that emphasize competition, the "striving for extremes that has been a mark of manhood" (p. 181). From this standpoint, an act is ethical if it corresponds with an abstract standard, a "rule or principle" (p. 184). An "ethic of relations," on the other hand, asks that human beings contextualize their decision making and "take into account the relations in which moral agents live and find their identities" (p. 184).[3] Noddings claims that an "ethic of principles" encourages us to see our enemies as "other"—as nonhuman entities whose concerns bear no resemblance to our concerns. If an "ethic of relations" informed political decision making, we would recognize connections with "others" and we would be less likely to "inflict pain on those we judge to be evil" (p. 196).

Ruddick (1989) supports Noddings's observations and addresses political transformations suggested by an "ethic of relations." Borrowing a term from Sandra Hartsock (1983), Ruddick argues that "a feminist standpoint is a superior vision produced by the conditions and distinctive work of women" (p. 129). Because women have served as caretakers, "a defining task of their work is to maintain mutually helpful connections with another person—or animal—whose separateness they create and respect" (p. 131). Ruddick summarizes her position that traditional "women's work" has informed the creation of a female-identified value system.

> Whether care takers are cleaning toilet bowls, attending to the incontinence of dying patients, or toilet training children; whether they nurse a baby, invent a sauce, or mash potatoes thin enough to allow a toothless, elderly person to feed herself, care workers depend on a practical knowledge of the qualities of the material world, including the human bodily world, in which they deal. (p. 130)

Ruddick argues that caretakers do not make decisions based on abstractions; rather, their decision making is grounded in the recognition of the particular needs and circumstances of the people they are helping. And so Ruddick proposes that a value system emphasizing caretaking—"a maternal resource for peace"—would thwart U. S. militaristic impulses that are "permeated with a distinctive blend of abstract fanaticism, professionalized bureaucracy, and complicated high technology" (p. 139).

Thus, if we turn to cultural feminists for direction in mapping a postmodernist feminist ethic for a new politics, three characteristics emerge that should mark political communication. A postmodernist feminist ethic, in questioning the privileging of reason and abstract standards in Enlightenment philosophy, foregrounds the roles that personal experience, context, and relationships play in moral decision making. These characteristics reflect challenges to the features of Enlightenment thought identified by Flax (1990). Although a debate rages among feminists concerning the cultural feminist approach mapped in this essay (hooks, 1984, 1990; Houston, 1992; Kerber, 1993; Spelman, 1988), we believe that the United States would be a better place if political communicators embraced the *values* identified by these theorists.[4] A postmodernist feminist standpoint, framed by respect for these values, would encourage dialogue among the diverse voices in U. S. culture. Some women, in their roles as political communicators, may serve as guides in articulating the postmodernist feminist standpoint articulated in this essay.

POLITICAL COMMUNICATION:
REALIZING A POSTMODERNIST FEMINIST STANCE

Women politicians are directly and indirectly revealing their commitments to the postmodernist feminist ethic outlined in this essay. When U. S. Representative Patricia Schroeder announced in 1987 that she would not seek the 1988 Democratic nomination for the presidency of the United States, she expressed frustration with political processes that asked her to "be separated from those I serve" (quoted in Weaver, 1A). She emphasized that she wanted to "talk to people" and maintain connections with them (quoted in Weaver, 1A). Throughout her career in the House, discussions with voters—their stories—have influenced her decisions concerning policy. In her book, *Champion of the Great American Family: A Personal and Political Book* (1989), Schroeder chronicles her dissatisfaction with a politics that is informed by Enlightenment values. She notes that traditional wisdom suggests politicians should overlook the "mundane" and address "big" issues—abstract issues. For Schroeder, the "big" issues are the ones that touch people's lives, and she urges politicians to think about their constituencies—to contextualize—when deliberating.

> Wanting the best child care for a sick child, needing to attend both a meeting at work and a child's school function, and trying to get by on a tight budget—these are the concerns of most constituents. Family issues aren't exciting, they are merely the stuff of everyday life. A person who talks family issues is perceived as dealing with the mundane, not with power. (p. 166)

Furthermore, Schroeder indicates that she values her own experiences in making public policy decisions. For example, when discussing the importance of improving child care in the United States, she refers to her own experiences and observes: "That first year in Washington I had a half a dozen different arrangements, including housekeepers, baby sitters, and a child care center. I needed a contingency plan for seven days a week, twenty-four hours a day" (p. 57).[5]

In 1987, Ellen Goodman chided Schroeder for her inability to understand the political game and said, "She couldn't repackage herself" (p. 23A). Goodman implied that Schroeder was naive to assume that she could transcend the expectations of politics as usual. However, in 1992, voters seemed to sense that women politicians have the potential to challenge "politics as usual." An article in *Time* noted: "Public opinion surveys indicate that when women politicians are compared with their male colleagues, they are perceived to be more honest, caring and moral; more responsive to constituent concerns; and more likely to engage citizens in the political process" (Smolowe, 1992, p. 35).

Campaign 1992 also signaled a new interest among women voters in seeking the "different voices" represented by female candidates. Ruth B. Mandel, director of the Center for the American Woman and Politics (CAWP) of the Eagleton Center for the American Woman and Politics, Rutgers University, said many women were prepared to voice their outrage concerning Professor Anita Hill's interrogation by the all-male Senate Judiciary Committee during the fall of 1991. She remarked that "Anita Hill emerged as a potent symbol of women's powerlessness" (quoted in R. W. Apple, Jr., 1992, A19). Mandel also observed that the rape cases involving William Kennedy Smith and Mike Tyson may have added to the woman voter's sense of moral outrage.

However, for our purposes in identifying a feminist postmodernist ethic, two concerns take us beyond counting what *Time* referred to as "a flurry of fresh female faces" on Capitol Hill (1992, p. 21). First, we seek transformations in political decision making—via transformations in political communication—to challenge the Enlightenment values questioned by postmodernist and feminist culturalist perspectives. From our perspective, it is irrelevant whether these values are female-identified or human-identified.[6] We do believe decision making grounded in personal experience, context, and maintenance of relationships would encourage political decision makers to move beyond abstractions in framing and presenting their positions for the American people. Terms such as "collateral damage," "frogfoot," "fur ball," "mort themselves out," "human remains pouches," and "Operation Desert Storm"—all euphemisms designed to distance U. S. citizens from the reality of the 1991 Gulf War—would be challenged by a postmodernist feminist thinker. Such terminology obscures the realities of war and permits U. S. leaders to frame the war as a "principled" crusade. When the terms are measured from the standpoint of personal experience, context, and relations, their function in promoting U. S. chauvinism and vilifying the "other," is obvious.

Postmodernist feminist values demand the deconstruction of such terms to expose what war means in real human terms. President Bill Clinton also has engaged in abstractions in justifying his policy in Somalia. From a postmodernist feminist perspective, we must ask the President and his advisers to explain what they mean by a policy of "constructive ambiguity." Officials in the Clinton administration define "constructive ambiguity" as a policy "to coax, squeeze and cajol [*sic*] the local warlords into cooperating with each other and the United Nations just enough that a functioning political authority will be in place by the time the United States wants to pull out" (Friedman, 1993, p. A12). What will a policy of "constructive ambiguity" mean for the Somalian people, the American people, and people of the world?

In closing, we address one additional concern regarding the practice of rhetorical criticism. Our postmodernist feminist ethic speaks to "the search for the partial, the other, the silenced" (Balsamo, 1987, p. 70). Popular and scholarly rhetorical critics examining political discourse must validate communication practices that honor the roles of personal experience, context, and relations in decision making. When Goodman mocked Schroeder for seeking a "different kind of politics," she validated "politics as usual" and cast Schroeder in the role of "outsider." Although the role of outsider may serve a politician rhetorically in election years such as 1992, a label provided by a columnist as powerful as Goodman may discourage voters from taking "different" politicians seriously. Scholars who analyze political discourse must also make an effort to recognize and validate transformations in approaches to political decision making.[7] In "the search for the partial, the other, the silenced," scholars must stretch the boundaries of rhetorical critical approaches to recognize voices—and approaches to political decision making—that have been marginalized by the "politics as usual" associated with Enlightenment philosophical thought.

NOTES

1. We have chosen to use the term "cultural feminism" to describe this particular approach to feminist theorizing. However, this approach is sometimes referred to as "the new moral feminist vision" (Donovan, 1992). We believe that feminist theorists, such as Gilligan, should be referred to as "cultural feminists" due to their direct responses to Enlightenment thought. Just as nineteenth and early twentieth-century feminists, such as Elizabeth Cady Stanton and Charlotte Perkins Gilman, proposed that a female-identified value system was morally superior to a male-identified value system, so do contemporary feminist theorists discussed in this essay. Donovan discusses "cultural feminism" and "the new moral feminist vision" as separate feminist approaches; we believe the two approaches are aligned.

2. The dualistic nature of her work has been criticized; however, she does not argue that *all* women operate in accordance with a "care" ethic nor that *all* men operate in accordance with a "rights" ethic.

3. Noddings (1989) does recognize that all ethical systems, to some extent, are "relational" in that "all ethical theories say something about how moral agents should relate to external entities" (p. 183). However, she distinguishes the type of relation posited by "an ethic of principles" as opposed to "an ethic of relations" (p. 183). She says: "Usually, however, an ethics lays out the relations between moral agents and certain principles. The object of this relation is sometimes to guide people in their actual human relations, but often the objective becomes a narrow guide toward an ideal life for the individual. An ethic of principles usually prohibits actively harming innocent others, but it rarely forces the individual to consider the role of others in supporting his or her ideal life. In contrast, relational ethics concentrates on the moral health and vigor of relations, not of individuals" (p. 184).

4. Feminist cultural theorists have been charged with "essentialism"—assuming *all* women are alike—and with "valorization"—arguing that women are morally superior and associating them with traditional female gender roles. For an excellent overview of the debate concerning cultural feminist thought, see Wood (1992).

5. For a detailed analysis of Schroeder's reliance on cooperation, context, and personal experience as a political communicator, see Sullivan (1993).

6. We agree with Tronto (1993) that it is irrelevant whether the values identified by cultural feminists are associated with women. Tronto argues that political argument should be transformed to correspond with an ethic of care in order to improve political decision making.

7. Two recent essays by feminist scholars in communication studies exemplify the approach we recommend in this essay. Foss and Griffin (1992) turn to Starhawk, a feminist writer, to argue for a revisioning of rhetoric that "would involve the use of symbols to maintain connection with and value all human beings" (p. 338). Griffin (1993) relies on feminist theologian Mary Daly to develop a feminist perspective that defines rhetoric in relational terms (pp. 158-177).

REFERENCES

Apple, R. W. (1992, April 29). Seeking fresh faces: Few turn out for Bush and Clinton, but voters flock to female candidate. *The New York Times,* p. A19.

Balsamo, A. (1987). Un-wrapping the postmodern: A feminist glance. *Journal of Communication Inquiry, 11* (1), 64-72.

Baudrillard, J. (1983a). The ecstasy of communication. In H. Foster (Ed.), *The anti-aesthetic* (pp. 126-134). Port Townsend, WA: Bay Press.

Baudrillard, J. (1983b). *Simulations* (Trans. P. Foss, P. Patton, and J. Johnston). New York: Semiotext(e).

Belenky, M. F., Clinchy, B. M, Goldberger, N. R., & Tarule, J. M. (1986). *Women's ways of knowing: The development of self, voice, and mind.* New York: Basic Books.

Cirksena, K., & Cuklanz, L. (1992). Male is to female as _____ is to _____: A guided tour of five feminist frameworks for communication studies. In L. Rakow (Ed.), *Women making meaning: New feminist directions in communication* (pp. 18-44). New York: Routledge.

Donovan, M. (1985, 1992). *Feminist theory: The intellectual traditions of American feminism.* New York: Frederick Ungar.

Flax, J. (1990). Postmodernism and gender relations in feminist theory. In L. Nicolson (Ed.), *Feminism/post-modernism* (pp. 39-62). New York: Routledge.

Foss, S. K., & Griffin, C. L. (1992). A feminist perspective on rhetorical theory. *Western Journal of Communication, 56* (4), 330-349.

Friedman, T. L. (1993, October 15). Somalia buzzwords: "Constructive ambiguity." *The New York Times,* pp. A1, A12.

From Anita Hill to Capitol Hill (1992, November 16). *Time,* p. 21.

Gilligan, C. (1982). *In a different voice: Psychological theory and women's development.* Cambridge: Harvard University Press.

Goodman, E. (1987, October 2). She couldn't repackage herself. *The New York Times*, p. 23A.

Griffin, C. (1993). Women as communicators: Mary Daly's hagography as rhetoric. *Communication Monographs, 60* (2), 158-177.

Hartsock, N. C. M. (1983). The feminist standpoint: Developing the ground for a specifically feminist historical materialism. In S. Harding & M. Hintikka (Eds.), *Discovering reality: Feminist perspectives on epistemology, metaphysics, methodology, and philosophy of science* (pp. 283-310). Boston: Reidel.

hooks, b. (1984). *Feminist theory: From margin to center.* Boston: South End Press.

hooks, b. (1990). Feminism: A transformational politic. In D. L. Rhode (Ed.), *Theoretical perspectives on sexual difference* (pp. 185-193). New Haven: Yale University Press.

Houston, M. (1992). The politics of difference: Race, class, and women's communication. In L. Rakow (Ed.), *Women making meaning: New feminist directions in communication* (pp. 45-59). New York: Routledge.

Kerber, L. K. (1993). Some cautionary words for historians. In M. J. Larrabee (Ed.), *An ethic of care: Feminist and interdisciplinary perspectives* (pp. 102-107). New York: Routledge.

Noddings, N. (1984). *Caring: A feminine approach to ethics and moral education.* Berkeley: University of California Press.

Noddings, N. (1989). *Women and evil.* Berkeley: University of California Press.

Rakow, L. (1985). A paradigm of one's own: Feminist ferment in the field. Paper presented at the annual meeting of the International Communication Association, Honolulu, Hawaii.

Ruddick, S. (1989). *Maternal thinking: Toward a politics of peace.* Boston: Beacon Press.

Schroeder, P. (1989). With Andrea Camp and Robyn Lipner. *Champion of the great American family: A personal and political book.* New York: Random House.

Schwichtenberg, C. (1992). Madonna's postmodern feminism: Bringing the margins to the center. *The Southern Communication Journal, 5* (2), 120-131.

Smolowe, J. (1992, May 4). Politics: The feminist machine. *Time*, pp. 34-36.

Spelman, E. V. (1988). *Inessential woman: Problems of exclusion in feminist thought.* Boston: Beacon Press.

Sullivan, P. A. (1993). Women's discourse and political communication: A case study of congressperson Patricia Schroeder. *Western Journal of Communication, 57* (4), 530-545.

Tronto, J. C. (1993). *Moral boundaries: A political argument from an ethic of care.* New York: Routledge.

Weaver, W. (1987, September 29). Speech: Pat Schroeder will not seek nomination. *The New York Times*, p. 1A.

Wood, J. (1992). Gender and moral voice: Moving from women's nature to standpoint epistemology. *Women's Studies in Communication, 15*(1), 1-24.

20

Gender, Communication, and Community

Helen M. Sterk and Lynn H. Turner

As editors of this volume, we have come to the conclusion that merely understanding and accepting differences between women and men will not be enough to move communication scholarship forward, either toward more meaningful basic research or toward assisting people in their lived experiences. Thus, we suggest that new paradigms are needed for thinking about gender relations. We must move beyond analyzing and critiquing what *is* and begin to suggest what *should be*. Women and men together form the human community, and major changes face, and possibly threaten, the entire community. We believe communication, language, and gender scholars are well suited to propose and develop new paradigms capable of responding to these changes, thereby encouraging human community. Further, we suggest that unless scholars engage themselves with future possibilities and take the risky step of advocating some human actions over others, they abdicate responsibilities to their students, discipline, and culture.

In this final chapter, we propose three objectives: (1) to outline the basic aspects of new paradigm thinking about gender relations, (2) to suggest a vision of reconciliation based on our common humanity, and (3) to offer a range of possible approaches for communication scholarship based on this vision.

NEW PARADIGMS NEEDED FOR GENDER-BASED THEORY

As many of the chapters in this book show, current theory in communication and gender studies allows ample discussion of the differences that separate men and women. We are able to demonstrate that differences exist, to pinpoint them, and to describe their magnitude (see most of the chapters in Part I). Further, we are able to critique current gender relations, in which the power to enforce cultural meanings is shown to belong to men and to the masculine point of view (see Part II). And we are beginning to develop ways of talking about gender reconciliation, ways in which women can have their meanings included in the cultural code (Part III). However, it is clear that work in gender and communication must attend to development of human community, in which gender diversity is seen as a resource and not a threat.

Despite the fact that the "longing for community is one of the oldest themes in our nation's young history" (Davidson, 1993, p. 113), contemporary American community is marked by estrangement--between racial groups, between economic classes, between age groups, and (certainly not least of all) between women and men. In 1994, for example, two gendered interpersonal events received much media attention in the United States, and thus were played out across the public consiousness, capturing our imagination. Lorena Bobbitt sliced off her husband John's penis, and skater Tonya Harding's bodyguard whacked fellow skater Nancy Kerrigan's landing leg. In each case, the gulf between women and men was widened by the perspective taken in sensational media stories and the comic uses that the stories were given on late night talk shows and other outlets.

Neither of these cases was presented solely as one person attacking another person for specific human reasons. Instead, the Bobbitt stories and jokes highlighted, for the most part, men's fears that women were out to castrate them. As just one example, on January 10, 1994, *Newsweek* magazine ran a "Hillary Rodham Bobbitt" cartoon on its "Perspectives" page, depicting a wakeful Hillary contemplating castration of an unsuspecting, sleeping President Clinton. Mainstream media, such as *Newsweek*, perpetuated the castration theme, enhancing it by tying the theme to the Clintons, our most famous case of the partnership between a powerful man and a powerful woman. The Bobbitt case gripped media imagination because it lent itself so well to deeply embedded, gender-based prejudices and fears. By exploiting these prejudices and fears, media fostered the perception of differences between women and men.

In the case of Tonya Harding, gender-based prejudice also played a role. Early in the development of the story of how Shawn Eckardt, Harding's bodyguard, and Jeff Gillooly, her ex-husband, arranged to harm Nancy Kerrigan's (Harding's chief rival) right leg, media reports maintained Harding knew nothing about the planning or executing of the event. It seemed as if journalists could not accommodate their thinking about women figure skaters to include the idea that competitive greed might drive one woman to contemplate physical harm to another. But, as the story unfolded, and Eckardt and Gillooly implicated Harding, media turned toward portraying Harding as not entirely a woman, as something less than feminine, featuring language uses such as Harding exclaiming publicly, "What a bitch!" about her mother (Starr, 1994, p. 52). Contrasts were drawn between Kerrigan's aristocratic looks and style and Harding's stockier, scrappier image. Gender-based prejudices intersected with class biases and colored the Harding/Kerrigan story. As long as gender angles—that is, what is feminine, what is wifely, what are "women" capable of and what are "men" afraid of—dominate our cultural stories, our chances of bridging the gender gulf seem slim.

Our cultural estrangement is not only seen in popular mass media stories, but also in the new ways Americans find themselves living and communicating. As a culture,

America faces a future with the technological capacity to further isolate people from each other. Consider this: in 1930, less than eight per cent of American households consisted of a single person, while today almost 25% of U.S. households consist of one person living alone (Shaffer & Anundsen, 1993, p. 4). Additionally, today that one person living alone may soon find no need to leave the house. Computers, modems, telephone technology, and the development of the information super highway have the capability of allowing a person to fulfill work obligations, to socialize, and to purchase goods and services without ever stepping out the door. These technologies possess the potential to further isolate (and alienate) people from one another by obviating the need for face-to-face communication.

Given the potent combination of human longing for a sense of community and the potential loss of personal interaction, we believe that academic disciplines concerned with communication need to propose new ways of framing human situations that can build bridges rather than drive wedges. Communication scholars may be able to supply the thread for mending the fabric of social life. We are situated uniquely to see, present, describe, explain, and evaluate communication which will presume "human" as the explanatory category, rather than "man" or "woman." Up to this point, communication and gender scholarship has focused almost exclusively on differences, a necessary focus, given the imprecision of gender stereotypes current in research literature before the 1980s. However, now that we know there are differences, we need to turn our attention to how these differences can inform understandings and cultural meanings for the word "human" in human communication. "Human" must include all aspects of humanity: sexual constitution, gender orientation, race and ethnicity, and class, as well as how humanity is given nuance and meaning by what people believe and how beliefs are put into action.

In this light, we advocate scholarship that works to increase the stock of knowledge about what it means to be human beings who use language and symbols to design cultural environments in which to live. This kind of scholarship will arch over differences, seeking to develop the human unity inherent in human diversity. So, we advocate a paradigm of scholarship in which attention will be paid to diversity, with care taken to place diversity within a larger, human and humane, context. We see this kind of scholarship as healing, as aimed at nurturing what is best rather than at further polarizing women and men.

Although we endorse a new paradigm in communication and gender studies, one locating "gender" quite obviously within the context of "human," this paradigm fits within a long and well-honored tradition of scholarship, especially critical work. Matthew Arnold, in "The Function of Criticism at the Present Time," suggested that the function of criticism (which we take to include not only scholarship recognized as critical, but also scholarship that comments in any way on current culture) is not only to create a climate conducive to creative thought, but also to nourish the "best ideas" circulating at a given time (Arnold, 1970, p. 452). Given the tendency of mass media to polarize people in order to create sensational stories, which arguably could be seen as among the "worst ideas" of our culture, it behooves scholars to work against the grain, finding and nurturing ideas which show how humans can live productively, in good health, and with mutual respect.

RECONCILIATION MUST BE GROUNDED
IN RECOGNITION OF OUR SHARED HUMANITY

A key challenge to communication and gender scholars is how to reconcile (gender-based) difference with (human) similarity. In particular, we believe scholars need to avoid the dangers inherent in even well-intentioned praising of diversity and valorizing women's qualities over men's. Naomi Wolf's *Fire With Fire: The New Female Power and How It Will Change the 21st Century* graphically discusses how such talk alienates people from feminism, rather than helping them to see women as human beings with valuable resources. For example, adding women's forms of thinking and moral reasoning into cultural understandings of education, ethics, philosophy, and communication has great value. However, claiming women's styles of thinking as *better* than men's and arguing for women 's moral *superiority* over men further separates and polarizes people.

Although psychologists have suggested that dividing the world into pairs of opposites may be a basic organizing structure for thinking, this habit limits the possibilities for change because it falls short of offering a way to synthesize the opposites. Further, as Carol Tavris (1992) cogently argues, "Framing [any] question in terms of polarities, regardless of which pole is the valued one, immediately sets up false choices for women and men. It continues to divide the world into *men* and *women* as if these categories were unified opposites. It obscures the fact that the opposing qualities associated with masculinity and femininity are caricatures to begin with" (p. 60). So, any study which assumes the utility and necessity of polar differences between the sexes runs the great risk of blindness to the wide continuum of human behavior and to the variety of causes which may have affected any given communication behavior.

We recognize that we are not alone in advocating for new, fresh ways of thinking about women and men that allow research and theory to escape from the sameness/difference debate that we discussed in the first chapter. Joan Tronto (1993), to name just one, forcefully argues that this debate locks participants into terms that have been set by those in power. Thus, questions about the terms themselves often are overlooked as debaters focus on the implications caused by those terms. Tronto suggests that "[s]olving a dilemma usually requires that we reject the terms of the discussion within which that dilemma emerged" (p.17). Although it is true, Tronto maintains, that race, socioeconomic factors, sexual orientation, and other "categories" determine power and influence in combination with a person's gender, the arguments about these differences often obscure "the fact that we have fallen into categories that use an absurd way to think about how we organize human society. . ." (p. 17).

What this means for communication and gender research is that we need to recognize that focusing on sex-based gender differences may not be good or useful because such a focus eliminates from discussion key questions such as: Are there genders other than "men" and "women?" What other factors influence what are now understood as sex-based gender behaviors? In what ways are women and men alike? What resources do each bring to communication? What sorts of communication behaviors mark gay and lesbian intimate relationships? We are sure there are many more such questions that do not reach the table because they are obscured by the assumptions embedded in research valorizing difference.

Consequently, we suggest that communication and gender scholars look at the world in different ways, ways that structure social order less in terms of absolute power (and the hierarchies that accompany analyses based on power differentials) and more in terms of interdependence and care. By placing research values and efforts in aspects of life that have a *community* payoff rather than in those that speak only to power acquisition, we may be able to help in the construction of vibrant communities, made up of varieties of fully functioning members.

In moving nurture and care to the forefront of cultural concern, communication and gender scholars may be able to show and to convince others as both Wood (1994) and Tronto (1993) indicate, that the distinction between public and private is not only arbitrary, but also misleading. Wood (1994) points out that a conceptualization of social organization that gives reverence to life can lead to defining those activities that nurture life as centrally important. Tronto unites the personal and the public by arguing that the "notion of care is not only a moral concept but a valuable *political* concept as well. Care helps us to rethink humans as interdependent beings. It can serve as a political concept to prescribe an ideal for more democratic, more pluralistic politics in the United States, in which power is more evenly distributed" (p. 21). Wood cites many examples where the personal is intertwined with public policy, such as parental leave and work leave for caring for elderly parents. Wood believes that the United States is suffering from a crisis because a variety of institutional constraints act as impediments to caring for others in this country. Only a re-visioning of what is personal and what is public will allow us to cope with this crisis.

Currently, we see a casual, care-less attitude reverberating in both private and public domains. A recent newspaper editorial (Jacobs, 1994) told the story of a group of Castlemont High School students who were ejected from an Oakland, California, theater for laughing during a special screening of *Schindler's List*. Jacobs argued that modern society is deadening our children's ability to show compassion for others. Further, as Jacobs points out, the first step to changing this unhappy state of affairs is to be able to "see clearly," a job which we see as belonging squarely to those of us who make it our business to analyze and evaluate human communication. We argue that part of this clear-sightedness is rooted in the ability to merge the public and the private spheres, rather than continuing to bifurcate them. As Wood (1994) argues, a major portion of the task lies in situating care on the public agenda. Current political debates led by Hillary Rodham Clinton concerning health care may be a sign that issues of caring will have a public hearing. Yet, much more remains to be done. And it should be done by those, such as scholars, who have access to public forums. If scholars avoid or ignore opportunities to speak publicly about what they have observed and concluded about gender-related issues of care, issues which affect all human beings, then scholars give away the debate to participants who are free to deal in innuendo, sloppy thinking, and propaganda.

This newer way of thinking holds great promise for no less than the transformation of both the communication disciplines and modern society. However, we recognize these as no simple tasks. One of the great challenges is to adapt the commitment and caring found in traditional communities to the rhythms and pace of our modern society (see Bellah, Madson, Sullivan, Swidler, & Tipton, 1985, for further development of this line of thought).

POSSIBILITIES FOR COMMUNICATION, LANGUAGE, AND GENDER STUDIES

Communication, language, and gender researchers can be instrumental in forging this new vision. Through research, we scholars can suggest necessary points of focus and avenues for change. The following represents our suggestions for research areas that envision reconciliation through sensitive attention to humanity's common values and search for community.

Language is an important and primary area of concentration. As Wood (1994) suggests, care has been described negatively in language that demeans the construct and connotes a lack of agency on the part of the caregiver. "Subordination," "passivity," and "submission" are words that need to be reclaimed or replaced in order to dispel negative associations. Critical studies of language and naming patterns can aid in integrating the notion of care into public discourse. In this volume, Watters, and Sullivan and Goldzwig contribute to this effort and help us see where the public and private interface.

In addition to language studies, *interdisciplinary work* can provide opportunities to integrate public and private concerns. Health communication research, by nature interdisciplinary, can be a site in which scholars explore the effects of public policies on interpersonal relationships. Further, researchers can examine how better avenues of care in health facilities as well as in public policy can affect communication among people. In this book, work such as that carried out by Kreps indicates possible directions in gender and health communication.

We need more communication scholarship to address *masculinity* and examine the ways in which this social construct is created. To this date, virtually nothing has been done in communication and language studies that treats masculinity as worthy of study. This is an example of disciplinary research falling into patterns which serve those in power. If only women have "gender," then men continue to be persons (with all the privileges accorded to persons), and women continue to be considered but a species of persons. In this book, Gilmore's chapter examines the ways in which language about sex constructs images of both masculinity and femininity. If humanity is to be understood, masculinity and its constraints need at least as much attention as femininity has received.

Further, the communication of *fathering* is an understudied area that could benefit from focused attention. The absence of work on fathering and the presence of studies on mothering suggests the normalcy of women bearing the burden of domestic, or private, work. Here again, language issues are critical, since a father's home-work is often labelled as "helping" his wife or "baby-sitting" his children. When scholars treat fathering seriously, they will have something to say to guide public discussion and debate on men's work in the home and policies relevant to home-work.

Family life in general provides a communication context rich in possibilities for examining how femininity and masculinity are constituted. Thus, as Chodorow (1978) argues, family can be the primary context for changing attitudes toward these constructs and toward caring. Chodorow asserts that "equal parenting would leave people of both genders with the positive capacities each has, but without the destructive extremes these currently tend toward" (p. 218). The need for just such work is emphasized by findings such as Pamela Cooper's in this book, who found literature on stepfamilies to be in serious disjunction with lived experience.

Scholarship that pays attention to *homosexual relations* is necessary. Most gender and communication scholarship seems to assume the only two gender categories are "men" and "women" and that these categories find meaning when their members are studied in relation to one another. What happens in intimate relationships where the partners are of the same sex? Do they share the same gender orientation? How do they talk together? How do they solve problems? Lacking the support of cultural rituals and norms that undergird heterosexual relations (such as marriage, tax status, parenting roles, benefit status, and so on), how do homosexual partners maintain commitment? This area of gender communication study is grossly underdeveloped. It warrants attention because it can increase knowledge and understanding of the diversity within humanity.

In line with consideration of sexual constitution's effects on gender communication is research focusing on the effects *body type* and *body image* have on people. This is a legitimate area of study for scholars concerned with symbolic constructions of reality, yet it has not seen adequate development. What effects on communication exist for men and women of various body types? What does it do to a person's communication prospects to be in a differently abled body? How do cultural admonitions to women to be beautiful and men to be strong affect us and our relationships with others? The questions are legion, yet, largely, remain unasked and unanswered.

While there is much research available on gender and *workplace communication*, this, too, is an area of study which could be expanded to the profit of our culture. We especially advocate communication research aimed at how women's concerns and communication patterns are changing (or should be changing) workplace norms. The organization communication research represented in this book (such as Berryman-Fink; Gayle, Preiss, & Allen; Case & Thompson; Krone, Allen, & Ludlum; and Case) forms a solid basis for the development of just such scholarship.

Culture's effect on gender constructs also deserves more attention. Facing as we do the transition of what are now considered "minorities" into the majority in the early twentieth century, it is necessary for North Americans to add racial and ethnic influences to an understanding of what it means to be human. This research must always be aware of our common humanity and common destiny (bound as it is by the condition of our planet), and needs to suggest how cultural awareness can add richness to shared life, perhaps by suggesting different, yet equally valid, ways of living. In this book, the chapters written by Hardman and Remlinger show material and communication resources available in non-American cultures and not acknowledged in mainstream American culture.

While other research areas may suggest themselves to readers of this anthology, the final one we will consider is the role *religion* or *faith traditions* play in the development of gender. Many cultural influences are carried through religious practices, so including consideration of such practices will enhance understandings of what it means to be human. We suggest removing some of the restrictions placed on such discussions by many feminist theorists, restrictions based on a preference for nonpatriarchal religious forms and practices such as goddess worship and ecofeminism. Conversations need to develop among faith-filled persons of goodwill. Out of these conversations, everyone will benefit when common resources emerge for self-esteem, community building, and global concern. Again, stress on what we hold in common will help us hear one another, whereas stress on differences will keep us deaf to one another (see Maguire, 1993 for some suggestions on the common moral core at the bases of most of the world's religions, including ecofeminism). Connections can become the foundation for community building.

Developing gender and communication research in these, and other, directions can only enrich communication disciplines and enhance the contribution these disciplines can make to a culture greatly in need of guidance in community building.

ADVOCACY SCHOLARSHIP

We close this chapter and this book by urging all who are concerned with gender reconciliation to engage in advocacy scholarship. This is scholarship with a cause, a motivating agenda. We endorse scholarship motivated by the agenda, or goal, of enriching the stock of knowledge concerning what it means to be human by exploring all aspects and nuances of gendered communication. Scholarship which promotes this agenda will not be satisfied with what Naomi Wolf, in *Fire With Fire*, has labeled "victim feminism" (or with endlessly analyzing the power structures that validate men and invalidate women). Instead, scholarship with a human agenda will fill in contours by showing how sexual constitution, race, culture, situation, setting, relationships, economic standing, and political power all factor into life. It will suggest ways in which public and private concerns can mesh. It will give honor to varieties of life choices. It will affirm whatever enhances human life and dignity.

And scholarship which advocates a human agenda will make itself heard outside the walls of the academy. This scholarship will appear in academic journals, in business consultations, letters to editors, opinion pieces, features in general interest magazines, community gatherings, and radio and television talk shows. Academics have talked only to each other long enough. If we really believe we know something that can help people create better, more caring and integrated communities, we must act on our beliefs and speak where we will be heard by the people who make up those communities.

Making moves such as these, attending to questions as yet unasked and unanswered, and making our work known outside academic and disciplinary circles, will help communication and gender scholars fulfill the promise their work holds. Human respect, dignity, and enhanced community may well be the outcome. And *that* is scholarship that *will* make a difference.

REFERENCES

Arnold, M. (1970). The function of criticism at the present time. In W. J. Bate (Ed.), *Criticism: The major texts* (pp. 452-456). New York: Harcourt Brace Jovanovich, Inc.

Bellah, R. N., Madsen, R., Sullivan, W. M., Swidler, A., & Tipton, S. M. (1985). *Habits of the heart: Individualism and commitment in American life.* New York: Harper & Row.

Chodorow, N. (1978). *The reproduction of mothering.* Berkeley: University of California Press.

Davidson, O. G. (Nov./Dec. 1993). What, exactly, is community? *Utne Reader,* 113-116.

Jacobs, J. (February 1, 1994). Who cares? *The Milwaukee Sentinel,* 10A.

Maguire, D. (1993). *The moral core of Christianity and Judaism: Reclaiming the Revolution.* Minneapolis: Fortress Press.

Shaffer, C., & Anundsen, K. (1993). *Creating community anywhere.* New York: Jeremy P. Tarcher/Perigee.

Starr, M. (1994, January 31). "Another skate drops." *Newsweek,* pp. 52-53.

Tavris, C. (1992). *The mismeasure of woman.* New York: A Touchstone Book (Simon & Schuster).

Tronto, J. C. (1993). *Moral boundaries.* New York: Routledge.

Wolf, N. (1993). *Fire with fire: The new female power and how it will change the 21st century.* New York: Random House.

Wood, J. T. (1994). *Who cares?* Carbondale, IL: Southern Illinois University Press.

Index

accomodation, 21
adolescents, 4, 85-91, 94, 95, 97
advertising, 123, 125-127, 197
advocacy, 126, 220
affirmation, 103
agriculture, 151, 159
altruism, 74-80, 82
assembly effect bonus, 68, 69
assertiveness, 62, 63, 73, 75, 77, 143
asymmetry, 3, 137, 144, 146, 188
attachment, 36, 37
avoidance, 15, 144

beauty, 119, 123-127
Bellah, Robert, 218, 221
bibliotherapy, 111, 112, 114
Brod, H., 41, 48
Bush, George, 211

campaign, political, 195-199, 201,
     209
career, 4, 35-40, 43-47, 49, 51, 86-
     88, 90, 95, 124, 126, 148, 208
career assessment, 36, 38
career development, 35, 37, 38, 45,
     47
Catholic Church, 195, 196, 199, 200
chi-square, 15, 21, 66, 67, 80, 94
class, 34, 39, 86, 94, 95, 97, 121,
     122, 124-127, 130, 141, 156,
     165, 171, 212, 214, 215

code mixing, 163, 168
code stasis, 166-168
code switching, 163, 166, 168-170,
     172, 173
coercion, 74-78, 81, 82
collaboration, 21
communal gender role, 62
communication competency, 6-9
community, 59, 146, 151, 153, 157,
     159, 160, 173, 178, 199, 200,
     213-215, 217, 218, 220, 221
competition, 19, 151, 188, 207
compliance, 73-79, 81, 83, 84
compliance-gaining, in management,
     73, 76, 79
complementarity, 46, 69
compromise, 15, 19, 21, 22
conflict management strategies, 13-
     15, 19, 80
confrontation, 82, 148, 171
conquest, 129, 134, 151, 152, 154,
     155, 157, 161
consumerism, 123-125
content analysis, 39, 121, 127, 139
context, xi, xiv, 4, 14, 24, 28, 29,
     36-39, 43, 46, 52, 53, 56, 58, 62,
     68, 69, 86, 121, 139, 143, 148,
     152,158, 163, 170, 172, 173,
     177, 192, 193, 195,196,198,200,
     205-207, 209, 210, 215, 219
contextualist perspective, 52

control, 3, 4, 9, 15, 33, 62, 82, 90, 91, 99, 103, 105, 110, 129, 132, 137, 146-148, 171, 173, 191

conversation, 4, 50, 52, 99-103, 105, 106, 130, 138, 153, 156, 159, 164, 166-171, 173, 174, 194

Critical Incident Technique, 27, 28, 33

culture, xii, xiv, xv, 3, 27, 48, 97, 127, 129-131, 135, 137-140, 147, 151, 152, 154-158, 160, 163, 164, 166, 168, 170-173, 177, 188, 192, 194, 195-197, 199, 200, 202, 204, 207, 208, 213-215, 219, 220

death, xii, 101, 105, 114, 152

Deaux, Kay, 61, 69

defensive communication, 137, 142, 143

denial, 189-191, 193, 198

derivational thinking, 152, 154, 157, 159, 160

derogatory, 137, 139, 140, 143-145, 147

dialectic, xv, 97, 187, 192-194

dichotomies, 58

difference, xi-xv, 7-9, 40, 44, 45, 51, 58, 60, 64, 68, 73, 80, 82, 84, 115, 119-121, 124, 126, 130, 134, 144, 145, 149, 160, 178, 187, 188, 190-194, 195, 204, 206, 212, 216, 217, 221

directives, 54, 56, 57

discourse, 52, 58, 119, 120, 130, 131, 134, 135, 163, 164, 166, 167, 177, 196, 204, 205, 209, 210, 212, 218

discourse analysis, 164

discrimination, 137, 139, 150

diversity, xii, 35, 70, 71, 151, 173, 178, 214-216, 219

domesticity, 119, 122, 123, 125, 198

dominance, 58, 62, 63, 70, 99, 105, 129, 132, 134, 139, 143, 146, 147, 174, 187, 190-194

Eagly, Alice H., 14, 15, 24, 53, 58, 59, 61, 62, 70, 75, 83

education, 24, 35, 47-49, 90, 94, 96, 135, 155, 159, 165, 171, 200, 212, 216

elderly, as health care consumers, 27, 32, 33

empowerment, 36, 84, 161, 196, 200

Enlightenment, 204-210

equality, x, 139, 151, 155, 193, 198-201

essentialism, 210

ethic of principles, 207, 210

ethic of relations, 207, 210

ethnography, 154, 173

evaluation, 5-9, 59, 64, 142, 143

expectancy theory, 13, 19

facilitator, 100, 103, 104

faith, 198, 220

family, 4, 23, 29, 38, 46, 51, 62, 70, 97, 109, 111, 112, 115, 117, 118, 120-122, 141, 151-154, 158, 165, 172, 194, 195-197, 208, 212, 219

father, 48, 114, 118, 152

feedback, 37, 38, 41, 47, 50, 145, 152

femininity, xii, xv, 119, 126, 127, 192, 193, 198, 201, 216, 218, 219

feminism, xii, xiii, xv, 51, 83, 106, 109, 124, 135, 177, 187, 189, 191, 194, 195, 196, 199, 201, 202, 203-212, 220; cultural feminism, 109, 110, 210

Fisher, Walter, 28, 33, 114, 116

Flax, Jane, 204, 205, 207, 211

Friedan, Betty, 127, 192
friendship, 113, 114

gender, xi-xv, 3, 4, 5, 9-11, 13-15,
    19, 23-26, 27, 28, 33, 34, 35,
    37-41, 43-46, 49-51, 51-55, 57-
    60, 61-63, 65, 67-71, 73, 75-84,
    85-88, 90, 91, 94-97, 105, 106,
    109, 110, 115, 119, 126, 130,
    137, 138, 141, 143, 145, 147-
    150, 151, 152, 155, 156, 161,
    163, 164, 170, 172, 173, 177,
    178, 189, 192, 193, 195, 198,
    202, 203, 204, 210-212, 213-
    221
gender reconciliation, 214, 220
gender relations, xiii-xv, 3, 109,
    110, 204, 211, 213
gender roles, 19, 26, 37, 49, 85, 86,
    94, 150, 155, 170, 172, 177, 210
gender schema, 61, 96
gender-linked language effect, 51-
    53, 59, 60
Gilligan, Carol, xiii, xv, 35, 49, 188,
    192, 194, 206, 210, 211
government, 6, 159, 160

health care, 3, 27-34, 122, 125, 217
hedges, 54-57, 78, 83
hegemony, xiii, xiv, 158
homosexuality, 219
hooks, bell, xiii, xv, 207, 212
hostile environment, 137-139, 146,
    147, 150

idea-person, 63, 68
identity, 23, 36, 46, 49, 51, 97,
    106, 109, 126, 141, 148, 152,
    159, 171, 173, 195, 201, 206
ideology, 127, 134, 172, 198
illness, 101
incompetence, 64
independence, 37, 188, 196, 217
India, 97, 163, 165, 169, 172

interdependence, 36, 37
interruptions, 4, 54, 56, 57, 99, 101-
    103, 105, 106
interview, 10, 28, 106, 110, 125-
    127, 130, 132, 145, 166
Ireland, 177, 195-202

Kramarae, Cheris, 191, 194

Lakoff, Robin, 105, 106
language, xi-xiv, 48, 51-60, 69, 71,
    99, 105, 106, 109, 110, 129,
    132-134, 137, 139-145, 147-
    149, 151-157, 159-161, 163-
    168, 170-174, 177, 178, 194,
    195, 204, 213-215, 218, 219

magazines, xiv, 109, 119-127, 220
management, xv, 6, 10, 11, 13-15,
    19, 22-26, 41, 43, 44, 46-50, 80,
    82-84, 124, 125, 137-139, 141,
    142, 145-149, 160
management strategies, 13-15, 19,
    80
managers, 4, 7, 8, 10, 23, 25, 36, 37,
    43, 46-50, 73, 76-84, 140-142
marriage, 50, 152, 153, 158, 165,
    219
masculinity, xii, xiii, xv, 41, 139,
    141, 192, 216, 218, 219
meta-analysis, 4, 10, 14, 19, 73-75
metaphor, 129
meta-rule, 189
military, 133
minimal response, 104
mortality, 34, 101
mother, 110, 111, 113, 117, 120,
    152, 165, 172, 198, 214
music, 115, 131, 134, 171, 172

narrative, 3, 27, 28, 121, 203
narrative paradigm, 28
nature, xiii, xvi, 5, 28, 37, 47, 50,
    51, 52, 55, 58, 59, 113, 120,

135, 137, 138, 142, 146-148,
154, 173, 177, 187-190, 210,
212, 218
newspapers, 119, 154
nurture, 48, 188, 217

objectification, 134
occupation, 85, 86, 88-90, 94, 95,
159
Operation Desert Storm, 209
organizational culture, 137-139
organizational influence, 76, 82
organizational socialization, 76, 77,
80, 81

paradigms, 177, 213
parents, 86, 90, 94, 112, 113, 116,
118, 122, 145, 146, 167, 169,
171, 172, 217
participant/observer, 101
patronymics, 152, 154
performance appraisal, 10
Persian Gulf War, 177, 209
personal development, 4, 36-38, 43-
47
personhood, 177, 196-201
persuasion, 23, 74-76, 79-81
pluralism, 198, 199
politics, xv, 125, 157, 171, 194,
195-197, 199, 203, 206-210,
212, 217
postmodernism, 203-205, 207-209
power, xii-xvii, 3, 4, 24, 36, 75, 77,
78, 80-84, 95, 99, 106, 138-140,
142, 146-148, 150, 151, 152,
155, 158, 159, 163, 171-174,
177, 187-191, 193, 194, 204,
208, 213, 216-218, 220, 221
prejudice, 139, 148, 214
promiscuity, 130, 131

questions, xiv, 5-7, 47, 51, 52, 54-
59, 64-68, 73, 88, 119, 120, 166,
206, 207, 216, 217, 219, 221

race, xii, 10, 11, 34, 90, 91, 94, 126,
138, 149, 192, 212, 215, 216,
220
radical, 195
reason, xiv, 3, 33, 53, 75, 114, 124,
146, 152, 158, 205, 207
relationships, xi, 10, 28, 36-39, 44,
48, 52, 53, 55, 58, 59, 75, 82,
83, 89, 91, 94, 95, 110, 117,
125, 130, 131, 137, 139, 146,
150, 163, 171-173, 177, 187,
191, 206, 207, 209, 217-220
responsibility, 8, 38, 39, 45, 46, 63,
105, 124, 188, 194, 199
ritual, 131
Robinson, Mary, 177, 195-202
Ruddick, Sara, 206, 207, 212
rule, 113, 125, 153, 189, 190, 197,
202, 207

schemata, xiv, 85, 87, 88, 96, 97
Schroeder, Patricia, 203, 208-210,
212
self-confidence, 97, 200
self-esteem, 119, 125, 126, 220
self-reflection, 37, 51
setting, 25, 33, 46, 60, 62-63, 76,
84, 120, 137, 148, 163, 164,
168-170, 192, 220
sex, xii, xv, 3, 5, 6, 8-11, 13-15, 23-
26, 29, 33, 43, 44, 49, 50, 51-60,
61-71, 76, 78, 80, 83, 84, 85, 88,
96-98, 99, 106, 109, 129-135,
138, 140, 141, 147, 149, 151,
152, 156, 165, 173, 174, 187,
189, 191-193, 216-219
sex differences, 9, 11, 24, 25, 44,
49, 52, 57, 59, 60, 61, 62, 69-71,
83
sex games, 130, 132-135
sex roles, 3, 9-11, 33, 68, 76, 78, 96,
97, 106, 191-193
sexism, 151, 154-158, 160, 161
sexual harassment, 138, 139, 141-

143, 145, 147-150
social roles, 61, 76-78, 80, 81, 189
socialization, 61, 62, 70, 94, 146
sociolinguistics, 106, 163, 173
solidarity, 99, 105, 139, 171, 172
speech patterns, 99
sport sex, 129, 134
Steinem, Gloria, 124, 126, 127, 192
stepfamily, 111-113, 115-117
stepmother, 111-116, 118
Stoltenberg, John, 50

Tannen, Deborah, xiii, xv, 50, 60,
    99, 102, 105, 106, 188, 194
task achievement, 38, 40, 44, 45
task specialist, 61, 64, 65
technology, 178, 207, 215
television, 4, 25, 29, 51, 60, 85-91,
    94-98, 172, 221

threat/punishment, 74, 75, 79
touch, 35, 37, 147, 177, 208
Tronto, Joan, 210-212, 216, 217,
    221
trust, 84, 145, 190, 193

values, xiv, 28, 34, 62, 66, 85, 111,
    137, 140, 141, 155, 157, 160,
    165, 172, 192, 193, 196, 198,
    199, 206, 208-210, 217-218
violence, 135, 193
vision, 48, 121, 177, 178, 195, 196,
    198-201, 207, 210, 213, 218

Wolf, Naomi, xii, xv, 123, 220, 221
womanhood, 123, 125
Wood, Julia, xiii, xv, xvi, 9-11, 61,
    62, 68, 70, 71, 196, 198, 202,
    210, 212, 217, 218, 221

Contributors

Mike Allen is an Associate Professor in the Communication Department at the University of Wisconsin at Milwaukee.

Cynthia Berryman-Fink is Professor of Communication Studies at the University of Cincinnati.

Susan Schick Case is an Associate Professor of Organizational Behavior at Case Western Reserve University.

Pamela J. Cooper is a Professor in the School of Speech at Northwestern University, Evanston, Illinois.

Barbara Mae Gayle is an Associate Professor in the Communication Studies Department at the University of Portland.

Sean Michael Gilmore is a graduate student in Communication Studies at the University of Illinois at Urbana.

Steven R. Goldzwig is Associate Professor of Communication and Rhetorical Studies at Marquette University, Milwaukee, Wisconsin.

Robert J. Griffin is an Associate Professor in the College of Communication, Journalism and Performing Arts at Marquette University in Milwaukee, Wisconsin, and director of its Center for Mass Media Research.

M. J. Hardman is Professor of Anthropology and Linguistics at the University of Florida, Gainesville, Florida.

Sara Hayden is an Assistant Professor in the Department of Speech Communication at the College of St. Catherine, St. Paul, Minnesota.

Gary L. Kreps is a Professor in the Communication Studies Department at Northern Illinois University, De Kalb, Illinois.

Kathleen J. Krone is an Assistant Professor in the Department of Communication Studies at the University of Nebraska at Lincoln.

John Ludlum is an Assistant Professor in the Speech Communication Department of Otterbein College.

Edward A. Mabry is an Associate Professor in the Communication Department at the University of Wisconsin at Milwaukee.

Lisa Merrill is Associate Professor of Communication Arts at Hofstra University.

Jasna Meyer is a graduate student in Communication Studies at the University of Missouri at Columbia.

Bren Ortega Murphy is an Associate Professor in the Communication Department at Loyola University, Chicago.

Linda A. M. Perry is Associate Professor of Communication Studies at the University of San Diego.

Rhonda Plotkin is a client service executive at Nielsen Media Research in Chicago, Illinois.

Raymond W. Preiss is an Assistant Professor in the Department of Communication and Theatre Arts at the University of Puget Sound.

Denise Quirk is an associate of Lisa Merrill at Hofstra University.

Kathryn A. Remlinger is an Assistant Professor in the College of Science and Arts at Michigan Technological University.

Shaikat Sen is a Senior Research Analyst for Corporate Research at The Signature Group in Schaumburg, Illinois.

Mary-Jeanette Smythe is a Professor of Communication at the University of Missouri at Columbia.

Carolyn J. Sorgel is an Associate Executive Director and Development Director for the Riveredge Nature Center in Newburg, Wisconsin.

Helen M. Sterk is an Associate Professor of Communication and Rhetorical Studies at Marquette University, Milwaukeee, Wisconsin.

Patricia A. Sullivan is an Assistant Professor of Communication at the State University of New York, College at New Paltz.

Lorraine Thompson is a graduate student in Organizational Behavior at Case Western Reserve University.

Lynn H. Turner is Associate Professor of Communication and Rhetorical Studies at Marquette University, Milwaukee, Wisconsin.

Kathleen B. Watters is Assistant Professor of Communication at the University of Dayton.

About the Editors

LYNN H. TURNER is Associate Professor in the Department of Communication and Rhetorical Studies at Marquette University. She has coauthored *Gender and Communication* (1991), and has written numerous articles for the scholarly and popular press on gender and communication.

HELEN M. STERK is Associate Professor in the Department of Communication and Rhetorical Studies at Marquette University. She has coauthored *After Eden: Meeting The Challenge of Gender Reconciliation* (1987) along with numerous articles for the scholarly and popular press on gender and communication.

Together, they have coedited *Constructing and Reconstructing Gender* (1992) with Linda Perry.